NATIONALISM AND THE CINEMA IN FRANCE

NATIONALISM AND THE CINEMA IN FRANCE

POLITICAL MYTHOLOGIES AND FILM EVENTS, 1945–1995

HUGO FREY

Published in 2014 by
Berghahn Books
www.berghahnbooks.com

Library of Congress Cataloging-in-Publication Data
Frey, Hugo.
  Nationalism and the cinema in France: political mythologies and film
events, 1945-1995 / Hugo Frey.
    pages cm
  Includes bibliographical references and index.
  ISBN 978-1-78238-365-9 (hardback) -- ISBN 978-1-78533-208-1
(paperback) -- ISBN 978-1-78238-366-6 (ebook)
1. Motion pictures--France--History--20th century. 2. Motion pictures--
Political aspects--France--History--20th century. 3. Nationalism in motion
pictures. 4. Patriotism in motion pictures. I. Title.
  PN1993.5.F7F765 2014
  791.43094409'034--dc23

                                                                2013044566

British Library Cataloguing in Publication Data
A catalogue record for this book is available from the British Library

ISBN 978-1-78238-365-9 (hardback)
ISBN 978-1-78533-208-1 (paperback)
ISBN 978-1-78238-366-6 (ebook)

Contents

Acknowledgements

I am wholeheartedly grateful to the many people and institutions all of whom have enabled this title to be completed. Firstly, special thanks go to all at Berghahn Books, in particular Marion Berghahn and the editors who have dealt with this title, Adam Capitanio and Mark Stanton. The exceptionally positive and valuable critiques provided by three anonymous reviewers of the manuscript were also greatly appreciated. All of their comments, guidance and sympathy for my approach, were very helpful. Finally, many thanks go to Charlotte Mosedale, also at Berghahn, who assisted in turning the manuscript into this finished book.

Much of the research undertaken in Paris, France, was kindly supported by the University of Chichester and its Research Coordination office, directed by Dr Andy Dixon and, for a period, Professor Sandra Jowett. Without their assistance in finding funds to support this research the difficult task of conducting primary data collection would have been made even more complicated. In Paris, the project was facilitated by the staff of the Bibliothèque Nationale de France and the Bibliothèque du Film at La Cinémathèque Française. The interest and encouragement of Emmanuelle Fiée at the Cinémathèque was greatly appreciated, and her willingness to intellectually engage with a visiting researcher from England made me feel welcome at one of the homes of French cinema.

For the past fifteen years, the archival holdings and the support and kindness of the staff of the British Film Institute Library, then located on Stephen Street, London, has been exemplary and made film history research a fascinating experience. Similar tribute is to be paid to the British Library, London.

In 2008, a very short period of initial research on newspaper press review files – to scope out some of the basic grounds for the project – was conducted on a brief visit to the Cinematek, Brussels. That visit was made possible because of the interest and support of Professor Jan Baetens, who has made nearby KU Leuven a centre of international importance for all those interested in cultural and visual studies. This support is just one very small example of his kindness and encouragement. In short, his repeated enthusiasm for and interest in my work has been quite remarkable and I have been honoured to work with Jan on parallel projects from which I have learned a great deal. It is therefore with some trepidation that I hope the book that follows lives up to his generosity of spirit and is, at the least, what it set out to be in essence – an original and thought-provoking treatment.

'Work in progress' papers from sections of some chapters were presented at the Annual Society for the Study of French History Conference (University of York, U.K., 2012), and at a Round Table on national historiography organized by Philip Daileader and Philip Whalen at the Society for French Historical Studies (Charleston, SC, U.S.A., 2011). Draft chapters of the book, and underlying ideas, were read by and discussed with Karen Adler, Jan Baetens, Ben Noys and Barbara Rassi. Their interest in and critiques of the material were greatly appreciated. Similarly, Professor Keith Reader kindly reviewed an associated grant application, for which I was also most grateful. I am also most grateful to Fabrice Leroy and Charles Drazin for kindly offering their reviews to help publicize the work.

As the research and writing went on, my appreciation of the few similar works in the field grew by the day: titles from Antoine De Baecque, Charles Drazin, Ginette Vincendeau, Jean-Michel Frodon, Keith Reader and Susan Hayward, among others, are all remarkable achievements, without which my own more narrowly focused endeavour would have been impossible. Besides these very real if also imagined 'textual' companions, Mark Daly read the work 'in progress' from start to finish, and made the dissection of French cinema always enjoyable to discuss and debate. His background as a journalist greatly supported my obsession with the minutiae of the film events that are discussed herein. Thanks also here go to Getty Images, London, for granting permission to use two images from the nationalist-spectrum that is discussed in this work: François Truffaut and his collection of model Eiffel towers; and Alain Delon with Jean-Marie Le Pen.

Finally, there remains a very genuine disclaimer. The views, analyses, errors or oversights to be found in the work are entirely the responsibility of the author.

From International 'High Art' to the Parisian Political Melee

Tate Modern, London, autumn, 2012.

The cinema is an art form equal to any other and as such it is appropriate to find examples of it displayed in esteemed galleries, often alongside a focus on photography, pop art or video installations. A helpful way into the themes addressed in this book begins at precisely one such exhibition: the autumn 2012 Tate Modern show dedicated to two artists known primarily for their photography, William Klein and Daido Moriyama. There, the first exhibition space is dedicated to the screening on a permanent loop of an early short film from Klein that is titled *Broadway by Light* (1958). This semi-documentary, semi-abstract work was produced by the famous French house, Argos Films, the production company better known for completing several classics from the New Wave, including works from both Alain Resnais and Jean-Luc Godard. Klein's short is a beautifully shot evocation of the passing of time from daylight hours to night as witnessed on the quintessential American city space, Broadway. For fifteen minutes or so Klein's camera focuses on the advertising hoardings and neon lights that are so prominent in central New York and which come to life just as the dusk settles in. For a visually aware spectator, much of this film hauntingly prefigures Godard's own filming of Paris in *À bout de souffle* (1960).

The visitor exploring the gallery is next treated to Klein's cinema through a second set-piece projection. Here Klein has created an installation film composed of edited clips from several of his major feature films, including many that were made in France. For example, the visitor glimpses scenes from his work dedicated to haute couture – *Who are you Polly Magoo?* (1966) – and there is a prominent inclusion of sequences from his psychedelic pop-art classic *Mister Freedom* (1969). Interspersed are further snippets from his documentary work including film from the demonstrations of May 1968. Again aligning himself with the New Wave, Klein selected pictures of his fellow directors Godard, François Truffaut and a bearded Louis Malle marching, with students and other youths, in protest against the Gaullist state.

Klein and his curators at Tate Modern are astute arbiters and purveyors of contemporary cultural taste. Featuring the 'French' cinema of Klein in the exhibition blends together both traditional and relatively new modes of understanding and representing the medium to an international audience. Thus, one can see that the filmic content of the Klein exhibition supports classic British and American perceptions that Paris is the home of art cinema, and that directors working there display special ingenuity, quality and intellectual content that merit acknowledgement via display in a contemporary art context. Similarly, inclusion of direct reference to May 1968 confirms many people's popular belief that, generally speaking, the cineastes occupy a position on the left of the political spectrum. They were free spirits, critical of commonplace or conventional political ideas, so the story goes. Moreover, the selection of Klein's work for a major multimedia show is also astute because his life and work evidence the current emphasis in film studies and film criticism on the themes of cosmopolitanism and transnationalism. Let us recall that since around the turn of the new millennium a significant amount of academic discussion of French and Western European cinema has underlined how filmmaking is productively analysed for being situated in an international and transnational context. Quite brilliant works of new scholarship have analysed how the cinema functions in global markets – how in the modern period of postwar economic growth the European film industries worked on co-productions with stars who developed careers in more than one national film industry; one thinks, for example, of Romy Schneider working in Austria and then France, or her sometime partner Alain Delon, an iconic French film star, but also famous for starring in the Italian work *Rocco and his Brothers* (Visconti, 1960). Vanessa Schwartz's persuasive account *It's So French!: Hollywood, Paris and the Making of Cosmopolitan Film Culture* and Mark Betz's *Beyond the Subtitle: Remapping European Art Cinema* exemplify the fascinating and high-quality contributions this school of interpretation has achieved.[1] Clearly, Lucy Mazdon's work on Hollywood remakes of French cinema, *Encore Hollywood*, merits note as an early landmark text, as, on similar grounds, does Peter Lev's *The Euro-American Cinema*.[2] Indeed, few scholars working in the humanities in the 1980s and 1990s would have ever foreseen how influential this approach would become. In Britain alone there is now a scholarly journal entirely dedicated to transnationalism and cinema (*Transnational Cinemas*), as well as edited 'Readers' of the writings considered to be the most influential texts. William Klein's selection for the Tate Modern show of autumn 2012 corresponds perfectly to this momentum. After all, Klein was an American living and making cinema outside of his country of birth. Similarly, his work focuses on international culture (the fashion industry being a very good example) and indeed also competitive sport, including a documentary on the world of professional tennis. Thus, *The French* (Klein, 1982) is not an anthropological dissection of Klein's adopted homeland but rather a loving celebration of the French Open tennis tournament. Here Klein's focus is the international cavalcade of players, coaches, mentors and their fans that descends on Roland Garros to compete in the world famous clay-court tournament.

A second visit to an exhibition is a rewarding opportunity to re-examine works and to review pieces with a fresh eye. Dwelling a little longer at the impressive installation of snippets from Klein's collected cinema, my attention was repeatedly drawn to the colourful and surrealistic clips from *Mister Freedom*. Although highly international (made by an American director, filmed in France, featuring stars from Europe and the U.S.A.), it can equally be read so as to take one directly into an encounter with the domestic politics of late-1960s France. Thus, the key protagonist, Mister Freedom (played by John Abbey), is a re-creation of an imaginary American comic-strip superhero, who is sent to France to 'bring freedom' and to assert American values in the face of French obstinacy and the threat posed by Soviet and Chinese Marxists. In light of a full viewing of the work on DVD (it is available for purchase at the Tate Shop that concludes the exhibition), one discovers that it is a bitter political satire on Cold War sensibilities that is quite as savage as Stanley Kubrick's *Dr Strangelove* (1964). In addition, Klein's narrative frame is informed by, and transmits, powerful French nationalist anxieties about Americanization, which were contemporary to its production. The work is a dramatic and colourful projection of the commonly aired fear that the nation was under threat from U.S. cultural imperialism, a theme much espoused from 1946 onwards when Franco-American trade agreements brought Hollywood back into the European film market. *Mister Freedom* is a work of frenetic and absurd pop art, but it is also a metaphorical expression of common concerns in Paris over the perceived erosion of sovereignty because of 'Americanization'. I consider that the work is productively reviewed in light of the arguments mounted in the major texts on French anti-Americanism, Philippe Roger's

L'ennemi américain or Richard F. Kuisel's *Seducing the French: The Dilemma of Americanization.*[3] It stands good comparison with the cinema of Fernandel or Jacques Tati that had earlier toyed with similar themes, albeit in a more whimsical fashion.[4] Indeed, Klein's film was viewed with some concern by French state censors precisely because of its very open playing with politics so soon after the events of May 1968.[5]

In a single snapshot the polysemic quality of *Mister Freedom* exemplifies much of what I aim to discuss using the larger canvas of this book. Just as in the case of the ambiguities of *Mister Freedom* it seems to me that it is enlightening to open up new readings of French cinema that discuss nationalistic subtexts, sometimes explicit, but more often than not nuanced in tone. In these pages the intention is to question how the narrative inflection of selected symbolically important works of cinema and their reception histories are coloured by nationalist discourses. Certainly the twentieth century offers numerous confirmations that peoples, ideas, cultures and art forms are hybrid structures reflecting productive multicultural syntheses, travels, journeys and complex exchanges. What is emphasized in this treatment is that these processes and their representations in visual culture occurred alongside and in dialogue with more fixed notions and expressions of pride in nationhood (1945 to 1995). The evidence marshalled in this historical treatment recalls where the residual and conventional national loyalties existed in cinema in parallel to the development of transnationalism.

Not of course that the basic fictional binary of a separation between 'transnational' and nationalist/ism can be fully sustained for very long, and that is also a subtext of this book. The cinema in which we are interested was being made in a context of decolonization that meant that the borders of France, Algeria, Indochina and elsewhere, were being reshaped and newly hewn throughout the period, and that the world of cinema was far from isolated from this shape-shifting phenomenon. Moreover, postwar France witnessed a relatively rushed process of modernization that was associated with Americanization. As Kristin Ross underlined so effectively in *Fast Cars, Clean Bodies*, culture and cinema were being made in a society that was highly permeable and in flux from pressures coming from within and without. France is a place that Ross so memorably describes as being characterized by 'exploiting colonial populations at the same time that it [France] is being dominated by, or more precisely, entering more and more into collaboration or fusion with, American capitalism'.[6]

To underline the complexity further with reference to the specific context of postwar cinema, it is the case that in some significant instances it was migrants to France who expressed some of the sharpest and most explicit political documents, including reflections marked by nationalism or Eurocentrism. Godard is the locus classicus, in the late 1940s making the short journey from Switzerland to the Hexagon. But there were also other important figures with international backgrounds, such as the prolific action-filmmaker Henri Vernueil, who in 1924, at the age of just four, fled with his family from Armenia to build a new life in France. Or, there is the life story recounted in the recent memoirs of the film critic Henry Chapier. In *Version originale* he explains that it was partly because he was an outsider in Paris (having grown up in Romania, born of Franco-Austrian parents, and living briefly in Israel) that he felt obliged to express strong loyalty to the idea of France and French cinema.[7] Thus, although the intellectual starting point for this study is the analysis of nationalism as expressed in and disseminated through cinema, that concept taken in naïve isolation is reductive.

To add further explanation, the book I am writing is not a critical re-evaluation of the state of contemporary French filmmaking (it focuses on film history and presumes not to speak to recent works from the past fifteen to twenty years). Similarly, it is not a chronological guide to the history of film after the Liberation (1944 to 1945). Great works already exist in this important style, so repetition would be redundant.[8] In any case, my preference for uncovering and analysing the subjects treated in this book is to adopt a more thematic form of organization. In these necessary preliminaries let me underline too that 'the nationalist question' offers no special hermeneutical key to unlocking the cinema, let alone organizing a modern society. On the contrary, the research that informs this study is conducted so as to add in some small way to a growing picture of rich complexity that is increasingly emerging as a defining quality of film studies and the writing of contemporary history in the twenty-first century. Nonetheless, it seems to me that now is a significant time to reflect on selected sites from postwar history and to tease out and relocalize analysis of the cinema around the politics of nationalism – not least because the archival documentation of film reviews from the French press is so rich and readily accessible to the researcher at three institutions:

Bibliothèque du Film (BIFI), Paris, the Cinematek, Brussels, and the British Film Institute (BFI), London. Their archives of extensive and sometimes digitalized dossiers of original press clippings offer the historian detailed reception documentation that capture when and how film was interpreted as a site of nationalism. Here, however, variation in archival practice differs quite significantly between the institutions. For instance, in Paris at BIFI it is exclusively film reviews that are held, and no press material relating to more general biographical information (about directors, stars or other filmworkers) is archived. Distinctively, in London the microfiche files cover a wider range of aspects relating to general biographical information, including news stories on romances, crimes and political interventions (broadly what the French dismiss as *faits divers*). In support of this wealth of documentation, the uniquely literary and literate culture of filmmaking in France in our period means the historian has access to more pages of testimony and reflection from that milieu than for perhaps any other place where cinema is made.

To review, this book aims to be a discussion about a place: the problematic and contested area that we call France, shaped externally as well as internally by migrations and changing geopolitical framing. It is also focused on a time: what is increasingly being called the postwar period, 1945 to 1995, the latter date coinciding with the centenary of the invention of cinema. And the primary evidence that I am working on is the cinema, ranging from analysis of important films from a variety of genres to press reviews, writings from the rich supply of specialist cinema periodicals, film festival events and other forms of reception. These documents are to be critically analysed through the tool of historical description and reconstruction to consider whether they have been explicit or implicit conduits for nationalism. The book does therefore take us some distance from interpreting cinema as a high art for exhibition in galleries. As the individual titles of chapters signal, the material focused on includes exclusionary, implicitly racist and anti-Semitic discourses. Acknowledgement of such hard nationalist material in some quarters of cinema is foregrounded in this book so as to openly debate and discuss its disturbing historical presence. This is not to imply that all French cinema is shaped or characterized by these perspectives, even in a period when such attitudes were relatively commonplace in the minds of many Europeans (1940s to 1980s). One should add that this theme is not entirely new or unexamined, just less familiar in existing English-language scholarship. Thus, the analyses that are developed on this subtopic in parts of three substantial chapters seek to expand on Jacques Siclier's nuanced discussions of the right and cinema and Pascal Ory's more wide-ranging interpretation in his essay, *L'Anarchisme de droite*.[9]

Filmmaking in France from 1945 to 1995 is a rich corpus indeed, and this author has identified what he believes to be some of the more significant issues and evidence for a reflexive discussion. As such, the work explores the influence of nationalistic dispositions and codifications in selected films from, and including, Michel Audiard, Claude Autant-Lara, Bertrand Blier, Marcel Carné, and many other once famous figures. A counter-filmography of directors and works that are distinctive from the more nationalist-sounding voices is a far more limited concern for this book. Certainly directors such as Claude Chabrol, Claude Lanzmann, Alain Resnais, Bertrand Tavernier, René Vautier and others stand out anew because their films differ greatly from issues and works discussed at length in this book. I suppose because I was still something of a structuralist at heart when I worked through the approach I wanted to develop in this study, it means there is a core discussion: the nationalist-cinema nexus; and there is a periphery: the works marked by more universal or antinationalist dispositions.

Two questions falling under the heading 'method and theory' are probably helpful to discuss further.

(1) What do we mean when using the term nationalism? Following Ernst Gellner and Benedict Anderson, it is helpful to underline that the national idea is a modern construct, perpetuated in the minds of people and disseminated through politics and culture (including in subtle and not so subtle ways through films and their reception, which is the underlying premise of this book), and inflected to preserve class positions.[10] Returning to the much used, but quite brilliant, phrase from Anderson, it is the case that France is an 'imagined community' and it is the hypothesis of this book that the cinema has contributed in part to that imaginary, added or played a role in perpetuating it. Furthermore, in twentieth-century France the basic content of the 'imagined national community' has been a contested and a disputed body of culture, opinion and knowledge. As the political historian Michel Winock so helpfully guides, two imagined Frances have existed in the modern period, these based on distinctive and competing notions dating from the divisions of the Revolution (1789) and subsequent revolutionary periods (1830, 1848 and 1870).[11] On the one hand, there is the Republican imaginary of France, which is

socially inclusive and founded on the notion that citizenship is about a loyalty to the constitution. On the other hand, organic or counter-revolutionary versions of France are commonly adumbrated in politics and culture. Herein, the notion of belonging is linked not to constitutional loyalty but rather to a perceived shared set of cultural values, including language (French), religion (Catholicism) and ethnic and cultural traditions and practice. At times, though not exclusively, of political crisis such as the Dreyfus Affair (1898) or defeat to Nazism in 1940, the exponents of this vision of France have espoused anti-Semitic views, and most political historians agree that this tradition of organic nationalism strongly informed Vichy's collaboration with Nazism (1940 to 1944) and that regime's complicity in the Holocaust. A further very important lesson from Winock is that the boundary between the two imagined 'Frances' is not fixed and that in some historical contexts it is exceptionally blurred. In practice constitutional nationalists can express and have expressed hard, more closed, nationalist opinions that might be more readily associated in a purely theoretical sense with the organic nationalist right wing. One thinks, for example, of no less a figure than General Charles de Gaulle whose writing, rhetoric and actions included loyalty to the Republic but were shaded with organic nationalism. In short, once one understands that 'France' in the twentieth century is a contested national identity, it is often best to explore focused and precise examples of expression of nationalism and to detail the specific micro-contexts because so often generalization is too simplistic. This is a perspective that this book follows ardently by recurrently underlining the importance of contextual evidence from film reception and through careful close rereading of symbolically important films or repeated patterning in sets of films of a similar type.

Further historical generalizations, which are necessarily problematic, are also still helpful to situate nationalism in our period. Firstly, the tensions of the 'two Frances' noted in the paragraph above were partly in abeyance in the decades we are addressing. Generally speaking, the political expression of royalism was marginalized after 1945, though maintained as a part of intellectual and cultural life.[12] Qualities of being French, the warp and weave of nationalism, are therefore less closely aligned in our period to an explicitly tense competition around the national brand, and are instead centred on softer more ambiguous concepts like 'being chic'; 'demonstrating intellectual refinement'; 'valuing traditional rural life over new forms of (foreign/American) urban modernity';

or even 'making great cinema', the latter trope being the subject of the first chapter of this book. It is also the case that after the Second World War there was slowly recognition that xenophobic nationalism in extremely hard forms was politically scandalous. For example, expressions of anti-Semitism in the postwar decades are relatively distinctive because of their more coded nature, as when compared to the 1930s or under Vichy. Secondly, to repeat from earlier, this was an era coloured by political violence around definitions of Frenchness mainly because of decolonization (1945 to 1962, with legacies and impacts long after). Thirdly, French patriots in the period imagined the rank of their country in contradictory and complex terms because in some respects this was a genuinely confusing time. The nation was rebuilding and growing in confidence after 1945 and there was a renewed sense of success: the early postwar decades were experienced as 'good times', *les trentes glorieuses*, and continue to be memorialized as such in today's news magazines and other pop-history memorabilia.[13] The people were at peace (when they were not fighting in the wars of decolonization); they were in employment and, depending on income, enjoying some of the gifts of modernity, including the leisure to enjoy art and cinema, as well as new technology ranging from the TGV super-trains to the mini-tel computer communication network (the French forerunner to email, which was much used for dating, and which ceased function in 2012). However, the French also found themselves being a reduced middle power, no longer as influential in the world as in the years before 1940 and learning to live with the two superpowers whose might was both admired and feared.

Much of the rest of this book will explore and specify as plausibly as possible how works of cinema exemplified and added to the very general context of nationalism described above. Nevertheless, this work does not propose that the cinema simply mirrors the larger societal and political trends that were occurring, as was developed in Siegfried Kracauer's classic study *From Caligari to Hitler*.[14] In fact, the idea of the 'cinema as mirror' or 'national barometer' or 'window on the national psyche' is for the most part avoided because of the lack of precision. Hence, we must ask a second question of a rather general, methodological, type.

(2) What are the intellectual tools needed for the analysis of our general theme to achieve a finely graded form of historical writing? For me, the valuable theoretical ideas that inform the research developed herein are 'political myth'

and the 'film event', the latter less familiar concept being first articulated by Marc Ferro in his *Cinéma et histoire*.[15]

The idea of political myth continues to be a useful way of grounding any reading of cultural products, including films and their narratives, that seeks to account for political subtext. Hence, for my political analysis of filmic content I follow the definition of modern political mythmaking provided by Christopher Flood in *Political Myth: A Theoretical Introduction*.[16] For Flood, political myth is when narratives in any form are coloured by ideological values of one kind or another or when these doctrines are communicated to audiences or readerships in narratives. Though drawing on Roland Barthes's still remarkably pertinent *Mythologies*, Flood is clear that he is not linking mythmaking to one dominant ideology (for example, bourgeois oppression and mythmaking to conceal that injustice) but rather that all political doctrines express ideas and values through narrative communication, including visual narratives such as films, and it is this that is political myth.[17] In short, a film can be 'mythopeic' when it carries overt or covert ideological narrative content that an informed viewer is likely to either identify and support (to believe in to greater or lesser extent) or to contest and therefore explicitly reject (because they hold different ideological opinions and hence recoil maybe in anger). Works of cinema clearly do communicate political myths, including variations of nationalism, but what I will often underline herein is how series of films with repetitious political subtexts make an impact on society, thereby shaping a common, and not random, nationalist-ideological mode. This occurs in highly complex ways; few films in our period work as crude propaganda that is easily interpreted or reducible to a single meaning or political message. The mythic content of many films is subtle, open to inferred reading, and also in some cases internal contradictions. This kind of approach does place great emphasis on analysing narrative and so plot summaries of films are presented far more often in this work than is sometimes common. To see the political subtexts one needs to describe how films narrate stories coloured by nationalist ideology. As such, the work that follows is close in style and tone (for good or ill) to two other myth-film discussions that also spend considerable time describing filmic content: Yannick Dehée's excellent general account *Mythologies politiques du cinéma français* and the well-regarded new analysis of the ideology of recent Hollywood movies, Laurent Aknin's *Mythes et idéologie du cinéma américain*.[18] For now, let us also add that for a form such as cinema it will also be important to consider the ideology of representations of space and backdrop, the mise en scène, as well as basic narrative structures.

Throughout the research for this analysis I have also become increasingly fascinated by how the release and distribution of films regularly provoked political melees, both large and small, around their meaning. This aspect of reception is what I am calling the 'film event' or 'film events' or as in the original conceptualization where Marc Ferro wrote quite simply 'le film crée l'événement' ['the film stimulates an event'].[19] Little theoretical work to date has been contributed on this concept because to some extent film history has been written from above, constituted by discussions of major aesthetic periods, or individual directors or landmark works. Nevertheless, we can say that film events or 'films making events' are when works of cinema promote societal interactions, where the cinema goes beyond a projection machine and a screen to meet real people with complex social-political needs, attitudes and reactions. It is hoped the reader finds that this book expands quite significantly on these areas by discussing some familiar and some new forms of this type of evidence in relation to expression and circulation of nationalism. Therefore it includes detailed discussions of competitions and the award of prizes at film festivals – notably Cannes, but also the César, Deauville, Venice and the Academy Awards – polemics and public disputes between directors, and even violent street protests against films, including the extreme right wing's attacks on *La Bataille d'Alger* (Pontecorvo, 1965) and their later protests against *The Last Temptation of Christ* (Scorsese, 1989). For me the term 'film event' has also opened up discussion of the accoutrements of official state promotion of the cinema and consideration of the ideological subtext around that kind of marketing-cum-heritage strategy. For example, in the first chapter of this book I focus in part on the Centenary of Cinema when in 1995 industry groups and state officials commemorated the invention of film in France (1895). Thus, a further contribution of this study will be to draw greater attention to the politics of these little researched types of historical event. An important sub-aim of this research is to enhance our understanding of their character and to begin an informed analysis of film events around the themes of nationalism.

Let me underline the significance of film events a little further because of their significance for the period that is treated herein. Going to the cinema between 1945 and 1995 was mostly a one-off experience, meaning a time-limited encounter with a work. This audience experience of film was far less mediated than it is today by the technologies of DVD, internet, wi-fi and so on. Without blogs, or social media, films were less 'invented' by fan-audiences and far more mediated by quite bold and traditional formats: mainstream press reviews; film festivals and reporting thereon; specialist periodicals, including public and trade publications; bureaucrats and politicians. Cinema was arguably itself more of an event in the postwar years than ever before or since because of these highly structured and controlled forms of public reception. All of which did of course mean that works of cinema could gain a genuine life in the minds of people, many of whom may never have actually even seen the work in question. It is a wager of this study that finding out how people talked about influential films (and the structures that made this talk socially legitimate – press columns, festivals, trade journals) is as valuable a historical task as conventional criticism of aesthetics or philosophy.

The book is a work of politically informed cultural history (or culturally informed political history, if you prefer) and not a sociological essay. Clearly, nevertheless, it reiterates some lessons taught by the work of Pierre Bourdieu. In particular, it is committed to reading film ('culture') for political values. Similarly, because so often the work is unpicking complex discourses that appear apolitical but which are actually very marked by patriotic values, it follows in the spirit of Bourdieu's clever deconstruction of the euphemistic discourses found in Martin Heidegger's philosophy. To some extent too, because so often films and film reviewers offer competing versions of nationalistic opinion one could consider the work to be a preliminary sketch of what Bourdieu might have called the tactics being pursued by different actors in the field of cinema.[20] However, the work does not pretend to offer anything close to a sociological map of a field, nor does it explore the social habitus of the players in the fascinating game of cinema creation in France. Neither is it of concern here as to how cinema gained in legitimacy as an art form in the period under discussion. Such an angle of analysis would make for a fascinating further work, since clearly even euphemistic claims to speak for the nation are potentially also subtle assertions of the importance of the whole field per se. What the approach developed does indicate is that the 'film event' opens up a scope of discussion too rarely developed in the wider historical literature. At the least, the work will show the many and varied actors all vying to discuss cinema and offer readings of films that carry political implications and inferences.

Finally, the practical organization of the work is thematic and is framed in two distinct parts. Thus, the opening part of this book, set out in the next three chapters, is a discussion of where the cinema can be said to have offered outlines of what French nationhood could be taken to be and where cinema offered ideals or models to maintain and sustain nationalism. In other words, these chapters deal with self-assertions, projections of myths about the grandeur and glory of France. The second part of the work is devoted to far more negative discourses and film events where cinema has expressed anxiety or concern about the influence, or role, of non-French Others. As we will see this thematic division of labour is useful to keep hold of a relatively large body of quite complex historical data. However, it is also the case that when cinema connotes a positive valorization of France it has an exclusionary subtext in the background. Likewise, when the cinema negatively depicts the Other there is an implied notion of the 'perfect nationhood' ordering that discourse.

French cinema (from 1945 to 1995) will always mean many different things to many different people and that is all for the good. This book is not even about French cinema in any totalizing or classical sense. What it does seek to map through for the first time is the complex modes of the cinema world's encouragement and dissemination of forms of nationalism, including extreme cases, as well as more implied attitudes and ambiguous undercurrents. That is a very different subject from where this chapter started and the world of film and the international art scene (a subject to which I hope to return in future research). What has been increasingly evident in the course of writing this book is that filmmakers are very subtle and sophisticated mythmakers of nationalism and that the localized public reception of works in press coverage, at festivals and through organized promotional activities, has been a space for contestation and debate. For some limited periods and in some quarters, there were instances of ferociously exclusionary discourses at work. It has been my academic duty to weigh that material as meticulously as possible and to describe its political dynamics. Such genuinely disturbing matters are inevitably a proportionately greater part of this book than in more general studies or thematic works dedicated to different questions.

Notes

1. V. Schwartz, 2007, *It's So French!: Hollywood, Paris, and the Making of Cosmopolitan Film Culture*, Chicago: Chicago UP; M. Betz, 2009, *Beyond the Subtitle: Remapping European Art Cinema*, Duluth: Minnesota UP.
2. L. Mazdon, 2000, *Encore Hollywood. Remaking French Cinema*, London: BFI; P. Lev, 1993, *The Euro-American Cinema*, Austin: University of Texas Press. For a different kind of comparative approach see the broad-ranging and original work, C. Celli, 2011, *National Identity in Global Cinema*, Basingstoke, Palgrave.
3. P. Roger, 2004, *L'ennemi américain*, Paris: Seuil; R.F. Kuisel, 1997, *Seducing the French: The Dilemma of Americanization*, Berkeley: University of California Press.
4. R.F. Kuisel, 2000, 'The Fernandel Factor', *Yale French Studies* 98, 119–34.
5. See L. Garreau, 2009, *Archives secrètes du cinéma français, 1945–1975*, Paris: PUF, 230–31.
6. K. Ross, 1996, *Fast Cars, Clean Bodies*, London: the MIT Press, 7.
7. H. Chapier, 2012, *Version originale*, Paris: Fayard.
8. See for example, C. Drazin, 2011, *The Faber Book of French Cinema*, London: Faber; J. Forbes, 1992, *The Cinema in France after the New Wave*, London, BFI; J-M. Frodon, 1995, *L'Âge moderne du cinéma français*, Paris: Flammarion; S. Hayward, 2005, *French National Cinema*, London: Routledge.
9. J. Siclier, 1997, 'Le cinéma', in J.F. Sirinelli (ed.), *Les Droites en France*, Vol.2. *Culture*, Paris: Gallimard, 293–324; P. Ory, 1985, *L'Anarchisme de droite*, Paris: Grasset.
10. B. Anderson, 1991, *Imagined Communities. Reflections on the Origin and Spread of Nationalism*, London: Verso; E. Gellner, 1997, *Nationalism*, London: Weidenfeld.
11. M. Winock, 1996, 'Qu'est-ce qu'une nation?', *L'Histoire*, 201, 8. For the wider current of 'organic' nationalism see P. Birnbaum, 1993, *La France aux Français: histoire des haines nationalistes*, Paris: Seuil.
12. R. Girardet, 1957, 'L'Héritage de l'Action française', *Revue française de science politique* 7 (4), 765–92; N. Hewitt, 1996, *Literature and the Right in Postwar France*, Oxford: Berg; F. Dufay, 2006, *Le soufre et le moisi. La droite littéraire après 1945*, Paris: Perrin; and Ory, *L'Anarchisme*.
13. For example, Historia-Paris Match, 2012, *1945–1975. La France Heureuse*, Paris: Paris-Match.
14. S. Kracauer, 1947, *From Caligari to Hitler: A Psychological History of the German Film*, London: Dennis Dobson.
15. M. Ferro, 1993, *Cinéma et histoire*, Paris: Gallimard-Folio.
16. C. Flood, 1996, *Political Myth: A Theoretical Introduction*, New York: Garland.
17. R. Barthes, 1970, *Mythologies*, Paris: Seuil.
18. Y. Dehée, 2000, *Mythologies politiques du cinéma français, 1960–2000*, Paris: PUF; L. Aknin, 2012, *Mythes et idéologies du cinéma américain*, Paris: Vendémiaire.
19. Ferro, *Cinéma et histoire*, 14.

20. Particularly interesting for a different methodology to that adopted in this history, see the classic sociological discussions around themes of legitimacy, cultural field and habitus in P. Bourdieu, 1993, *The Field of Cultural Production*, Cambridge: Polity; while for examples of Bourdieu's skill at unpicking political euphemism in discourses that seek to deny their implicit political values, see P. Bourdieu, 1991, *Language and Symbolic Power*, Cambridge: Polity; as well as the more extensive P. Bourdieu, 1988, *L'ontologie politique de Martin Heidegger*, Paris: Éditions de Minuit.

CHAPTER ONE

The Cinema of Self-promotion
Patriotic Subtexts in 'Films about Films'

This chapter provides a new analysis of selected major works of French cinema that focus on the process of filmmaking itself. The opening pages describe the mythic content and reception of François Truffaut's *La Nuit américaine* (1973). It is a work that exemplifies how the cinema can be plainly international in intention and format but also function to contribute to the circulation of implied nationalist values or myths. This work is then compared with the films and film events dating from the Centenary of Cinema, which was celebrated in 1995. The working hypothesis of the chapter is that modernist meta-film is a significant vector for asserting nationalistic-sounding value judgements, albeit quite gently and with high levels of sophistication and euphemism.

Patriotism in the International World of the Cinema: *La Nuit américaine*

For readers unfamiliar with the plot, Truffaut's *La Nuit américaine* recounts the making of the melodrama, *Je vous présente Paméla*. Though seemingly quite convoluted, the basic structure of Truffaut's script is relatively straightforward to summarize. Leading man Alphonse (Jean-Pierre Léaud) is in love with script girl Liliane (Dani); however, she prefers English stuntman Mark Spencer (Mark Boyle). Emotionally unstable Hollywood star of the film Julie (Jacqueline Bisset) pities him and he instantly falls in love with her, telephoning her husband to tell him the good news that he is soon to divorce. Just when that mess is seemingly resolved, veteran actor Alexandre (Jean-Pierre Aumont) dies in a car accident. Despite these trials and tribulations, the director, Ferrand (played by Truffaut), and his assistants, script girl Joëlle (Nathalie Baye) and props specialist Bernard (Bernard Menez), successfully complete *Paméla*. It is a bittersweet ending but as the professionals depart from the set they know they have finished the work: a new piece of cinema is born.

La Nuit américaine is a transnational work aimed at French and North American film markets. Warner Brothers, London, produced it and its cast includes international stars with careers in Hollywood and Europe. References to American cinema proliferate. Truffaut noted that besides admiring *Le Schpountz* (Pagnol, 1938), he appreciated Vincent Minnelli's *The Bad and the Beautiful* (1952) and Stanley Donen's *Singing in the Rain* (1952).[1] The film is dedicated to Lillian Gish and it also cites work from Howard Hawks and Raoul Walsh.[2] Aumont was cast because he had the 'perfume of Hollywood' about him.[3] Furthermore, when discussing how to market the film, Truffaut emphasized its clever title. He suggested that the best way to sell his picture was as an encounter between France and the U.S.A., a 'nuit d'amour franco-hollywoodienne, entre Léaud et Bisset'.[4] That was a far more commercial reading of the film's title than explaining the technical filmmaking term, *nuit américaine,* that is used to describe shooting film 'day for night'.

In their private correspondence Jean Renoir told Truffaut how he was greatly looking forward to this picture. After watching it, he praised him for learning English, explaining: 'Nowadays, one can fly from Paris to Los Angeles in about ten hours. Our audience is international and we are working for the audience.'[5] *La Nuit américaine* captures precisely the international mood to which Renoir referred. Following its release at Cannes it was widely distributed and dubbed into English to maximize audience revenue in the U.S.A.[6] When it was shown there Truffaut toured to promote it, attending screenings at the New York film festival where it was a huge success, grossing more than all of Truffaut's combined previous sales there.[7] The American success of the work was not over and when the moment came Truffaut was delighted to be awarded an Oscar for the work. At the same ceremony at which the veteran Cinémathèque director Henri Langlois also won a special award, Truffaut purred in gratitude to his hosts: 'I am very happy because *La Nuit américaine* speaks about people from the cinema like you, it's your award. But if it's ok with you I will keep it for you.'[8] In Paris, film trade magazine *Le Film français* greeted the news with pride. Following Luis Buñuel's success the previous year with *Le Charme discret de la bourgeoisie* (1972) the victory was further great news. Editor Robert Chazal wrote that the triumph meant that from then on Truffaut would be able to make films with complete freedom from producers. Truffaut and Buñuel were successful because their subjects were universal themes (bourgeoisie, the cinema) that were unrestricted by a national context. Chazal highlighted further that the strategy the French should learn was to tackle universal subjects but through the original French style.[9]

However, the work and its reception history are quite complex. It seems to me that there is sufficient evidence to regard Truffaut's film as being as patriotic as it is cosmopolitan. In fact, it was Truffaut himself who explained this duality in the preface to the published script where he writes, 'I wanted to make a French film, exclusively so, but even so I wanted one to strongly sense the presence of Hollywood'.[10] Alongside all the universal, Hollywood-related themes, throughout *La Nuit américaine* Truffaut made a series of nuanced nationalistic assertions.

Let us turn first to content and a narrative analysis of nationalist political myth. The script hints at the patriotic subtext that was a part of the work. Let us review in close detail: it is the case that all of the threats to the making of *Paméla* come from non-French people. It is English stuntman Mark Spencer who steals Liliane from French film star Alphonse. It is English Hollywood star Julie Baker who is described as being psychologically unstable and who sleeps with Alphonse. She goes to his room and is the predatory protagonist at the beginning of the evening. It is the American film producers who demand *Paméla* be completed quickly. In a further short scene Ferrand (Truffaut) complains that all that is on in the cinema in Nice is Francis Ford Coppola's *The Godfather*. Other foreigners intrude too, notably, when a funny German film producer pesters Ferrand to make more politically informed works, or erotica. One can continue: Alexandre dies in the car accident after picking up his non-French friend from the airport; the insurance agents who are sent to adjudicate on financing the movie arrive from London, the novelist Graham Greene featuring in a cameo role. Ferrand, Joëlle and Bernard work against all these foreign threats to complete their film. The only sexual liaison on set that does not cause chaos is between Joëlle and Bernard, who quickly make love with each other just off the roadside. The perils ranged against *Paméla* are all non-French, or to be precise, are caused when French and non-French people come into collaborative, and romantic, contact with each other. One might conclude that through light comedy Truffaut is sketching out the political myth of clash of civilizations, between the French and the non-French. These encounters conclude happily, although they are complicated and stressful and provide the mythopeic force, or narrative core, for the development of the work.

In his public statements about the work, Truffaut emphasized that *La Nuit américaine* and the fictional *Paméla* were similar: they are both about identity and paternity.[11] And, from what we know of Ferrand's film, *Paméla*, the same implied nationalism is evident. Paméla is an English girl whose marriage and love affair with a French father and son bring tragedy. She is the foreigner from Yorkshire who destroys the French family. This is a plot line that inverts Simone Signoret's casting as a femme fatale in the Yorkshire-set *Room at the Top* (Clayton, 1958) where the French actress is used to signify exotic danger. And, to digress, coincidentally, twenty years later Louis Malle's *Damage* (1993) unintentionally remade *Paméla*. Malle's little-appreciated love triangle changed round the nationalities that featured in *Paméla*. In *Damage* (again, following *Room at the Top*) it is the French vamp (Juliette Binoche), working for Sotheby's in South Kensington, London, who destroys the British upper-middle-class family by seducing son and then father (Jeremy Irons).[12]

If one explores further, there is an anti-American subtext to other Truffaut films of this period. For instance, in *Domicile conjugal* (1970) Truffaut wittily satirizes American corporate life (see further on this in chapter 4). Similarly, *La Peau douce* (1964) includes two symbolically significant scenes that are comparable to the ideology of *La Nuit américaine*. Therein the air hostess Nicole (Françoise Dorléac) makes fun of an American traveller who has been so frightened of turbulence that he makes himself sick from the whiskey he drinks to steady his nerves. Secondly, her lover, Pierre (Jean Desailly), is disappointed when she sports blue jeans and so she changes quickly into a skirt to please him. *Une belle fille comme moi* (1972) provides further amusing material. Therein Truffaut mocks an Americanophile Frenchman who is unable to make love without listening to the engines of the Indy 500 car race.

On several different occasions in his career Truffaut had expressed his own reservations about working in cooperation with Anglo-American cinema. Let us recall that he found filming *Fahrenheit 451* in London taxing (1966), and his diaries from that time were published together with the script of *La Nuit américaine*. When in 1963 he contemplated directing *Bonnie and Clyde* he planned on casting the Canadian French speaker Alexandra Stewart to assist him.[13] Jacqueline Bisset who he used for *La Nuit américaine* was an actress who was fluent in French. Despite the title, no significant U.S. actors were employed on *La Nuit américaine*.

Truffaut's treatment of his alter ego, Ferrand, suggests a kind and caring man, the father of the film, whose love of cinema could not be any greater. He is portrayed taking everyone forward together to achieve a successful picture. He is able to calm his anxious, romantic and chaotic stars. Against the odds, he completes the work on time, adding the aesthetically pleasing touch of the critical final scenes for *Paméla* being shot in fake wintery snow. The film offers a catalogue of examples of Ferrand's/Truffaut's creative brilliance. The director is shown to be ingenious, quick-thinking and artful. *La Nuit américaine* added to his international reputation as a French filmmaker of the highest rank, a status that for many people also signified French grandeur. Jean-Michel Frodon was right to call the film a publicity spot for Truffaut.[14] It is also the transformation of film director into something akin to a national hero.

Truffaut quotes freely from well-known works of French cinema throughout the film. For instance, according to Truffaut, his film was made in the tradition of Prévert. Also looking back to the 1930s, it is a part reworking of Jean Renoir's *La Règle du jeu* (1939), and there are citations too from Truffaut's own *La Peau douce*.[15] Characters in the film are named Chagrin and Pitié, after the banned television documentary about Clermont-Ferrand under Nazi rule. Reference is made as well to the long-forgotten Georges Simenon adaptation about a country under foreign occupation, *La Neige était sale* (Saslavsky, 1954). The tragic car accident theme echoes the real-life death of Françoise Dorléac. This intertextual material all referring to French film history gives audiences the chance to engage with the work on a level deeper than that of its comedy plot. The references establish a link too between the artist and the domestic audience, creating a shared set of knowledge that belongs to the national community who are able to read the references and decode them correctly. The effect underlines the impression that Truffaut is the master artist, a figure representative of French art at home and abroad. The inference generated is that he is a cinephile in complete command of his métier.

Using conventional measures of state power (demography, economy, military security, imperial stretch) the French twentieth century is one of relative decline. As Paul Kennedy illustrated in his famous work, its relative ranking as a great power was year on year being curtailed.[16] Outward forms of conventional power had been lost in the trenches of the First World War. Full control of the geographical territory without external influence was obliterated with Nazi occupation in 1940 and Indochina and Algeria fell within twenty-five years. In place of conventional measures of national power, patriots, politicians, diplomats, artists, intellectuals, including filmmakers, turned to culture and the arts to imagine that their nation's grandeur continued unaltered. Literature, philosophy, ideas, was the ground where national pride could be constructed. H. Stuart Hughes explains:

> [A]s the French withdrew from foreign commitments to the cultivation of their own garden, the nation's sense of cultural primacy became, if anything, still more pronounced. For an assertion of the artistic or philosophical pre-eminence served as psychic compensation for the relinquishment of an active international role. ... Paris might have lost its position as the hub of international doings, but it still ranked as the cultural capital of the West.[17]

In a small, and localized, way *La Nuit américaine* contributed to this same process, providing compensation for decline by demonstrating the skills of its leading cineaste.

Certainly, the style of filmmaking depicted in *La Nuit américaine* is biased towards commemorating French practice. The picture lovingly praises how a small group of people working together can complete a film. That the actors and actresses stay together throughout most of the shoot suggests the idea of a theatrical company united in a single artistic aim. Following Ferrand's leadership everyone is dedicated to a collective project. This is achieved through a shared passion for the art of cinema, and is not regulated by trade unions, law or capitalist dictates. Truffaut highlights ingenuity and craftsmanship. For instance, Ferrand praises the prop man (Bernard Menez) who has developed a candle that neatly projects light in the correct direction for the photography of a key scene to work. Later in the film the Victorine set-designers create a window frame and a perch for actors to stand on, thus avoiding expense but creating a perfect illusion for shooting part of *Paméla*. Such techniques were standard in France from the 1930s to the 1950s, and Truffaut's film reveals them one by one as if they are exhibits in a museum.[18] These images of Ferrand and his work are utterly implausible. Truffaut and the other New Wave directors made their significant films offset and had done more than anyone to undermine traditional studio shooting. Truffaut was misrepresenting his own past. He had not made films in the manner depicted in his meta-film but all the same he wanted to celebrate a national industry and its heritage.

The setting used, the real Victorine Studios, is promoted throughout as a site of national importance. Scenes in which they feature recall how the studios are central to the history of French cinema and they evoke the memory of famous works that were made there. For example, the first postwar success, *Les Enfants du paradis*, was completed there between 1943 and 1945.[19] *La Nuit américaine* commemorates this heritage and in so doing asserts hope for future productions. The film shows off the place that had once been imagined as the nation's own version of Hollywood.

Where Truffaut's film deviates most radically with a work he admired greatly – *La Règle du jeu* – is in its deeply positive gloss on society, its celebratory mode of imagining the nation as being happily at work.[20] Truffaut's perfect (fake) world of work is corporatist. When viewed out of historical context this ideological myth is quite charming. However, when one returns to the early 1970s there is a deeply conservative effect. This was a period of industrial unrest when working together in harmony to achieve an economic goal was unusual. For instance, in early 1972, a security guard working for Renault killed the factory worker Pierre Overney. Protests followed that were supported by film industry colleagues from the left wing: Simone Signoret, Yves Montand, Chris Marker, Jean-Luc Godard and Jean-Pierre Gorin. One hundred thousand people attended Overney's funeral. Comparable social tensions continued through 1971, 1972 and 1973: dockers went on strike in sympathy with British workers; there were police–student confrontations in Paris, a month-long strike at Pechiney-Noguères and a factory occupation at Lip. The former action ended in a police raid, injuries and arrests. *La Nuit américaine* patches over the sociopolitical tensions France confronted after May 1968. Truffaut's film offered conservative audiences respite and reassurance from events they watched on the television news and read about in newspapers. It provided corporatist happiness and enthusiasm for filmmaking. Cinema is magic, to borrow Truffaut's slogan, and it is also a conduit for political mythmaking, and Truffaut's film turns worklife into entertainment. The one historically plausible threat to *Paméla* – strikes, political protests – is never considered.

Let us turn to reception; what events or ripples did it make? After seeing the picture in May 1973, crime novelist and scriptwriter Jean-Patrick Manchette wrote in his diaries: 'It is enjoyable. Too gentle as usual, but distracting and funny.' A fair judgement, and he went to watch it again the following Wednesday.[21] Others on the left wing despised the work: famously, Jean-Luc Godard loathed it, writing privately to Truffaut to tell him. Truffaut replied at length and was blunt: 'in my opinion you have been acting like a shit'.[22] Shortly before Truffaut completed his film, Jean-Luc Godard and his collaborator Jean-Pierre Gorin had just finished a film that had implicitly attacked Hollywood and all middle-of-the-road commercialism. Godard, radicalized, condemned conventional filmmaking as being a part of the bourgeois system. His point had already been suggested in his own earlier film about cinema *Le Mépris* (1963) and now it was elaborated further in *Tout va bien* (1972).[23] Therein, Yves Montand and Jane Fonda were cast to play a film and a radio journalist who are captured in a workers' protest and held prisoner with the factory boss. Montand, a reified signifier of the cinema, is placed under the control of the workers – he and Fonda are used in the work to develop a critical argument against commercial cinema. On the set itself Godard treated the stars with provocative contempt. Even when Jean-Pierre Gorin visited Fonda to ask her to work on the film, he had already been abusive. Fonda's partner, the director Roger Vadim, recalls: 'He harangued her for three hours … "No third degree in my home," I said to Gorin. … He pretended to believe I was joking.'[24] *La Nuit américaine* functioned in a domestic French viewing context to counter Godard's political imagination and action in this period. It revised his anticapitalist, anti-Hollywood perspective. In interviews Truffaut noted that not enough French films mythologized filmmaking, and that remark was clearly an indirect swipe at Godard's contributions.

The press pack at the Cannes Festival 1973 adored *La Nuit américaine*, calling it a national triumph. They sold the film to their readers based on its being a work shot by a French director and set at a famous French studio. Although it was screened outside of the competition, many journalists suggested it was the best film that year. Several compared it favourably to Fellini's *Otto et mezzo* (1963). Henry Rabine writing for *La Croix* was angered that Truffaut had not been more competitive and allowed his work to be entered in the competition. He told his readers that for once France had had a fantastic chance of winning the Palme d'Or and it was frustrating that this would be denied because of Truffaut's sense of fair play.[25] Other commentators suspected that a conspiracy had been cooked up between Cannes officials and Warner Brothers to keep Truffaut's work out of the competition because these parties wanted an all-American winner. *Le Canard enchaîné* alleged that the competition in 1973 was rigged; that because it was the fiftieth anniversary of Warner Brothers, everything had been agreed beforehand so an American picture would take the Palme d'Or. Despite the fact that Warner had distributed Truffaut's work it was too French to fit the bill. *Le Canard enchaîné* described it as 'un film purement français' and asserted that everything had been arranged to insure that the 'totalement américan' *L'Épouvantail* (*Scarecrow*, Schatzberg, 1973) won the main prize that year.[26] All evidence that seems to me to illustrate how the festival is far more than a happy, apolitical meeting point for international artists and producers. Details from 1973 that show that for the Parisian press, cinema there was presented along nationalist lines and in reportage that included suspicions of U.S. over-involvement in the occasion. That is a minor historical addition to the perspective argued by Vanessa Schwartz in *It's So French!: Hollywood, Paris, and the Making of Cosmopolitan Film Culture.*

To review, *La Nuit américaine* is a celebration of international cinema. It revises Godard's radical critiques of commercial, Hollywood, cinema, replacing those views with far more positive internationalist material. Equally, Truffaut glorifies the specifically French tradition of making cinema. He mythologizes the idea of the French director, the New Wave genius. The film also underlines the idea that the Victorine Studios were an important home for cinema. Without making explicitly didactic points, Truffaut suggests that French artists struggle against outside forces but still win the day. The preeminence of French cinema is implied, while Hollywood's significance is accepted. Roger Crittenden explained, 'Truffaut was fond of pre-empting his critics; whenever possible he would weave the perceived criticisms into his films'.[27] Truffaut employed this weaving strategy to balance the international, pro-Hollywood, aspects of *La Nuit américaine* with his intelligent but conservative promotion of France. Some of the reception at Cannes and elsewhere even constructed the film as a national champion, a perspective that added to the longstanding belief in French primacy in cultural affairs.

The Centenary of Cinema (1995): Official Commemorations and Ambiguous Mavericks

In 1995, France commemorated the centenary of cinema. A century earlier, the Lumières brothers from Lyons had perfected a projection device that allowed moving images to be watched on screens and hence the modern form of cinema was established. First projections occurred in spring 1895, with the new device being tested for scientific-business groups in Paris, and on 28 December 1895 the Salon Indien at the Grand Café hosted the first ever paying film show.

The public commemorations organized to mark the anniversary of cinema in 1995 encouraged renewed national pride. Three years earlier, the Ministry of Culture and the Centre National de la Cinématographie (CNC) created the association of the Premier Siècle du Cinéma. Michel Piccoli, Alain Crombecque and Serge Toubiana oversaw its practical operations and the association developed a portfolio of popular and scholarly projects. The Post Office issued four commemorative stamps dedicated to the anniversary and the Bank of France printed a specially designed two hundred franc note. Parisian museums mounted exhibitions relating to cinema, and coincidental anniversaries connected to filmmaking added to the celebrations.[28] Marcel Pagnol was remembered because it was the one hundredth anniversary of his birth. His popular comedy, *La Femme du boulanger* (1938), was rereleased and at La Défense an impressive exhibition was dedicated to him. The previous year, Jean Renoir's works were given a retrospective on the same grounds that now justified renewed interest in Pagnol. Further restored classics were rereleased, notably Jacques Tati's *Jour de fête* (1946). In Lyons the Institut Lumière hosted a major international conference where Bertrand Tavernier, Thierry Frémaux, Sylvie Burgat and the Institute welcomed cineastes from around the world.[29] They watched restored Lumière films and witnessed the laying of the first stone for a new building on the location of the Lumières' factory. In Paris the Ministry of Culture and the Association Premier Siècle du Cinéma organized a second international colloquia.

The popular film of the main anniversary weekend was Claude Lelouch's modern adaptation of Victor Hugo's *Les Misérables*. It was premiered at the capital's then largest cinema, the Grand Ecran on the Place d'Italie, where Lelouch and stars from his film joined the paying public.[30] Lelouch explained that he had wanted the release of his work to coincide with the century of cinema and he had included in it visual references to earlier important films. Jean-Paul Belmondo played Jean Valjean, and in playing that role evoked previous contributions from other stars such as Harry Baur, Jean Gabin and Lino Ventura.[31] Lelouch's film meant that audiences were offered a classic from French literature on the anniversary date of the nation's invention of cinema. This was not flag waving, military marching, nationalist display; it was a subtle form of cultural patriotism, an expression of pride in the country's achievements.

Two official works of cinema were completed to mark the anniversary: a drama by Agnès Varda, *Les Cent et une nuits*, and a film of famous extracts that gathered together over three hundred iconic scenes, *Les Enfants de Lumière*. These films provided sophisticated celebrations of cinema that trumpeted France as the home of the medium. They promoted national pride in France being first to offer film projections to paying audiences and for achieving greatness in cinema ever since. Following Truffaut, and the subtext of *La Nuit américaine*, they represented the cinema as an important part of the nation's heritage. One should add here for greater contextual understanding that such state support for works or gala public-screening events was nothing new to 1995. For example, as is discussed in the next chapter of this book, in 1981, the election of the socialist president Mitterrand signalled an ambitious and politically informed set of investments in cinema-making and wider promotion, not all of which were as successful as ambitiously intended (see the political confusion that developed around the history film *Danton* [1983] described in chapter 2). Similarly, we can very generally comment that such political manipulation of the arts was not unique. For example, it was also in 1995 that international press stories started to fully uncover how the U.S.A., and in particular the CIA, had during the Cold War sponsored intellectual life (conferences, periodicals), and at an even more concealed distance, assisted touring fine-art exhibitions and selected film productions such as the British-made animation-adaptation of George Orwell's *Animal Farm* (1954).[32] The French state's funding and extended 'film event' promotions of its cinema and relevant heritage material was open and without pretension to mislead or conceal anyone involved – producers or audiences.

Like *La Nuit américaine*, Agnès Varda's *Les Cent et une nuits* uses a discourse of positive internationalism alongside an assertion of the unique qualities of French cinema. Starring Michel Piccoli, the president of the Premier Siècle du Cinéma – the organization that managed the centenary commemorations, it offers a fantasy journey through key moments in the history of cinema. Piccoli plays a personification of cinema, Monsieur Simon Cinema. At one hundred he is feeling his age and so he appoints a young female film scholar, Camille (Julie Gayet), to assist him with his recollections. She makes visits to his chateau to talk with him about film. Simon's best friend, the Italian actor Marcello Mastroianni, is a frequent visitor. Wandering around his spacious house are the Lumières brothers, played by two actors, looking a little like

Dupond and Dupont from the Tintin books. Whenever Camille arrives at this veritable house of cinema a new star visitor is present or Simon (Piccoli) recollects another moment from film history and a clip is flashed up, including one from *La Nuit américaine*.

Camille meets Alain Delon and Jean-Paul Belmondo who both visit (Delon landing his helicopter on the front lawn of the chateau). Later Catherine Deneuve and Robert de Niro feature, boating together on the chateau's lake. Simon Cinema attends the Cannes Film Festival, walking up the famous red carpet into the congress hall. He waves to a startled Clint Eastwood (Varda edited original documentary footage from the Cannes Festival to film this section of her work).

There is little by way of a plot to hold the film together. Varda juxtaposes Camille's visits to Simon Cinema with her boyfriend's (Mathieu Demy) work to make a new film, possibly a gangster thriller. She intimates that these younger characters are going through a difficult phase in their relationship. To keep the loose narrative moving forward it is next suggested that Camille wants Simon Cinema to feature in the new film that is being made. Eventually, he agrees to contribute. However, Camille's life remains uncertain; Varda implies that she will break up with her filmmaker boyfriend.

Les Cents et une nuits celebrates world cinema and its importance. Monsieur Cinema visits Hollywood; he has encounters with American film stars Harrison Ford, Robert De Niro and Clint Eastwood.[33] Japanese visitors tour his chateau, which when they arrive has posters from their cinema on its walls (Kurosawa, Ozu). The episode is rather clichéd, the Japanese depicted in stereotypical tourist mode, bussed in and waving cameras about. Simon Cinema is also a friend to Italian Marcello Mastroianni. *Les Cents et une nuits* is therefore an international commemoration. However, it is also a glorification of French cinema and to some extent France. Simon Cinema is French, played by the president of the centenary committee, Piccoli, and he lives in a French chateau surrounded by typical French countryside. The implication is that the cinema and the nation are synonymous with each other. Furthermore, the film being shot in *Les Cent et une nuits* is absolutely made in France. Camille's boyfriend is working on his film in and around the thirteenth arrondissement, where Jean-Pierre Melville lived and worked. He and his friends are passionate about cinema and are not only looking backwards but are instead advancing the medium with consummate ease. They are carefree and easygoing professionals who are able to make films with great confidence. The images seen from their work suggest their gangster film resembles Quentin Tarantino's *Reservoir Dogs* (1992). In showing this Varda implies that French teenagers can achieve his work as if it were child's play. At least that is how one can read those scenes, though of course they are also acknowledgement of the young American's then recent impressive debut.

Varda's inclusion of a subplot about Camille's private life is an exemplary slice of French intimate melodrama. They are young and seemingly in love, yet Camille is also attracted to another man. Varda demonstrates that even through only snippets of this storyline she can make the audience care for her fictional characters. This aspect is a celebration of French cinema since its plot could have been taken from any number of works from directors specializing in intimate subjects (Rohmer, Sautet, Lelouch, Varda herself; see also chapter 3 herein). It underlines Varda's own talent as a filmmaker for here she shows off that she can also still achieve the necessary illusion to make an audience care about characters and their lives, even while fulfilling the official heritage function of the film.

Varda produced a similarly sophisticated double discourse to that seen in Truffaut's classic film about cinema. She acknowledges the great cinema tradition in the Western world, Hollywood, as well as other selected nations with strong traditions for making films. All the while, French filmmaking is praised too and with far more panache and emphasis. The comparison being run in *Les Cents et une nuits* between U.S.-Hollywood film and French production flatters the European side. The positioning of French film as an equal if not better to Hollywood is a very positive reading, commercial data from the two nations' film industries evidencing the French industry in relative decline for most of the century, whereas for long periods Hollywood was in the ascendancy. On the screen the picture Varda presented is the opposite. One should not be surprised by the lightness of touch through which the celebration of French cinema was pursued at the expense of a realistic analysis of Hollywood's economic dominance. As David Bellos underlined in his groundbreaking study, *Jacques Tati: His Life and Art*, it was common in the postwar period for some in French cinema to elaborate ambiguous attitudes towards the U.S.A.[34]

Varda's careful celebration of French cinema was far subtler than other recent works of meta-film. In 1988, Italian director Giuseppe Tornatore, working with Philippe Noiret and fellow French actor Jacques Perrin, completed *Cinema paradiso*. French film critics adored it, revelling in its nostalgic vision of childhood and filmgoing in Italy.[35] Varda eschewed such simplistic representations. She offered an intellectually rewarding, cosmopolitan but patriotic, commentary. This was perhaps to be expected since she was a skilled practitioner of making works about cinema. In 1991 she had filmed *Jacquot de Nantes* about her late husband, Jacques Demy's youth, and just prior to working on *Les Cent et une nuits* she completed a documentary on one of his works, *Les Demoiselles ont eu 25 ans* (1993).

The second official film for the centenary *Les Enfants de Lumière* is a catalogue of the greatest moments from French cinema. With a voiceover from Jacques Perrin, it is organized thematically to reflect all the achievements of the nation's cinema. Its opening section is a sequence of clips from classic productions. Here there are memorable images from the 1930s, *Le Quai des brumes* (1938), *Hôtel du Nord* (1938), alongside images from Pagnol's *La Femme du boulanger* and Berri's version of Pagnol, *Jean de Florette* (1986). The New Wave is highlighted as another key period, with early clips selected from *Pierrot le fou* (Godard, 1965) and *Jules et Jim* (Truffaut, 1964). The rest of the film is sequenced by genre and theme, sweeping through extracts from costume dramas, including Gance's *Napoléon* (1927), Renoir's *La Marseillaise* (1938) and Depardieu in Wajda's *Danton*. Next there are snippets relating to crime films, war, the depiction of war and the Holocaust, as well as images of sex symbols, Brigitte Bardot and Béatrice Dalle.

Les Enfants de Lumière imagines cinema as a part of the nation's lifeblood. It celebrates how France has found success in this field. Implicitly the message is that France invented cinema and has excelled by contributing great works. Unlike either *La Nuit américaine* or *Les Cent et une nuits* there is no pretence to address Hollywood or other non-French filmmaking. Not a single foreign film is included to acknowledge the presence of imported works that French audiences watched in their droves. Big grossing hits in France such as *Jaws* (Spielberg, 1975), *Star Wars* (Lucas, 1977) and *Rambo II* (Cosmatos, 1985) are utterly ignored. So too are popular genre films that had had long runs in French cinemas, cult films such as *The Texas Chain Saw Massacre* (Hooper, 1975) that were enjoyed in France and promoted in glossy fan magazines like *Mad Movies*. Favourite foreign stars are also overlooked, even though many people admired them.

However, the clips do acknowledge when French history has been difficult or ethically tainted – scenes are included from the Holocaust documentaries *Nuit et brouillard* (Resnais, 1956) and *Shoah* (Lanzmann, 1985), as well as *Au revoir les enfants* (Malle, 1987) and *Lacombe Lucien* (Malle, 1974). However, these images are now placed into the history of cinema and are projected as examples of how important cineastes have addressed difficult themes. Colonial history is ignored altogether with the only relevant clips coming from nationalist films like Pierre Schoendoerffer's *Le Crabe tambour* (1977) and the glossy heritage film Régis Wargnier's *Indochine* (1992). No time is devoted to *La Bataille d'Alger*, the film that explained the war from an Algerian point of view and which was censored for four years and then brutally attacked by extreme right-wing thugs (see also chapter 5). French-made films that were critical of the nation's record in the wars of decolonization are also forgotten: thus, no time is devoted to *La Question* (Heynemann, 1976) or *Avoir vingt ans dans les Aurès* (Vautier, 1972).

Les Enfants de Lumière added to a form of self-confident nationalist mythology: the idea that France had primacy in the visual arts. The record of one hundred years of cinema presented is a positive one, and by analogy it was glorious and great to be French. In 1995, this message was important. The period witnessed the end of the fourteen years of Mitterrand's presidency. There had been uncertainty as to whether Balladur, Chirac or Jospin would win in that year's presidential elections. Moreover, unemployment was exceptionally high, the macro-economy managed entirely to peg the franc to the deutschmark in preparation for a single European currency. The cinema filmed as patriotic heritage provided an uncontroversial and positive national identity in a time of anxiety. Because of the meta-film tradition, and the longstanding reputation of the New Wave period, the cinema was an area where it was taken for granted that the French had excelled and there were grounds to believe that this would continue. In his explicitly critical journalistic survey, *On the Brink: the Trouble with France*, even the cynical Jonathan Fenby conceded, 'France still cuts a distinct dash with its well subsidized and protected national film industry which has built up a record of popular success'.[36]

Although it was fashionable to discuss the 'death of cinema' because of emerging digital technology, and the more general *fin-de-siècle* malaise of the 1990s, all efforts were made to be positive in the 1995 anniversary of 1895. The film history proposed in *Les Enfants de Lumière* provided a sense of continuity and unity. The French experience of the twentieth century had been one of political division, relative decline and social instability. However the implication of the film was that whatever the year, or the political crisis occurring, directors had made works of a high standard and audiences had gained pleasure from watching them. The implicit message was that France excelled in this field and that the people should feel good about that achievement. The centenary (and the two official films deconstructed herein for their mythic content) implied that there was a collective national community who shared a love of the cinema. It established this idea of national unity when French society was in reality fragmented; as of course is the film industry, being highly hierarchical, often internationally co-funded, and subject to commercial pressure.

Finally, we should add briefly, for reasons of space and to keep focus on primary argumentation, that the cinephilia expressed in the public events and official films of 1995 was a high point in a longer and deeper postwar tradition. Underpinning 1995 there were at least four decades of intellectual and public legitimation of film in the wider intellectual and literary culture. Grosso modo, the rise of film clubs, specialist journals, published interviews, scripts, novelizations and so forth created what the historian Antoine de Baecque describes in his work *La Cinéphilie* as an entire intellectual culture of love for the cinema. Furthermore, the films about films discussed in this chapter projected to audiences a variation of a discrete preexisting literary genre. Thus, it was in 1958 that Jean Cocteau published to much acclaim his 'making of' essay devoted to the creation of *La Belle et la bête* (1946). A small number of works have followed (and it is a genre that travels with several similar works being published in the U.S.A.).[37]

More maverick films about cinema came out around the time of the centenary and these merit a new analytical discussion in this chapter. Contracted for the British Film Institute's series of television films, 'Century of Cinema', Jean-Luc Godard and Anne-Marie Miévielle made *2x50 ans de cinéma français*. In addition, Bertrand Blier directed and/or scripted several works where cinema was the subject. These began with *Merci la vie* (1992), continued with *Grosse fatigue* (1994) – directed from a Blier script by Michel Blanc – and culminated with *Les Acteurs* (2000). All these works provided a more critical reflection on French cinema; however, they also contributed further to the idea that France was a uniquely special place for making films because it was where a good discussion was to be had about all things cinematic. Godard and

Miévielle's and Blier's contributions to the commemorations were far less critical than they seemed or were intended to be.

2x50 ans de cinéma français is a direct riposte to the reverential mode of *Les Enfants de Lumière* and *Les Cent et une nuits*. Here, Michel Piccoli plays himself, President of the *Premier Siècle du Cinéma* project. Godard films him in and around a banal hotel setting, and then fires off random provocative questions at him that try to undermine the point of the centenary. Piccoli does his best to answer them. Next, Godard films Piccoli discussing the history of cinema with staff of the hotel (all played by actors). He asks them about famous films from French cinema – Renoir's *La Grande Illusion*, Jacques Becker, Jean Gabin, *Touchez pas aux grisbi* (1954). The staff answer that they know nothing of Piccoli's idea of cinema. All they are interested in is Madonna, Arnold Schwarzenegger and Boris Becker, not the historically important director and sometime assistant to Renoir, Jacques Becker. Thus, Godard implies that France is too Americanized, too saturated with television, for the centenary of cinema to achieve anything. For him the battle is already lost. Piccoli, who puts in a fine performance, is supposed to look silly commemorating the invention of cinema.

Godard gave interviews and made press statements explaining his scepticism about the celebrations. He mocked the official commemorations and saw much of the anniversary as self-congratulatory. Furthermore, he questioned the historical interpretation on which the commemoration had been established. He did not agree with the state, or the vast majority of French film historians, that one could really identify the birth of cinema with the Lumière brothers. He found the use of the first commercial screening at the Grand Café (28 December 1895) as the birth of cinema highly inappropriate. Identifying this episode as the birth of film too greatly associated the idea of cinema with commercialism and capitalism.[38] For the media looking for new angles on the centenary, these provocative perspectives proved attractive. Godard was able to air his views in magazines and on television and the radio. He offered a contrast to the official celebrations. He gave the media a new angle on the anniversary of the invention of the cinema by being critical about it.

Ironically, Godard's work contributed to the zeitgeist that implied that France was the home of cinema and of debating its meaning. Paradoxically, *2x50 ans de cinéma français* added to the very mood of commemoration that it criticised. Piccoli's brave decision to feature in the film served his cause more than Godard's. His presence on the screen outweighs Godard's baiting of him.

Godard had declared that he would not participate in the centenary, but by making an interrogation of the symbolic figurehead of the commemorations, Piccoli, he did engage with it. He gave the director of the centenary a rough ride but he had granted him the chance to feature in an intellectual product that was all about the century of cinema. The film had a nostalgic element too, which was nowhere near as critical as the director perhaps intended. 2x50 ans celebrates French film critics, concluding with an image of Henri Langlois.[39]

Godard and Miévielle reassured the international intelligentsia that they could still think of France as a site of innovation and achievement precisely because they were not lulled into maybe banal heritage exercises. Their intervention advanced the myth that French cineastes are especially clever, that the country is a home of intellectuals and free thinkers. In the international arena, his interventions were probably more influential than Varda's because they evoked the popular external stereotype of France being an elite intellectual space, uniquely capable of achieving success in the fields of philosophy, art and ideas. Art films being a neat synthesis of all of these areas, neatly packaged for export, in this case by the BFI in London.

The ambiguity of 2x50 ans looked forward to Godard's long and arty documentary series, Histoire(s) du cinéma (1997 to 2000). Here, Godard was again ambivalent about the contribution of France to cinema history. His episodic musings suggest that the French have achieved not so much. Instead, Godard emphasizes American, Russian, German and Italian cinemas as examples of when national communities and filmmaking have melded successfully together to achieve perfection. Thus, French film is not included among the classic cinema-nations, as determined by Godard. Nevertheless, he does not ignore France altogether or reduce it to the rank of a minor power. He speculates that the New Wave, coinciding with decolonization, is a genuine cinema. This hypothesis is however attenuated when Godard highlights filmmakers' inability to depict the Holocaust, to draw attention to Nazism's crimes, which means that the medium never survived 1945.[40] Histoire(s) du cinéma therefore downplays the status of France. However, its very quality as an impressive and complex francophone documentary undermined its own argumentation. That Godard is the author of this provocative and unique history of world cinema supports the idea that France is a preeminent home for making and thinking about film. This Swiss who made his career in Paris evidences the intellectual calibre of French cinema.

Bertrand Blier's image of filmmaking in France is as ambiguous as Godard's but is, one has to say, far more fun and funky. His fascination with film is developed through a series of works in the 1990s. Therein Blier pokes fun at French cinema, underlining its power dynamics and the consequences of being an individual living inside a star system. In his many meta-films, Blier highlights how horrible it can be to 'live in the world of films', to be an actor constantly performing and being treated by everyone as a character from a film. Nonetheless, Blier's provocative interpretation asserts national pride in the domestic industry. The framing assumption that the French industry was a superior sector is continued in his work and also in its reception.

Merci la vie is an intricate and multilayered film. Two teenage girls go on a road-movie style adventure. The conservative Camille (Charlotte Gainsbourg) observes and tries to help the more rebellious Joëlle (Anouk Grinberg) as they wander from deserted beaches to a small provincial town. Joëlle, who has enjoyed an active sex life, is suffering from AIDS. These characters are in fact stars in a movie that is being shot about France during the Nazi occupation. When they walk down a road the camera moves back to illustrate that they are protagonists in a film. The girls confront a malicious doctor (Depardieu) and Nazi thugs, and witness their own conception, Camille observing her father (Michel Blanc) impregnating her mother (she encourages him along). These scenes could be for the purposes of completing a new film or films. In one famous scene Camille proclaims that life is terribly unfair: why is she living in a world of two films at once, where there is the threat of AIDS and the brutality of Nazism. That isn't right!

Two actors play film directors (François Perrot and Didier Benureau), one working on the modern film in which the girls star, and the other responsible for the period film set under the Nazi Occupation. One of these figures is called Maurice, a reference to the filmmaker Maurice Pialat.[41] Through his representation of the film directors, Blier implies that they are the ones imposing miserable plots and experiences on the two girls. The camera is implicated as a force for conservative control, framing and cutting the action. When Camille is crying because of her plight the director cynically declares his optimism for success at Cannes. In a more disturbing but also symbolically important scene, Camille's father is made blind, his eye removed and then carried by Nazi doctors through a series of corridors to be inserted into a vagina. Avant-garde, the metaphorical suggestion is that vision, sight, film, is oppressive, a defilement that adds to the misery of the world, be that in the 1940s or the 1990s. Cinema is associated with torture and rape. The two stars Camille and Joëlle are pushed, prodded and bossed around. They star in films that they do not want to be in. When Joëlle is filmed being deported to a concentration camp she stands naked, shouting at the actors who are playing Nazis, 'I want to go to Hollywood'. Nothing could be further from *La Nuit américaine* than the implications of that scene. In fact, Blier explained that he had wanted to invert Truffaut's earlier vision. He considered that *La Nuit américaine* was limited to illustrating the perspective of a director. For him the value of *Merci la vie* was as an exploration of the role of actors, a vision of their experience of being in a film.[42]

Besides blurring reality with 'film within a film' fictions, Blier uses a myriad of shooting techniques. He employs black and white, tinted sepia, shades of grey and blue, and then conventional colour film. These forms of representation are quickly interchanged, coordinated with the rock-music soundtrack that is used in the film (featuring memorable songs from Arno). *Merci la vie* is a tour de force of how the cinema can manipulate images and sounds to achieve impressive effects. All of which makes it as much a statement on the power of film as it is a questioning of the experience of acting. Perceptively, Gilles Anquetil identified this theme in his review for *Le Nouvel Observateur*: 'il sera beaucoup pardonné à 'speedy' Blier tant réalisateur nous offre dans ce 'Huit et demi' à la sauce très piquante, une leçon de vitalité cinématographique'. ['There is lots to forgive 'speedy' Blier, for as a director he is giving us an 'Eight and a half' with a very spicy sauce, a lesson in cinematic vitality'].[43] Blier underlined the point too by declaring his pride in being a French filmmaker when he presented his work to journalists in Paris. On the release of his film, he suggested to them that it was only in France that a film like *Merci la vie* could be made.[44]

In *Grosse fatigue* (scripted by Blier and directed by actor Michel Blanc) Michel Blanc plays himself, and a lookalike character who steals his identity. Eventually the fake Blanc becomes the real one and the real one is relegated to unemployment. The thesis behind the film is that through stardom actors lose their identities, quite literally. At the end of the movie Blanc implies that many other French stars have been replaced by their doubles. Because of the triviality of the star system French cinema is now a world of fakes. Nonetheless, there is also a patriotic and anti-American subtext to this self-critique. The film concludes with a conversation between the real actors Blanc and Philippe Noiret. Chatting with each other they bemoan the negative influence of Hollywood on their industry. Standing over the tomb of the unknown soldier at the Arc de Triomphe, Noiret laments that Hollywood has beaten France: 'Le voilà, il est là-dessous! … Maintenant, c'est le soldat inconnu, le cinéma français … Au mort' ['There, cinema is under there … Now, French cinema, it's the unknown soldier…Dead']. As they walk down the Champs-Elysées, Blanc and Noiret are discovered by Roman Polanski, who offers them new work. Despite everything, it is concluded that French cinema is alive and well, being made by Polanski, controversially living in exile from Hollywood.

Blanc confirmed his nationalist, euphemistically anti-American, beliefs when he promoted his film. For example, he asserted to readers of *Télérama*:

Hollywood, actuellement, ressemble à cette nourriture de grand hôtel qui, à force de ne vouloir déplaire à personne, n'a plus aucun goût. C'est ni mauvais ni bon. Ça ne rend pas malade, c'est tout ce qu'on peut dire. Eh bien, je préfère risquer une chiasse et manger un bon poulet au curry, voilà! On dit toujours du cinéma français qu'il est franchouillard. Et le cinéma américain est-ce qu'il n'est pas américanouillard, peut-être? Avec ses clichés et ses tics.[45]

[Currently Hollywood is like food from a big hotel, which without wanting to upset anybody, has no taste. It's neither good nor bad. It doesn't make you ill, that's all you can say. Well, I prefer to risk the runs and eat a good chicken curry, so there! People always say that French cinema is narrow-mindedly French. And American cinema, isn't that maybe typically American? With its clichés and its mannerisms.]

When Blanc's film was reviewed in the U.S.A., Georgia Brown repaid the compliment with the barbed comment in *Village Voice*, 'the Americans are the rapacious usurpers, the uncouth pretenders … the small hitch here is that there's been no French cinema to usurp for 20 years'.[46]

In the further meta-film made shortly after our main period of interest, *Les Acteurs*, Blier brings together all of the main male film stars working in France in the contemporary period to offer another work on the perils of stardom. With limited plotting, they do turns to camera that reflect aspects of their lives and their star image. Superficially resembling both *Les Enfants de Lumière* and

Les Cent et une nuits, it is a series of star performances to celebrate the industry. Speaking about his work, Blier underlined that he had wanted to promote domestic cinema:

> *A certains égards,* les Acteurs *est un film de patrimoine. Je crois que je le dois à Alain Resnais et à* On connait la chanson. ... *On a ce problème d'identité dans le cinéma français: est-ce que ça existe encore, est-ce que ça vaut la peine? La réponse est oui, mais il faut être très hexagonal et rester auteur, c'est ça le secret. Ou alors faire du cinéma d'attraction, façon* Titanic.[47]

> *[In some respects,* Les Acteurs *is a heritage film. I think I owe a lot to Alain Resnais and* On connait la chanson ... *we have this problem of identity in French cinema: will it still exist, is that worth the trouble? The answer is yes, but one must be very French and stay an auteur, that's the secret. Otherwise make spectacular work,* Titanic *style.]*

Les Acteurs is a highly nostalgic tribute to the male stars who feature in it. It is a clever recital of famous faces and evocations of previous works from national film history. For example, the sequence that features Jean-Paul Belmondo is telling: therein Blier repeats the famous death scene that he had originally shot for Godard in *À bout de souffle*. The ghosts of Jean Gabin and Lino Ventura are also invoked, and Blier recalls memories of his father, Bernard Blier. Still, the stars seem a little wooden and the material becomes repetitive. Critics identified that it was more troubling and provocative than it first seemed. Michel Boujut explained to readers of *Charlie Hebdo* what he thought Blier was trying to say.[48] Boujut realised that it was not a superficial commemoration of cinema: it was a work of brutal self-criticism. Boujut noted that when Blier made his actors do their star turns to camera there was an absurdist subtext. The stars lost all individuality and were reduced to their simplistic public image. Through the cinema they had lost their own personalities, selling themselves for art and fame. As well as offering nostalgia, Blier was therefore describing the shallowness of stardom, as he had already suggested in his script for *Grosse fatigue*.

Conclusion

It seems to me that a very important part of the film–nationalism encounter is where films about cinema assert the greatness of the French industry. They suggest that France is the home of cinema and that the nation can be proud of the achievements of its directors, technicians and actors. This is not a blunt propaganda machine. Instead, as in the classic *La Nuit américaine*, the technique adopted is often a highly sophisticated form of implied political communication and achievement of a duality of voice, balancing note of the greatness of all cinema, including Hollywood, with support for domestic production. To repeat, in these works praise for France is interwoven with acknowledgement of Hollywood, Italian or Japanese cinema.

In and around the one hundredth anniversary of cinema, the deliberately provocative cineastes, Godard and Blier, made sarcastic films about cinema and the treatment of stars yet in so doing they also asserted the grandeur of French filmmaking. It was the cleverness of their meta-films that signalled the vibrancy of French art. Though both men were critical about the industry in which they were situated, their very wry commentaries on film heritage added to the audiences' sense that France was a leading cultural force.

All these meta-films, ironic, maverick or otherwise, perpetuate a form of what political scientist Michael Billig describes as banal nationalism.[49] It is not militaristic, nor is it an aggressive pursuit of a polished political argument. However, the works reviewed often advanced the longstanding stereotype that France is a uniquely qualified society to achieve greatness in the arts. This trend developed originally when the nation's sources of hard power went into decline. The mode is plainly inward looking and self-regarding. For example, in a work such as *Merci la vie*, Blier drew on other meta-films, Truffaut's *La Nuit américaine*, as well as his own earlier career, citing *Les Valseuses* (1974) and *Notre histoire* (1984). This kind of self-obsession is quite normal amid the wider body of films about films. Besides the examples noted herein (Truffaut on Truffaut, Varda on Varda, Blier on Blier), one quickly thinks of Jean-Pierre Mocky's *Mocky Story* (1994) an anthology of clips from the comedy director's thirty-five year career. Not to mention, from more recent times beyond the scope of this book, the documentary *Retour en Normandie* (2007) in which Nicolas Philibert revelled in his recollections of working on *Moi, Pierre Rivière* (Allio, 1974), the far better, unsentimental, earlier film.

It is also worth highlighting that the standard political divisions and debates on French national identity disappear from view in most of these selected works. In the fantasies of filmmaking by Truffaut and Varda, France is reimagined as an apolitical place where there is seemingly consensus about everything, not least the idea of France itself, which is viewed as simply a great place for cinema. Racism, colonialism, anti-Semitism, multicultural society, immigration, themes treated elsewhere in the later chapters of this book, are entirely missing from the superficially impartial world of the films about cinema, circa 1973 or 1995.

Incidentally, one can underline that the idea of the 'film event' has been expanded on through the discussions developed in this chapter. We can see now that these reception events are far more than a simplistic promotional device in any conventional sense. Press reports of festivals and films, government-funded commemorations, each function to give audiences fully formed modes for understanding and valuing film. Mediation of films through reportage creates in the public mind their status as national products, sometimes competing with other countries for recognition. The material herein debated also indicates variations of scale and temporality. Film events in this period range in form from single newspaper reviews to huge investments in individual films and heritage sites, conferences, museum exhibitions, quasi-organized intellectual discussions, and so on. Obviously 1995 was a unique anniversary but as noted above individual directors such as Renoir, Pagnol and Tati were also being feted as sites of cultural value in comparable ways. In other words, by the early 1990s film heritage was a growing field and it can be seen as a maximal offshoot of the more everyday press discussion of significance and value of an individual work. Film events though recurrent are also clearly time limited and hence sometimes overlooked by academic historians and film specialists. They coincide with direct responses and discourses around the release of significant works, or festivals or major anniversaries and commemorations. They therefore superficially look singular, one-offs. As such for this postwar period, film events do appear more structured, regulated and static than what was to follow when film reception entered the digital period of fan sites, endless DVD extras or an extended multiplatform visual culture. Nevertheless, if the buzz (or debate) became extended or prolonged, then the event could quite easily stretch beyond the release schedule of a given film; moreover, journalists repeat their biases in series of reviews. As one will also discover in the next chapter, despite their apparently controlled singularity, film events are both repetitious and quite anarchic in that political contestations around the meaning of works can move in quite unpredictable directions, very different than intended by filmmakers and their sponsors, private or state.

Notes

1. See F. Truffaut, 2000, 'Avant propos', *La Nuit américaine, scénario, suivi de journal de tournage de Fahrenheit 451*, Paris: Cahiers du Cinéma, 6 [first published, Seghers, 1974].
2. J. Monaco, 1976, *The New Wave*, New York: Oxford University Press, 89.
3. R. Crittenden, 1998, *La Nuit américaine*, London: BFI, 36.
4. A. de Baecque and S. Toubiana, 2001, *François Truffaut*, Paris: Gallimard, 583.
5. J. Renoir, 1994, *Letters*, London: Faber, 517, 521.
6. M. Betz, 2001, 'The Name above the (Sub)Title: Internationalism, Coproduction, and Polyglot European Art Cinema', *Camera Obscura* XVI/1, 3.
7. de Baecque and Toubiana, *François Truffaut*, 612.
8. de Baecque and Toubiana, *François Truffaut*, 613.
9. R. Chazal, 1974, 'Éditorial', *Le Film français*, 5 April, 1.
10. Truffaut, 'Avant propos', *La Nuit américaine*, 8.
11. Truffaut and D. Maillet, 1973, 'Entretiens', *Cinématographe* 3 (1973), 14–18; A. Insdorf, 1994, *François Truffaut*, Cambridge: CUP, 192.
12. *Damage* is an adaptation of the novel of the same title by Josephine Hart.
13. M. Harris, 2008, *Pictures at a Revolution: Five Movies and the Birth of the New Hollywood*, London: Penguin, 94–95.
14. Frodon, *L'Âge moderne*, 391.
15. Insdorf, *Truffaut*, 94–100, 190.
16. P. Kennedy, 1988, *The Rise and Fall of the Great Powers*, London: Fontana, 624–31.
17. H. Stuart Hughes. 1968. *The Obstructed Path: French Social Thought in the Years of Desperation, 1930–1960*, New York: Harper, 3.
18. Frodon, *L'Âge moderne*, 391.
19. A-E. Dutheil de la Rochère, 1998. *Les Studios de la Victorine, 1919–1929*, Nice: AFRHC, 9.
20. Insdorf, *Truffaut*, 100. Truffaut was aware of the fantasy element to his film and by implication this was toned down when the script was published alongside the shooting diary of *Fahrenheit 451* that records the jarring reality of filming that work.
21. J-P. Manchette, 2008, *Journal, 1966–1974*, Paris: Gallimard, 557–59.
22. F. Truffaut, 1989, *Letters*, London: Faber, 384.
23. For a further analysis of *Le Mépris* see chapter 4 herein.

24. R. Vadim, 1986, *Bardot, Deneuve, Fonda: The Memoirs of Roger Vadim*, London: New English Library, 324–25.
25. H. Rabine, 1973, 'Cannes: Bravo Truffaut', *La Croix*, 16 May. Page numbers for some periodicals are unavailable as they are either cut from microfiche or removed from digital copy at BFI and BIFI, respectively.
26. 'Coups de Cannes', 1973, *Le Canard enchaîné*, 6 June.
27. Crittenden, *La Nuit américaine*, 31.
28. The Centre Pompidou hosted a collection on cinema from the Pathé studios. The Musée du Cinéma Henri Langlois worked with Gaumont on a similar project. The Carnavelet hosted a celebration of the cinema houses of the capital. The Bibliothèque Nationale exhibited film materials from the 1920s and 1930s.
29. S. Dacbert, 1995, 'Le cinéma fête un passé plein d'avenir', *Le Film français* 2550, 17 March, 23–24; J. Breschand, 1995, 'Lyon fête ses Lumières', *Cahiers du cinéma* 49, 18–19.
30. The author attended and just about recalls that the atmosphere was festive and reverential. The Grand Écran has since closed down and been converted into a shopping mall.
31. M-C. Arbaude, 1995, 'Claude Lelouch, entretien', *Le Film français* 2550, 20–21.
32. See F. Stoner Saunders, 1995, 'Modern Art Was CIA Weapon', *The Independent*, 22/10. See online: http://www.independent.co.uk/news/world/modern-art-was-cia-weapon-1578808.html (last accessed October 2013); F. Stoner Saunders, 2000, *Who Paid the Piper? The CIA and the Cultural Cold War*, London: Granta.
33. Harrison Ford knew Jacques Demy, Varda's husband, when he had worked in Hollywood.
34. D. Bellos, 2001, *Jacques Tati: His Life and Art*, London: Vintage. See also chapter 4 herein.
35. The other significant contemporary film is *The Player* (Altman, 1992).
36. J. Fenby, 2002, *On the Brink: The Trouble with France*, London: Little Brown, 27.
37. A. de Baecque, 2002, *La Cinéphilie*, Paris: Fayard; J. Baetens, 2013, 'Writing the "Making of", a New Literary Genre?' research paper presented L'Aquila, 17/11, forthcoming.
38. A. de Baecque, 2010, *Godard, biographie*, Paris: Gallimard, 735.
39. de Baecque, *Godard*, 737.
40. See M. Witt, 2000, '"Qu'était-ce que le cinéma, Jean-Luc Godard?" An Analysis of the Cinema(s) at Work in and around Godard's *Histoire(s) du cinéma*', in E. Ezra and S. Harris (eds) *France in Focus: Film and National Identity*, Oxford: Berg, 23–41.
41. B. Blier, 1991, 'Merci qui?', *7 à Paris*, 13 March.
42. B. Blier, 1991, 'Entretien avec Danièle Heymann', *Le Monde*, 14 March.
43. G. Anquetil, 1991, 'Attention, ceci est un hold-up!' *Le Nouvel observateur*, 14 March.
44. Blier, 'Entretien'.
45. M. Blanc and P. Murat, 1994. 'Plus Blanc que Blanc', *Télérama*, 28 May.
46. G. Brown, 1995, 'Film', *Village Voice*, 18 July.

47. O. Séguret, 2000, 'Bertrand Blier autour de son 13ᵉ film', *Libération*, 5 April.
48. M. Boujut, 2000, 'Ils font acteurs chez Blier', *Charlie Hebdo*, 5 April.
49. M. Billig, 1995, *Banal Nationalism*, London: Sage.

CHAPTER TWO

The Search for National Unity through History

For the past twenty-five years the question of how modern France understands its own past has received extensive and sustained attention from political and cultural historians. Scholars interested in themes of collective memory, representation and politics have addressed this subject in groundbreaking works including publications that focus on the role of history films. One thinks immediately of Henry Rousso's *Le Syndrome de Vichy*, Sylvie Lindeperg's *Les Écrans de l'ombre* or Shlomo Sand's *Le XXᵉ siècle à l'écran*.[1] This chapter returns to the fascinating question of how works of cinema project selected slices of positively read national history to relay to audiences a sense of pride and shared respect for the past. Its intended contribution to the scholarly discussion is essentially threefold. (1) It details and describes how cinema and film events worked consistently until the early 1970s to assert national pride through images of the wartime resistance. This mythmaking is important for our subject, and its scope and shape merit a new analysis herein – analysis concluding on Jean-Pierre Melville's *L'Armée des ombres* (1969). (2) As this is a complex area, it is necessary to introduce and be open about contradiction, and so the chapter also underlines where resistance filmmaking sparked division among journalists and audiences and how cinema perpetuated more cynical views of the occupation (already an influential strand of works by the mid 1950s). (3) It focuses in, for comparison, on the politics of representation of the Revolution in the 1980s, from *Danton* to the fears and anxieties this work prompted in the run-up to the bicentenary (1989). What is proposed therefore is an argumentation that discusses how historical film was a force for patriotic unity, at least circa 1945 to 1970; but readers will also learn how making patriotic historical works was a tense and contested process, dare one say even divisive.

From Myth to Fracture: Projecting a Nation of Resisters (1945–1969)

René Clément's *La Bataille du rail* (1946) is the first major work of cinema to commemorate the resistance and as such is the appropriate starting point for our discussion. In it, Clément implies that French people came together to fight for a better world than that offered by living in a subjugated state inside Nazi-controlled Europe. His heroes of the resistance are presented as young, virile and dynamic men (only one woman is briefly glimpsed working with a guerrilla band). They are mainly industrial railway workers, although white-collar engineers who run the company are also in support of the cause. Importantly the resistance is shown achieving great success. The inference suggested throughout is that France fought with the allies to defeat Germany. In the political imagination of this film the people had been solidly behind the resistance, not Pétain's Vichy regime (1940 to 1944).

Publicity for the film was enormous and is illustrative of how a film's release can take on a powerful social role through its marketing and distribution. Thus, it was premiered on 11 January 1946 at the theatre of the Palais Chaillot in Paris, 'sous la présidence' of the President of the Republic, General de Gaulle, and with a member of his Provisional Government, Jules Moch, in attendance.[2] Across France, decorations announcing the work were to be seen in shop windows and cinemas themselves prepared their frontages with advertising material to mark the release. Marketing emphasized the originality of Clément's documentary-style aesthetics and the heroism of the resistance fighters he depicted. It was one of the highest-grossing works of 1946 and in the railway towns of Nancy and Limoges it did especially well. A journalist covering Toulouse explained that it had been years since anyone had witnessed such enthusiasm for a film.[3] Furthermore, *La Bataille du rail* was selected as one of six official French entries to the first ever Cannes Film Festival (1946). At the end of the competition, it was crowned with the Prix Spécial du Jury and Clément was awarded the Grand Prix International de la Mise en Scène. To mark Clément's victory, the film magazine *L'Écran français* devoted its cover to a still from the film showing a railway resistance fighter.[4] After all, the film had triumphed over important works from the other national delegations and the Cannes jury had preferred it to Roberto Rossellini's *Rome, Open City*.

Like *Les Enfants du paradis*, which had been released a year before, *La Bataille du rail* was presented in the press as demonstration of a renewal of

THE SEARCH FOR NATIONAL UNITY THROUGH HISTORY · 45

national confidence, a marker that French cinema could achieve greatness and be influential around the world. Praise was heaped on it in the press, including in the periodicals read by intellectuals and those who aspired to such a role. Writing for *Esprit*, André Bazin compared it favourably with Sergei Eisenstein's *Ivan the Terrible* (1944). In 1953, the historian and lecturer at the national film school, Institut des Hautes Études Cinématographiques (henceforth IDHEC), Georges Sadoul reflected: 'It really reached epic proportions in several of its episodes ... The film equals in value the Swiss *The Last Chance* or Roberto Rossellini's famous *Rome, Open City*, although it is somewhat less in quality than the latter's *Paisa*.'[5] Moreover, the film was also the source for a novelization written by Clément and his scriptwriter Colette Audry, which no doubt prolonged its influence on the wider reading public. Published in 1949, it recounted the story found in the original film in a literary style close to neorealism: it is a text written as a 'roman documentaire', using the past tense and third-person narration. As Jean-Marie Clerc has underlined, this novelization foregrounds the historical narrative implied in *La Bataille* and does not draw explicit attention to the filmmaking itself.[6]

The high point for resistance mythmaking through cinema followed closely after the promotion of *La Bataille du rail*. Throughout the late 1940s and early 1950s, cinema contributed greatly to retrospectively finding national honour in the war years.[7] For example, *Jéricho* (Henri Calef, 1946) narrated the war experience in Amiens and critics presented it as an admirable work. Similarly, *La Révue du cinéma*, forerunner to *Cahiers du cinéma*, recommended Jean Grémillon's *Le 6 juin à l'aube* (1945); like *La Bataille du rail*, it experimented with neorealism. Further glorifications followed, notably, the Jean-Pierre Melville adaptation of Vercors's resistance novel, *Le Silence de la mer* (1948) and Robert Bresson's *Un condamné à mort s'est échappé* (1955). Clément contributed again on the subject of the war with *Les Maudits* (1946) and *Jeux interdits* (1951). Further interest in the resistance was revived when de Gaulle returned to the presidency (1958 to 1969) and in particular it was with the twenty-fifth anniversary of the outbreak of war in Europe, and by 1966, that a spate of new works was released. For instance, Chabrol's *La Ligne de démarcation* (1966) and Astruc's *La Longue marche* (1966) were both completed that year, as was René Clément's new international coproduction, *Paris brûle-t-il?* Therein he employed an array of international film stars to tell the heroic story of the liberation of Paris. His impressive cast included: Alain Delon, Jean-Paul

Belmondo, Simone Signoret, Leslie Caron, Jean-Louis Trintignant, Yves Montand and Anthony Perkins, playing a GI, not a psycho. Paris welcomed the completion of this work with a spectacular premiere gala. There were fireworks at significant locations around the city, and despite the rain which apparently did dampen spirits a little, Yves Montand was scheduled to croon the 'Chants des Partisans', perched high up on the first floor of the Eiffel tower.[8]

Grosso modo, these films and their well-organized reception events, which were staged for their promotion to the public, invited the French to honour those men who had made the ultimate sacrifice. In addition they encouraged the retrospective belief that everyone had fought off the occupying German powers and that this had been a mostly unified society working together and where class differences did not matter and even narrowed. The films emphasize that, although material losses were terrible, the nation had retained a sense of independence and a military force. They implied that France had always supported the Allied struggle for freedom from fascism. In particular, French people were highlighted for having acted bravely and having made sacrifices that contributed to victory. In that sense, the works used history to offer repeatedly reassuring images of a victorious masculinity. Clearly, the films compensated hugely for the military collapse of 1940 by showing dramatic feats of arms. Resistance heroics offered some reassurance too for any future conflicts that might arise in the Cold War. Future wars were not to be feared since the military record, as imagined in resistance cinema, was favourable. This perception also helped gloss over the defeats in the wars of decolonization, which were occurring almost exactly when these military glorifications were being released in cinemas. Indeed, some prominent advocates for defence of French power overseas often linked their own role in the resistance to their new struggles for defence of Empire. Initially de Gaulle's own return to office in 1958 was in part based on this general understanding. Georges Bidault, present at de Gaulle's side during the liberation of Paris, and who then became a supporter of Algérie Française, wrote his memoirs and titled them *D'une résistance à l'autre* (1965).

Through much of the cinema of this type there are repeated political myths that imply that most people from different political and social backgrounds were ultimately drawn together to combat Nazism. For example, Claude Chabrol made much of this aspect in *La Ligne de démarcation*. Here the resistance is slowly gathered together, composed of people from all manner of walks of life. At the end of the movie, the Pétainist aristocrat (played by Maurice Ronet, an actor whose offscreen politics were right-wing anarchist), kills two Gestapo agents, and the good French gather together to defiantly sing a rendition of 'La Marseillaise'. Speaking comparatively, *Paris brûle-t-il?* was a more nuanced work because it acknowledged that there were tensions between the different factions in the resistance. This matter of historical fact could not be hidden – after all the film was an adaptation of an internationally recognized history book.[9] Nonetheless, it is the transition from internal disputes inside the resistance to a collective position of unity on how to liberate the capital that is emphasized throughout the film's plot. Over two and half hours of film, the different parties in the Parisian underground slowly resolve their differences to then free the city. One telling scene is when a resistance leader confronts his opposite number in the German military. Here the German baits him by asking which group in the resistance he represents. The Frenchman replies that for him there is no difference between communist and non-communist resisters, a statement that exemplifies how these films wanted to use history to by implication unify present-day France, itself fraught with Cold War tensions between communist and anticommunist political parties.

Histories that sat uncomfortably with the ideas of victory and unity were overlooked in this form of cinematic mythmaking. The fact that very few people really heard de Gaulle's first call to resistance on 18 June 1940 is studiously avoided. The communist party's neutrality, because of the Molotov–Ribbentrop Pact (1939 to 1941), is also very conveniently forgotten and the role of women in the resistance is not focused on in any meaningful way. Intricacies of Vichy policy disappear and often the regime might as well never have existed from what one witnesses onscreen. Similarly, the films cemented over the colonial dimension to the Second World War. For example, no one reimagined in film the Pétainist regime that Admiral Decoux ruled over in Indochina (1940 to 1944), even though his published memoirs were serialized daily in *Le Monde* and were for a period a relatively prominent work.[10] The role of colonial troops did not figure in mainstream resistance cinema of this period, although as Karen Adler highlights in her perceptive analysis of the detailed historical backdrop to the recent film *Indigènes* (2006, Bourchareb), their contribution was not absent from the military's own printed publications of the early postwar years.[11] The fact that Algiers was for a short period the de facto political capital of Free France is nearly entirely forgotten, let alone inclusion of an event like the Sétif massacre (1944) where the French forces violently suppressed Algerian independence protests. It is true however that *Paris brûle-t-il?* did include a shot of black resistance fighters, but they are only onscreen for a couple of seconds and they do not have a single line to deliver. Regional variations in experiencing the war are similarly partly repressed in cinema (for example, one learns nothing of the repeated Allied carpet-bombing of Lorient, home of an impregnable German submarine base). Nor, for that matter is any information gleaned about the forced conscription of Alsatian men into the Wehrmacht. That many in the resistance were not French but foreign refugees from Nazism or the Spanish Civil War is also negated: eventually they are represented in Guédiguian's *L'Armée du crime* (2009). Extreme images of death and violence were also very limited and, when compared to Rossellini's *Rome, Open City*, there were few grotesque scenes of torture.

Following Rousso, Lindeperg and others, one can conclude that Vichy's complicity in the Holocaust is treated most obliquely. Cinema through the 1950s and 1960s focused on resistance martyrs and was not concerned with the history of the Holocaust or many specificities about who was selected for extermination and why.[12] The first documentary made on the Holocaust in France, Alain Resnais's *Nuit et brouillard*, was censored to remove reference to French concentration camps. At the 1956 Cannes Festival it was shown only outside of the main competition, which was a diplomatic decision taken to not insult the West German delegation. At the same festival other works, including war films likely to cause tensions between delegations (such as *A Town Like Alice*) were also sidelined, though this did not stop a series of walkouts and protests.[13] It should be added that very few nations wanted to make cinematic comment on the Holocaust in this period. A problematic film like *Nuit et brouillard* was nevertheless in advance of works from elsewhere (including Britain; the USA; and Germany and Israel).

It is likely that director Clément's curriculum vitae was considerably tidied up for the release of *La Bataille du rail*. In 1943, when contributing to the Artistic and Technical Centre for Young Film Makers ('Centre de jeunes') in Nice, Clément directed a seemingly Vichyite propaganda short, *Chefs de demain* (1943). That film portrays the recruits, their dedication to improve themselves and their assistance in agricultural work. It depicts the oath of loyalty sworn by the students: a trainer asks, 'Etes-vous prêts à vous mettre au service de la jeunesse?' ['Are you ready to give yourself in the service of youth?'] The class reply 'Oui!' Historian of documentary film Steve Wharton summarizes: 'From its very beginning, this film puts in place the Vichy tenets of teamwork, discipline and service to the nation ... The system of the new order must be staffed by those knowing the true way, which is why schools such as those filmed here were created.'[14] More recently than Wharton's research, Olivier Curchod writes in *Postif* that a similar work from Clément, which he dates as from 1942, was only superficially propagandistic and was instead founded on deconstructive 'ironie sur corde raide'[irony on a tightrope or on a knife-edge]. Similarly, Alain Weber has noted that some resistance filming took place under the auspices of the Young Filmmakers Centre, not least pointing to chief operator, Henri Alekan, filming espionage material while working on the Clément piece, *Ceux du rail* (1943).[15] In any case, Clément's Vichy-era work avoided discussion in 1946 maybe because it was relatively common and understood that people switched allegiances and that the immediate past was best not too closely scrutinized. Other filmmakers' careers under Vichy were glossed over in a similar mode, quite different from the world of literature where authors who had collaborated were named and shamed in public blacklists. For instance, Louis Daquin directed the Pétainist mountaineering film, *Premier de cordée* (1943) but by 1944 he was the communist Secretary General on the Comité de Libération du Cinéma. He claimed that the making of the mountain film for Vichy had concealed his resistance work, a position that the historian Evelyn Ehrlich doubts holds up very well.[16] Similarly, Marcel Carné's *Les Enfants du paradis* had begun production under Nazi occupation only to be released after the liberation with the extreme right-wing sympathizer, actor Robert Le Vigan, leaving the production. In 1945 Marcel Pagnol rereleased *La Fille du puisatier* (1941) in which a radio broadcast from de Gaulle now replaced the original soundtrack, which had featured Pétain. And, one should not be naïve enough to think this was an especially French experience – again some international comparison sheds a side light on the above process of postwar professional integration. Thus, one can briefly underline that comparable issues marked the apprenticeships of the Italian directors Roberto Rossellini and Michelangelo Antonioni, both of who, before making careers as international artists in the postwar era, had worked under Italian fascism.

It is also worth underlining in these discussions of absences that resistance cinema was reticent in portraying de Gaulle. The only fictional film to treat the subject was a planned Hollywood propaganda film from 1942 written by

William Faulkner. His *De Gaulle Story* remained on the drawing board because Free French representatives in the USA were unhappy with its portrayal and studios preferred to make a pro-Soviet film instead.[17] However, Jean Gabin did play the title role in Henri Verneuil's political intrigue *Le Président*, dating from 1961, so made just shortly after the General's return to high office in 1958. In a script by Michel Audiard the inspirations are evidently a mix, including Clemenceau, Briand and Herriot, and de Gaulle. Nonetheless, Verneuil used location footage of de Gaulle's own countryside retreat, La Boisserie, in the village Colombey-les-Deux-Églises. Furthermore, the idea that Audiard employed in his script of a retired politician operating in the wings of mainstream politics corresponded with de Gaulle's recent career when he had played precisely that role (1953 to 1958). De Gaulle's image from newsreels of the liberation of Paris and other news broadcasts was therefore dominant, and it seems that directors did not want to appear stupid by making a fictional representation that failed to live up to the existing iconography. After de Gaulle's return to power in 1958 they were also probably discouraged by a fear of state censorship. A common approach was therefore to reuse original historical footage – this was the technique Clément deployed for *Paris brûle-t-il?* However, one alternative was to find non-French footage that was less censored than would be available at home. When Audiard turned to make his far more critical, quasi-racist, and anti-Gaullist satire, *Vive la France* (1973), he is said to have used the archives of the BBC to circumvent the domestic political controls.

With so much of history left out, it is maybe unsurprising that the best way to achieve a popular national vision was to remove all serious content in favour of a resistance imagined through the genre of light comedy. Comedy film provided the most adroit path to apoliticism, as well as box-office success. Let us recall that *La Grande vadrouille* (Oury, 1966), starring Louis de Funès and André Bourvil, portrays how two ordinary Frenchmen assist a downed British airman (Terry Thomas). The film rides on having great fun with national stereotypes: the Germans are laughed at for their orderly behaviour and general nastiness, British airmen are all clichés too and the two French, one more upper class than the other, represent social stereotypes that are made amusing. Nothing is too serious, nor is anything political explicitly referred to. The two Frenchmen eventually end up working together and they are on the side of the resistance, if not members in an organized underground movement.[18]

Thereby Oury's work gave audiences a less serious view of recent history than that offered by Clément, Melville, Bresson or Chabrol, but it was one everyone could feel empathy towards because this was a resistance where anyone and everyone had been a hero.

Oury provided a past with which audiences could identify because nothing really painful ever happened. In his work there is only a nice, funny, society that had repelled Nazism. History was therefore exclusively an entertainment and no one in France was compromised: 17.2 million people enjoyed the film, making it the highest-grossing work of its day and for many years to come.[19] However, for all its simplicity and seeming apoliticism, it did retain the theme of unity between the classes through its stereotypical lead male protagonists. This, then, was an ideological feature that ran through much resistance cinema and which projected a sense of corporate unity as opposed to political tension. Clearly this approach patched over the sense of political division experienced in the 1930s and 1940s (as well as in the present), and it also provided a convenient and applicable myth that corresponded directly to modern France's own perceived narrowing of class divisions, or at least improving working-class and lower-middle-class status during the *trente glorieuses*. None of these films were about economics but they offered a nationalist myth that argued for male lower-, middle-, and upper-class harmony and (importantly) collaboration through endeavour. As we have seen, this was a narrow kind of unity that did not invite many others into its storyline, and that is also probably why ultimately these films went into some decline: they did not speak to enough groups and did not have an open enough treatment of history, for fear the realities would complicate the myth. It is also the case that the teaming up of leftish and rightish characters, workers and middle class, for the male heroes, meant that these films would gain support from Gaullist and communist audiences and critics, since both sides were configured equally together and not in conflict. These were images that therefore glossed over the postwar reality where each side was often labelling the other as being a fascist or a totalitarian group. In that sense unity in depictions of the past was deeply reassuring for the Cold War present, where real divisions and fantasies of division, existed; as de Gaulle himself polemically warned: Moscow was only two stages of the Tour de France from Strasbourg.

Be that as it may, Oury's success inspired numerous other wartime-set comedies, which were produced long into the 1980s. Over the years their content became more and more absurd and, as each new work sought to outdo its predecessor, all the more extreme. For instance, *L'As des as* (Oury again, 1982), starring Jean-Paul Belmondo, mixed light-hearted antifascist heroism with a plot about rescuing a German Jewish family. Therein history becomes complete farce: it concludes with the resister and the Jewish refugees accidentally visiting Hitler's Berchtesgaden retreat, where lederhosen and cuckoo clocks abound. It closely resembles aspects of the material discussed later in this book where our attention is placed on trivializations of the Holocaust as an anti-Semitic trope (see chapter 6).

The liberalization of society in the late 1960s, the decline of de Gaulle's popularity, and no doubt part of the younger generation's scepticism about exuberant nationalism, meant resistance epics went slowly out of fashion, though as one can see comedy remained viable. The famous work from the later 1960s, Jean-Pierre Melville's *L'Armée des ombres*, adapted from the reportage by Joseph Kessel, provided a final solemn image of history that clearly responded critically to the frivolity of the *La Grande vadrouille* mode and aimed to achieve a distinct discourse on the past. As readers will recall, Melville's film narrates the experiences of a small group of resistance fighters, who find that their network has been betrayed to the Gestapo by one of their own number. On discovering the traitor they capture and execute him. Similarly, the film concludes when the resistance fighters decide they must kill a brave colleague, female resistance fighter Mathilde (Simone Signoret), because she is feared to be a liability. The film's denouement shows how the leader of the resistance (Lino Ventura) must assassinate her, a friend whose heroism has been second to none.

What is important about this film is that it achieves a patriotic tribute to the resistance but avoids the clichés of the genre. It certainly does offer a nationalistic myth because it is this kind of historical episode that it focuses on, and the characters are again strongly imagined as national heroes. However, this is so carefully rendered, with an awareness of where earlier films had exaggerated or been too simplistic in representing history, that it stands out today as being exceptionally sophisticated. It is for this reason that it is useful to focus on further for a final case study.

For Melville the standard simplistic moral judgements about the heroism of the French and the evil of the Germans are removed because repeatedly the resisters are represented eliminating traitors within their own ranks. This narrative emphasis revises the two principal ideological subtexts of the tradition: that the resistance was united and that despite losses there would be a victorious male hero, more or less untarnished. This however is not its only revisionist aspect. For example, it also gives far greater acknowledgement to the heroism of women and offers a far more convincingly balanced narrative by this measure alone. Furthermore, Melville even includes images of French police controlling a concentration camp and thereby opens up the question of the scale of state collaboration with Nazism. In fact, Melville includes scenes that restores to view almost the precise picture of a French policeman at a concentration camp gatehouse that the state censors had concealed in Resnais's *Nuit et brouillard*.

Melville's film critiques its own genre's by then long-established conventions, yet at the same time it achieves a work in which the resistance is remembered with distinction, through an aesthetic that blends realism with the menace of film noir. There is a coldness and solemnity to the work that makes one think of Bresson's oeuvre. Nevertheless, because of the above radical shifts in content and tone, it is a genuinely original work. It is also a difficult work to analyse in light of our main theme as it is ambiguous and highly nuanced in texture. Because of the content I have summarized quickly above, it is difficult to label the work 'nationalistic' in any conventional sense for it reveals the horrors of war, a divided people, and a part of the country working in collaboration with Nazism. The resisters are convincingly portrayed and are driven by fear and riven with self-defeating intrigues. It is therefore on the grounds of the competence and seeming accuracy of the historical representation that one gains admiration for the resistance and not because of any run-of-the-mill glorification. This is the cleverness of Melville's work: its deep patriotism is achieved because the resistance struggle is presented in a harsher and more complex light than in many other examples. The heroes are genuine because they are alone, terrified and fearful of one another. When searching for a convincing intertext one returns to Bresson because his earlier work, *Un condamné à mort*, points in this direction through its aesthetics, if not its plot.

Although *L'Armée des ombres* is often regarded as a failure because *Cahiers du cinéma* was critical, this negative attitude was far from unanimous. Several contemporary reviewers astutely underlined how Melville was changing the genre in this work and saw the film in a similar way to that described above.

Thus, a critic at *Journal du dimanche* informed that the film challenged 'poncifs du genre' ['clichés of the genre']. Robert Chazal explained that Melville was breaking with convention because there was none of the lightness one might associate with other action films. Albert Cervoni sensed the revolutionary tone as well. He highlighted that *L'Armée des ombres* destroyed old moral certainties and underlined how it included references to collaboration, the concentration camp holding communists, Christians, Jews, resistance fighters and veterans of the Spanish Civil War, and how these prisoners were held captive by 'des gendarmes français'. Cervoni concluded, 'Les équivoques et les pénibles réalites d'une époque sont donc rendues, retenues, rappelées'. ['The ambiguities and terrible realities of the time were therefore returned, kept in and recalled']. Writers on *Le Figaro* and *Carrefour* identified the same revisionism. Michel Duran, who in 1966 had been so critical of *Paris brûle-t-il?*, was delighted that cinema was finally getting closer to his preferred idea of history. He described it as the most truthful, the most beautiful and least complacent work on the subject.[20] Writing on *L'Armée des ombres* in 1975, the novelist Philippe Labro astutely identified it as one of the first of many works to offer more critical depictions of twentieth-century history. Labro believed the bleak image of the resistance had prepared the way for subsequent works that highlighted how ambiguous the war years had really been for France. Melville was anticipating Louis Malle's *Lacombe Lucien*, Costa-Gavras's *Section spéciale* (1975) and Michel Drach's *Les Violons du bal* (1974).[21]

Others writing about the film were repelled by Melville's revisionism, a feeling that also confirms his originality. *La France catholique* described the picture as 'sec et cruel' ['dry and cruel'] and claimed that it was inauthentic to the tradition of writing and filming about the resistance. Likewise, Marcel Martin of the communist *Les Lettres françaises* was disappointed. In his review he questioned whether the resistance had really only spent its time assassinating traitors and rescuing friends and he warned that the film was 'plat comme un roman feuillton' ['flat like a serialized novel'].[22] As noted, *Cahiers du cinéma* did not understand the originality of the portrayal of the resistance. They mocked Melville because of his fleeting, positive depiction of General de Gaulle. Jean-Louis Comolli sniped, 'le premier et le plus bel exemple cinématographique de l'Art gaulliste, fond et forme' ['the first and the best cinematographic example of Gaullist art, content and form'].[23] In hindsight the General's shadowy presence is only one small aspect of a far more important work that was able to commemorate the resistance without denying the horrible context that warranted its existence.

It is important to underscore that glorification of resistance was never hegemonic in the world of cinema and that the mixed reception of Melville's late work was not as unusual as one might think. Myths were made but they were also questioned and provoked counter-responses. Let us recall that, according to the historian Tony Judt, by 1948 to 1951, in the literary-political milieu the resistance's association with communism meant that its reputation was quite tarnished.[24] In the cinema the resistance theme also proved divisive, even when so ardently seeking unity. Thus, L'Écran français journalists welcomed La Bataille du rail and its success, but they also used its premiere gala evening to score points against the sitting provisional government. Reporting on the premiere at the Palais Chaillot, the critic complained that the film had not been given sufficient recognition by the government. De Gaulle had preferred to be on holiday on the Côte d'Azur, rather than at the important commemorative event. André Malraux, Minister of Information, was also absent and similarly chided.[25] Not all film critics were seduced by Clément's social-realist film on railway resistance. At L'Écran français, for example, the reviewer regretted the Manichean presentation of the work. Writing on it for La Révue du cinéma, Alain Spenlé highlighted that the material was exaggerated.[26] One can add here that the reception of Melville's Le Silence de la mer was also marred by some political controversy. Its director had alienated the film industry because he had worked on the picture without the trade unions. Ginette Vincendeau explains in her account of the director's life and work, Melville: An American in Paris, that the 'projection box had to be cordoned off to prevent the print being seized'.[27]

Another example is when Paris brûle-t-il? reached the cinemas and René Chateau interviewed its director Clément for the men's magazine Lui.[28] Therein Chateau asked Clément what he had done during the liberation of Paris and the director replied rather limply, 'J'ai regardé, voilà ce que j'ai fait' ['I watched, that's what I did']. Next Chateau suggested that Paris brûle-t-il? was an exercise in Gaullist and communist propaganda, stating: 'Gore Vidal scénariste du film, a déclaré avant le tournage: "Beaucoup d'éléments du livre, qui sont pourtant authentiques, ne peuvent être utilisés: si l'on offense De Gaulle nous n'aurons pas les rues, si l'on offense les communistes nous n'aurons pas les électriciens et le machinistes"' ['Gore Vidal the scriptwriter on the film has said that before shooting, "Lots of elements of the book, which were all authentic, could not be used: if one offended de Gaulle we would not have access to the streets, if we offended the communists then we would not have electricians or grips'"]. Clément retorted that Gore Vidal's views were wrong and that he did not understand what he had meant. Next Chateau probed Clément as to whether or not *Paris brûle-t-il?* was a copy of *The Longest Day?* The director was angered and snapped, 'Ce n'est plus une interview, c'est de la polémique' ['This is no longer an interview, it is a polemic']. Nevertheless, the conversation continued when Chateau followed up with the pointed question, 'During the war were you not tempted to film for Continental?' Clément admitted that he had been invited to work for the Nazi production group but that he had declined. In his rather elegant (and maybe cruel) manner, the interviewer systematically destroyed Clément's claim to have any authenticity behind representing the resistance and the liberation. One can add that the director did not argue with Chateau or claim that he had pursued discourses of irony at the Vichy academy, the current explanation offered in *Positif* for his career under the occupation.

Others found different faults with the same film. At *Le Canard enchaîné*, Michel Duran highlighted that Clément had omitted Georges Bidault altogether from the reconstruction of the liberation. He told his readers that this was a disgrace, a complete misrepresentation of the liberation of Paris. Duran implied that resistance hero Bidault had been removed because of his subsequent opposition to de Gaulle's Algeria policy and for Duran this was a ridiculous approach to historical cinema.[29] In other words, one is highlighting that the complexities of the subjects being depicted meant that these resistance films were not always successful at finding a welcoming set of reviews. History was politics and so historical films generated politically divided and nuanced film criticism.

(To digress, meanwhile, Clément's *Chefs de demain* was overlooked in the Paris press that I have consulted. Strangely the producers, Paramount, did note it in their English language publicity material, which is today archived at the BFI, London. There, the English language biography for Clément, released by the Publicity Director's Office, Paramount, London, notes, 'During the Occupation he was in Nice at the Artistic and Technical Centre for Young Film Makers where he directed a propagandistic short entitled 'Chefs de demain' [1943] ['Leaders of Tomorrow'].[30] It is difficult to ascertain if this was included

THE SEARCH FOR NATIONAL UNITY THROUGH HISTORY · **57**

to avoid accusations of a cover-up or if the press officer responsible was an exceptionally diligent film buff.)

A limited number of films tried to offer ironic interpretations of the war years, often by focusing on the 'little man' with no time for the politics of either resistance or collaboration. Let us underline: no work of cinema adapted the frequently published neo-Pétainist memoirs and histories being written through the 1950s and 1960s by several former Vichy politicians, coming from the Albin Michel, Plon and Grasset houses, among others. However, one can discern in their place a cinema that did capture a different (but also nationalistic) image of the war from that which was found in the resistance mythmaking films. This was achieved obliquely by raising themes such as the prisoners of war captured in 1940; the world of the black market; and the violence of war, including the Allied fighting during the liberation. Because each of these works is quite different, it is difficult for a historian to make many generalizations about their nationalist mythic content, and they were deliberately presented as being apolitical. What can be said is that their ideological subtext was to question the legitimacy of the dominant Gaullist-Communist emphasis on heroic resistance, and that they emerge from a milieu close to the cultural-literary world described in Pascal Ory's *L'Anarchisme de droite*.[31] Thus, the most politically explicit of these films were derived from right-wing novels, produced by figures who were part of a postwar intellectual clique still relatively sympathetic to Pétain, deeply anti-communist and shocked by the purge trials held against collaborators. Two writers were especially influential on this variant form of the nationalism–cinema encounter: Marcel Aymé and Antoine Blondin. Thus, the infamous example of this subculture is the adaptation of a Marcel Aymé short story, *La Traversée de Paris* (Claude Autant-Lara, 1956). It focuses on how two men smuggle a pig carcass across Paris. It is a popular film that was suffused with a challenging black humour delivered by Jean Gabin and Bourvil (who would later star in a similar role in *La Grande vadrouille*). There is no comment on resistance and the work seems made to suggest that France survived because everyone was wheeling and dealing, not supporting de Gaulle or communism. In it there is an especially unpleasant scene, which is rarely discussed, where the two Parisians joke about a hidden Jewish girl whose presence in a café interrupts their black-market dealings. It was Gabin again who starred alongside Belmondo in another wartime comedy of a similar tenor, *Un singe en hiver* (Henri Verneuil, 1962), based on the novel of the same title by Blondin. Without having space to summarize it in full, it includes an ironic commentary on the D-Day landings that concludes by gently mocking a commemoration organized on the beaches by Allied veterans. Suffice it to say this was not an early *Saving Private Ryan* (Spielberg, 1998).

The theme of escaping and returning prisoners of war was almost a subgenre of its own, begun with a portmanteau film *Retour à la vie* (1949, directed by a group of artists including H.G. Clouzot).[32] Much later, Fernandel starred in a comedy by Verneuil that took up this variation of historical theme and used it for humour in *Le Vache et le prisonnier* (1959). For what it is worth, Renoir turned in a mainly serious dramatic treatment on the same material when adapting Jacques Perret's novel *Le Caporal épinglé* (1961). In some symbolic regard, the French prisoners of war were the historical antithesis of the resistance. These were the soldiers who had been captured during the fall of France (1940) and who had been held in Germany, and used in Vichy's propaganda to justify collaboration. (Certainly de Gaulle himself had added to the discourse when mocking General Giraud for being captured. Giraud had recounted at length to impressed American generals of his heroic escape, when de Gaulle interjected that it would have been preferable to have avoided capture in the first place.) Through no fault of their own the prisoners were a central element in the justification of collaboration. It meant that to film on this subject, even via fictions about escape, was an implicit reminder that national history had been a complex and difficult matter, not simply a past peopled with resistance heroes. To draw this discussion to a close, first, clearly the rhetorical use of some comedy in these ideologically ambiguous films was important to their success with the public, and this is arguably precisely what director Oury grafted onto *La Grande vadrouille*. Secondly, the barbed humour was also a means of concealing otherwise offensive and disrespectful attitudes that were out of line with mainstream political and intellectual life, but which did have some traction in the 1950s literary arena.

For completeness one can note too that, although only rarely, there were major works that were pacifist, without a hint of even coded neo-Pétainism. Two very different styles of film of this variation are evident: Resnais's *Hiroshima mon amour* (1958) and *Weekend à Zuydcoote* (Verneuil, 1964). *Hiroshima mon amour* is a complex and ambiguous film that does not map easily into an analysis of the nationalist-film encounter which is the main subject of this book. Here subject and style were in direct opposition to the epic cinema treatment of resistance (à la Clément) and to the reactionary right-wing comedies (in the mode of Aymé). For those readers unfamiliar, the film explores a love affair between a French woman and a Japanese man. He speaks of the bombing of Hiroshima; famously asserting that no one without direct experience can understand what occurred. She reveals that she has spent the war in Nevers and has had a relationship with a German soldier for which she was publicly humiliated at the liberation, her hair being shorn as a punishment. The focus here is on a woman and not a man, and the liberation is pictured as a period of anguish and humiliation, not patriotic vitality. History is imagined as a transnational dialogue between Japan and France, not as a uniquely French possession, and relatively recently a Japanese director has made a counterpoint work, *H-Story* (Suwa, 2001). Made in 1964, *Weekend à Zuydcoote* shares the generally pacifist subtext of Resnais's more famous work, but little else. Starring Jean-Paul Belmondo, it depicts the defeat of France in 1940 and the experience of French and British soldiers awaiting evacuation at Dunkirk. The film is also a vehicle for an open discussion of the morality of war when, in an especially brutal passage, amidst the chaos of retreat two French soldiers attempt to rape a young woman (Catherine Spaak). This harrowing critical material captures the brutality of combat, and the depiction of the local girl who is raped, which is clichéd and sexist, nevertheless, openly portrays how women have commonly been the victims of men during wartime.

Resistance cinema as mode for nationalist mythmaking did, then, have rather frayed edges and, by the end of the 1960s, was internally reforming itself with *L'Armée des ombres*. I do not treat cinema's depiction of collaboration here because I do not see it working in any primary, or conventional, nationalistic fashion, although one could say that some *mode rétro* films were rather soft on collaborators, too unfair on the resisters, and that this representation very loosely corresponded with the new right-wing D'Estaing government. (Broadly generalizing, this was Michel Foucault's argument when writing his 'Anti-Retro' piece for *Cahiers du cinéma* and this is something that we will return to in chapter 6 when considering potential anti-Semitic subtexts in postwar film.) For now, one should underline that the state did continue to try to suppress works that were challenging to the resistance mythology and to do this for some time. For over a decade (1971 to 1981) the planned television documentary series *Le Chagrin et la pitié* (Marcel Ophuls, made in 1969 and shown exclusively for cinemas in 1971) was prohibited from audiences in the format that it was intended. The Office de radio et television française (ORTF) director Jean-Jacques de Bresson justifying this by saying the work was unhelpful for society because it destroyed myths that were still needed.[33] It was only after cinemas had screened Ophuls's work, and Malle's *Lacombe Lucien* had been a hit film in 1974, that, in 1975, President d'Estaing paid some official recognition of French collaboration when writing to *Le Monde* of his personal memories of witnessing the French police's anti-Semitic roundup (the Vel'd'hiv, 1942) and offering the same text for the credits of Joseph Losey's *Monsieur Klein* (1976, produced by Alain Delon), which the director declined.[34] That was an overeagerness that would lend plausibility to those who like Henry Rousso argue that the later post-1970s fashion for self-criticism and obsession with Vichy in cinema and culture was an exaggeration of history comparable to, and mimetic of, the earlier overblown representations of resistance.

In summary, from the 1950s to early 1970s depicting the resistance in the cinema was a standard mode for asserting national pride, and film after film indicated that most people had done their best. Similarly great emphasis was placed on the political unity of the resistance and the notion that the people from different classes had been united. It is noticeable that this theme is as much present in the works of Clément as of Oury, where social unification is an element despite the comedic frame. From inside the tradition of resistance film, it was Melville who brought about the greatest changes in representation with *L'Armée des ombres*. His work was one of the most sophisticated and its importance here is because it recounted a plausible historical-factual backdrop, while also commemorating heroism. In particular, Melville removed two clichés: the unity of the resistance and the implication that heroism would be rewarded with victory and not terrible personal loss. With the benefit of hindsight, resistance filmmaking was never without controversy because the past was so ambiguous, complex and subject to competing political interpretations. Consequently, there was a cinema that reflected politically critical attitudes towards de Gaulle and the Communists, although only indirectly. Typically, these films glorified in depicting how idiosyncratic individualists (embodied by a Gabin or a Bourvil) retained their spirit, and that even if high politics was not their particular bag they had jollied along.

The Challenge of Filming the Revolution: From *Danton* (1983) to the Bicentenary (1989)

When the Socialists gained office in 1981, the subject of the revolution returned to cinema for the first time in any meaningful way since the 1930s when Renoir had shot *La Marseillaise* (with due acknowledgement to Sacha Guitry's postwar works). Shortly after taking power, President Mitterrand's government engaged in an ambitious policy for cinema. The first history film to be made under these auspices was the Franco–Polish *Danton* (Wajda). Starring Gérard Depardieu and Patrice Chéreau, it received extensive funding from the new Minister of Culture, Jack Lang. The figure reported was between 2.5 and 3 million francs, as well as production funds from the state television company, TF1, Gaumont, and the Polish film fund. The strategy was to make a powerful European art film that demonstrated the prowess of cinema under the new government. It was assumed that the film would bring a socialist interpretation of the Revolution to the fore: a celebration of Revolution and, liberal, nationalism. The next paragraphs explore how this did not occur and how and why *Danton*, when read as a film event, illustrates that historical filmmaking is deeply problematic for nationalist mythmaking because, to repeat, the past inspires multiple and divisive interpretations.

The history of this film event recalls that nothing went to plan for Lang and Mitterrand. In its content Wajda's *Danton* presents a negative interpretation of revolution. The idea of revolutionary virtue is attacked for being inhuman, resulting in totalitarianism. *Danton* begins with ominous images of the guillotine. Next, Robespierre's son is beaten for misquoting the revolutionary tract, the Rights of Man. He cries in agony as he tries to remember the human rights the revolutionaries insist he memorize. Similarly acidic images end the film: Robespierre (Wojciech Pszoniak) has executed Danton (Depardieu) and he recognizes that the Terror is unleashed. The boy stands at the bed and he is now able to recite the Rights of Man. However, his words are meaningless, the implication being that the Terror has commenced. The screen fades to white. Further passages are similarly polemical. For example, Wajda includes a cynical depiction of the national anthem. He shows duplicitous revolutionaries singing 'La Marseillaise' to silence debate. It is possible to read all of this as a sharp rejoinder to Renoir's classic celebration from 1938, which focused on a positive account and use of the anthem.

As Robert Darnton underlined, Wajda used eighteenth-century history to critically analyse the meaning of revolution in Europe: Bolshevism, Stalin's purges, and the role of the Communist Party.[35] In Poland in December 1981, a military coup lead by General Jaruzelski had taken power and it had cracked down severely on the Solidarity movement. Journalists in Paris identified Wajda's Robespierre as a symbol for Jaruzelski and his Danton as a surrogate for Solidarity leader, Lech Walesa. Wajda refrained from making this direct comparison himself. However, in the press conferences he gave he stated that his film was about contrasting 'Western' and 'Eastern' European models of socialism and revolution.[36] Scriptwriter Jean-Claude Carrière however said that there were parallels between the depiction of late-eighteenth-century France and the contemporary crisis in Poland.[37]

When *Danton* premiered at a gala event hosted by the Cinémathèque, President Mitterrand hastily departed, avoiding having to give his views on it. Next, following private screenings in parliament, Socialist Party politicians lined up to criticize the film.[38] Pierre Joxe, president of the socialist group in the parliament, described *Danton* as a work of art and of no significance for the interpretation of history or politics. For Joxe the film overlooked the leftist *hébertistes* revolutionaries who had pressured both Danton and Robespierre; it omitted the context of the civil war and the war with the foreign powers. The Leader of the Assemblée, Louis Mermaz, explained that the film was historically inaccurate. He argued there should be no analogies made between the revolutionaries of 1789 and the present government.[39]

One must note further context here because it is also instructive as to what was going on when *Danton* was being attacked in Paris. In the autumn of 1981 at the Socialist Party congress in Valence, divisions had emerged between those calling for a slowdown of the government's reforms and the left wing of the party who wanted swifter change. Rhetoric from the revolutionary period was used at the congress to speak about this dispute. Paul Quilès employed historical analogies relating to Robespierre and the Revolution when discussing reorganization of industry, banking and the civil service and was quoted in the media: 'It is not enough to say heads must fall. We must say which ones and do so quickly.' In 1983 Quilès was now standing as the socialist candidate against Jacques Chirac for the office of Mayor of Paris and his words in Valence remained notorious in that campaign. Socialists feared *Danton* was re-highlighting the reformist-radical split at Valence by recalling Quilès's rhetoric.⁴⁰ Historical metaphors of guillotines, reform or revolution were sensitive for socialists because they echoed contemporary politics and many did not want to be associated with revolutionary extremism, which did not seem to play well with voters.

The communist response to *Danton* was especially scathing. For three weeks its daily newspaper, *L'Humanité*, relentlessly undermined the film. Firstly, Gérard Vaugeois stated it was far too simplistic a treatment that misused historical metaphors to erroneously comment on contemporary Poland. For him the director's attempt to represent Danton as a precursor to Lech Walesa and Robespierre to indicate President Jaruzelski rang false. Vaugeois explained that this rhetorical ploy oversimplified modern Polish politics.⁴¹ In the same issue of the newspaper the academic historian Michel Vovelle concluded with a defiant message to Wajda:

> *Non la révolution n'est pas une fatalité, un délire, ou un gouffre. La Révolution c'est nous de la rêver, de la construire à l'image de notre temps, de notre pays, de nos exigences de démocratie qui doivent être immenses … Car si l'on me permet de citer encore une fois Jaurès: 'Je suis avec lui [Robespierre] et c'est a côté de lui que je vais m'asseoir aux Jacobins'.⁴²*

> *[No the revolution is not an accident, or madness or an abyss. The Revolution is for us to dream, to construct in the image of our time and our country, from our needs for democracy that must be great. … For if you permit me to cite Jaurès one more time: 'I am with him (Robespierre) and it is next to him that I will sit with the Jacobins'.]*

Vovelle aspired for a better, more French and more socialist film of the Revolution. Seven days later Martine Monod took up the cause again. *Danton* was not a good film because it falsified revolutionary history. Wajda had no sense of the grandeur of the historical events and he had erroneously reduced the Revolution to the status of a *faits divers*. Just in case any members of the communist party or fellow travellers had not understood that Wajda's treatment of 1789 and Polish history was erroneous, *L'Humanité* invited another commentary when poet Jean Marcenac aligned himself with Robespierre and criticized Wajda's attack on the great revolutionary. He added that the film was weak from an aesthetic point of view. He reported that on the morning after his visit to the cinema he had placed red roses at the feet of the bust of Robespierre located in the communist-run suburb Saint Denis.[43] Others on the left wing further shunned Wajda's contribution. For instance, Emile Breton, writing in all sincerity, implied in *Révolution*, a weekly communist publication, that the media marketing campaign that was commercially promoting *Danton* was equivalent to Soviet bloc censorship.[44] This was an especially odd judgement in light of the Polish regime's ongoing repression of Solidarity, and the imposition of martial law that had meant that *Danton* was filmed entirely in France, rather than in both countries as once planned. One hopes for greater nuance in the specialist film reviews; however, this was not the case when in *Positif* Jean-Philippe Domecq accused *Danton* of being marred by conservative ideology. He described the film as reactionary because it associated 1793 France with the Soviet Gulag. He highlighted errors of fact that were found in the movie and considered the presentation of Danton as a Christ-like figure to be just wrong.[45]

A little surprisingly, one or two right-wing intellectuals were upset as well. Notably, Thierry Maulnier preached that history was not about making up a good Danton and a severe Robespierre. He recalled that Danton was involved in instigating revolutionary massacres in 1792 and that he was one of the executioners of Louis XVI. Maulnier concluded, 'Danton killed with more eloquence, Robespierre with more calm'.[46] For Maulnier the representation of the past in the film was not critical enough.

In Poland, Wajda used the completion of the film to attack the sitting government. Shortly after finishing the work he resigned his position as president of the Polish film group. He signed a petition calling for the release of the seven leaders of the Solidarity movement who were being held prisoner. The state promptly stopped the Polish premiere of *Danton*, the regime claiming that there were technical problems with subtitling. Few believed this, especially when the Polish government prohibited a screening of the French-language version at the French cultural institute in Warsaw, where a copy was ready for screening on 13 January 1983.[47]

In summary, commissioned by the ruling French socialists, Wajda wanted to use film to comment on revolution in general and by implication this also meant on the status of Soviet power in Poland. A negative image of the French Revolution was used to speak implicitly about the failures of the Soviet and Polish system. The analogy functioned as a two-way process and hence the failures of the 1917 revolution threw a negative light back onto the origins of the French Republic. The socialists felt betrayed by the man they had hired and worried his film would deepen preexisting rifts within their party. The communist intellectuals counterattacked what they considered pernicious reactionary propaganda. The left political and media classes designated the film to be a negative work and did all they could to undermine it and its director. The historical content of the film was boldly rejected, expelled from the nation. As Pierre Joxe remarked in public, the message was that Wajda's work had nothing to do with French history or identity.

VSD magazine reported that the government was so dismayed with *Danton* that they had already developed a new policy for monitoring future works. Any films being made for the bicentenary celebrations planned for 1989 were to be vetted.[48] When 14 July 1989 eventually came, the cinema was relatively marginal to the bicentenary. A series of academic and cultural events linking cinema and revolution were prepared, but these were low-key. The Mission du Bicentenaire de la Révolution Française, in cooperation with other groups, organized a retrospective of films dedicated to the Revolution. A collection of photographs, 'Ciné-images de la Révolution Française', and posters, 'L'affiche de cinéma et la Révolution Française', were exhibited at the Centre d'Action Culturelle in Montreuil, near Paris. In the capital, the Cinémathèque (directed by Jean Rouch) honoured the bicentenary with a cycle of films that were banned in various parts of the world.[49] This season was scheduled for five years and was intended to end with the bicentenary of the cessation of slavery (1994). Paul Carpita's *Le Rendez-vous des quais* (1953), a film about Marseilles dock strikes against the French war in Indochina, was used to open the season.

Similarly, the Cannes Film Festival (1989) supported the bicentenary through a number of symbolic devices, but these were controlled and relatively modest. Thus, a special day in the festival fortnight was dedicated to 'the liberating forces of the cinema throughout the world': this was branded as the *Journée: cinéma et liberté.* [50] The official poster for the festival featured the symbol of the Republic, Marianne. *Première* magazine, a more popular monthly than *Cahiers du cinéma*, themed its issue with the cover slogan 'Cannes '89: Révolutionnaire!' However, one should underline that the Palme d'Or went to *Sex, Lies and Videotape* (Soderbergh, 1989), an American film with no link to domestic national history.[51]

The two-part film *La Révolution française* was released in the autumn of 1989; Robert Enrico directed part one of the project, 'Les Années lumières', and its sequel 'Les Années terribles' was handed to the American Richard Heffron. The films represent five hours of spectacle, supported by a generous budget of 300 million francs. In addition, on 31 October 1989, the TV channel Antenne 2 broadcast a 'making of' documentary about it. *La Révolution française* received official state support, as do most films. Soldiers were drafted into the project to play extras in the crowd scenes. The Minister of Defence, Jean-Pierre Chevènement agreed the cooperation on the understanding that the film be shot on location in France. State buildings were used as sets, Lang granting the use of Versailles and Laurent Fabius permitting access to his ministerial residence, Hotel de Lassay.[52] The huge budget for the film also corresponded to a recent Lang directive that French and European filmmaking must challenge Hollywood by making 'super-productions'. Furthermore, information-cum-promotional material was circulated to schools to encourage young people to watch the film and learn about their history. To the same end, a special educational-ticket tariff was given to school pupils. Huge posters were plastered on the walls of cities, proclaiming the arrival of the big-budget epic. Robert Enrico described his work as the only French film on the Revolution in 1989 and he hoped that it promoted the national cinema. He added: 'I also think that this kind of film can help promote the image of French cinema in other countries. It is a pretty visiting card.'[53]

The content of the film was meant to bring consensus and not produce another *Danton*-like controversy. Generally speaking, 'Les Années Lumières' offers a positive view that the Revolution had been worthwhile and that France is a better nation for being a republic. Enrico's film is however also kindly to Louis XVI, who is still presented benevolently for being a good person, albeit incarnating a political role that was out of date. Although the work promoted a political myth of consensus, the press were sceptical about the film and its interpretations of history. They acknowledged the film's ambitions but were critical of the end result. Similar to responses to *Danton*, the left-of-centre press considered it offered too conservative a treatment. In *Libération* François Reynaert complained that the second film, 'Les Années terribles', was far too conservative. He noted that the film's special historical adviser was Jean Tulard who was, 'l'historien le plus à droite sur la période'.[54] Directeur de l'Institut d'histoire de la Révolution, Marxist historian Michel Vovelle added new apercus of his own. Vovelle explained that while he was less perturbed than after watching *Danton* in 1983, he was disappointed nonetheless that the film gave such credit to Danton. Its overall emphasis on the leaders of the Revolution meant that it overlooked the role of the people. He considered Renoir's *La Marseillaise* the definitive film of the Revolution, expanding, 'tout en regrettant que les cinéastes français n'aient pas été inspirés par leur histoire comme les cinéastes sovietiques' ['Also sorry that French cineastes have not been inspired by their history in the way that the Soviet filmmakers were]'.[55]

Populist fare also failed to live up to the bicentenary of summer 1989. In 1988, Philippe de Broca made a romantic, fictional melodrama, *Chouans!* Starring Philippe Noiret and Sophie Marceau, it narrates a love story set in the chaotic civil war conditions of eighteenth-century Brittany. Its implicit politics did not conform to a straightforward celebration of republican values but did again seek some retrospective unity, albeit with some royalist preference. Throughout, de Broca implies that extremists existed on each side of the Revolution, Royalist and Republican, and that the whole period was horrendous for the nation. He claimed that his work spared neither side from criticism.[56] However, as the film develops, the emphasis shifts to highlight Republican atrocities and to excusing Royalist actions. In one important sequence a Republican firing squad takes aim to kill a young child and the massacre is stopped only when a young woman throws herself in front of the bullets, sacrificing herself. Royalist violence is never portrayed to this extreme. *Chouans!* concludes by implying that the true France is located in a combination of *ancien régime* and republican values. When the friendly aristocrat Savinien (Philippe Noiret) raises the tricolour, a Republican guard guns him down. He falls to the ground gripping the flag of the Revolution, pulling it to his chest where he sports the badge of the counter-revolutionaries. The symbols of the revolution and the *chouans* blur together in this powerful conclusion. De Broca conjoined in his final imagery an implied sympathy for both royalism and republicanism. This was a logical interpretation to use to celebrate France without being politically divisive. It was not however in line with the official bicentenary celebrations that were more strictly republican.

Conclusion

Resistance cinema of the 1950s and 1960s promoted the idea that the French had acted honorably and contributed greatly to the victory against Germany. They concealed much of the shabby complexity of the *années noires*, including the complicity of politicians, civil servants and others in the Holocaust. The films gave France national heroes and legitimated the political dominance of former resisters, notably de Gaulle and the communists. The subtexts to the films were about male cross-class unity, and, as we have seen, that spoke to contemporary society and its politics, as much as to any accurate reflection of history. Resistance film included national myths of unity to guide present-day audiences that greatness could be achieved if men united in a worthy cause and were not divided by class position, differences in social rank or party-political affiliation. However, this vision of the past was plainly a highly simplified one. And, one can conclude too that it was regularly questioned in works that were already being made in the final years of the 1950s.

The cinema's treatment of the Revolution is a complex, usually controversial, matter because of the longstanding differing interpretations that are made about this founding moment for the Republic. Already in the 1930s there was a huge desire to make a great national epic on the Revolution but no consensus could be won because none fully existed. The socialists' disappointment with Wajda's *Danton* is illustrative of the continued difficulty of making national unity out of a contested political history. They had hoped to fund a positive vision of national history, while what they watched in the completed film was a systematic argument against the idea of the Revolution and an implied critique of the Polish government.

In short, and possibly rather crudely, there was no shortage of attempts at nationalist mythmaking via films on important parts of the history of the Republic, antifascism and the foundation period (the Revolution). It was the subgenre of the cinema on resistance that was nearer to achieving a sense of unity through exemplary imagery of people working together for success against the German occupation. But even in its heyday, films, including the two Clément classics, were critiqued and controversial. It is tempting to conclude that the cinema–nationalism–history nexus discussed in this chapter was far less successful at maintaining positive ideas of Frenchness than the meta-films discussed earlier in chapter 1. The latter were more convincing precisely because they avoided all explicit politics that are necessary (even in the background and always in selection of viewpoint and content) in all but the most banal history films, and instead used celebration of art as a means to claim glory.

The chapter has also assisted in some development of the understanding of the qualities of film events. What is striking here is how the reception of works analysed is so consistently about issues of the ownership of meaning. The disputes, public controversies and debates about both cinema depicting the resistance and the Revolution occurred when the filmic symbolism of a work escaped the control of production and entered the public sphere where meanings were open to interpretation, claim and counterclaim. Since politicians and the state often supported these works (from the premiere of *Bataille du rail* to the bicentenary), this invited political opponents to watch and use the films against their sponsors. The film event becomes a full paradigm at the point when content of a film is read and re-mediated, where the producer of a work ceases to have control over how it can be read and is subject to first a director's creative initiative and then journalistic representations and disputes over its content. This becomes all the more evident when different parties receive a film in contradictory ways, thereby sparking disagreement and competing claims around the real meaning to be found.

Finally, the issues discussed in this chapter shed some new light on the recent, more theoretically inflected, work of Michael Rothberg. In his study *Multidirectional Memory* it is highlighted how memories and representations of the 1940s were commonly established in France so as to also speak or react to the crisis of decolonization.[57] As I have noted in passing this was true in a general sense and evident too in discussions around individual resistance films (for example, the presence/absence of Bidault in *Paris brûle-t-il?*). However, it is also precisely because the French imagined 1789 as a universal event (certainly the Marxist view) that this aspect of history was similarly transnational and dialogic and so open to multi-perspective, international usages and responses. As the case study of *Danton* illustrates so well, because French history could speak to other nations' politics and patterns of development, this history was free and open for reinterpretations inscribed from these very locations. Also, we might add, that because the cinema was commonly discussed as being in explicit competition with US film imports, on this further meta-level several works functioned as national icons mediated by the press as being in commercial rivalry with Hollywood.

Notes

1. H. Rousso, 1987, *Le Syndrome de Vichy*, Paris: Seuil; S. Lindeperg, 1997, *Les Écrans de l'ombre*, Paris: CNRS; S. Sand, 2004, *Le XXe siècle à l'écran*, Paris: Seuil.
2. '"La Bataille du rail" a été gagnée', 1946, *L'Écran français* 30, 23 January, 3; J-P. Bertin-Maghit, 1986, '"La Bataille du rail": de l'authenticité à la chanson de geste', *Revue d'histoire moderne et contemporaine* 33, 280–300; M. O'Shaughnessy, 1995, '*La Bataille du rail*: Unconventional Form, Conventional Image', in H.R. Kedward and N. Wood (eds), *Liberation: Image and Event*, Oxford: Berg, 15–28.
3. Nationwide 5,727,203 viewers watched the film. See S. Simsi, 2000, *Ciné-Passions*, Paris: Dixit, 4.
4. Cover photo of *L'Écran français*, 1946, 68, 26 October.
5. A. Bazin, 1997, '"Battle of the Rails" and "Ivan the Terrible"', *Bazin at Work*, London: Routledge, 197–203; G. Sadoul, 1953, *French Film*, London: Falcon Press, 118.
6. See J-M. Clerc, 1998, *Littérature et cinéma*, Paris: Nathan, 97, 99. With special thanks to Jan Baetens for drawing attention to this material and first identifying an exciting new genre in his researches.
7. Rousso, *Le Syndrome de Vichy*, 242.
8. J. Planchais, 1966, 'Paris brûle-t-il?', *Le Monde*, 26 October; 'Feu d'artifice pour Paris brûle-t-il?',1966, *Le Monde*, 18 October. See also S. Lindeperg, *Les Écrans de l'ombre*, 356.
9. L. Collins and D.L. Pierre, 1966, *Is Paris Burning?*, London: Penguin.
10. J. Decoux, 1949, *A la barre de l'Indochine*, Paris: Plon.
11. K.H. Adler, 2013, 'Indigènes after *Indigènes*: Post-war France and its North African Troops', *European Review of History*, 20.3, 463–78. Wherein Adler highlights the regular and 'tenacious' representation of colonial troops in the military periodical *Revue d'Information des Troupes françaises d'occupation en Allemagne* (1945–1950).
12. See Sand, *Le XXe siècle*, 329.
13. See 'French Asked Not to Show Film at Cannes', 1956, *The Times*, 19 April; R. Raskin, 1987, *Nuit et brouillard: On the Making, Reception and Function of a Major Documentary Film*, Aarhus: Aarhus University Press; E. Van der Knaap (ed.), 2006, *Uncovering the Holocaust*, London: Wallflower Press; G. Pollock and M. Silverman (eds), 2011, *Concentrationary Cinema*, Oxford: Berghahn. For Cannes Festival controversies see also H. Frey, 2011, 'Cannes 1956/1979: Riviera Reflections on Nationalism and Cinema', in S. Berger, L. Eriksonas and A. Mycock (eds), *Narrating the Nation: Representations in History, Media, and the Arts*, Oxford: Berghahn, 181–206.
14. S. Wharton, 2006, *Screening Reality: French Documentary Film during the German Occupation*, Oxford: Peter Lang, 74–76; see also P. d'Hugues, 2005, *Les Écrans de la guerre. Le cinéma français de 1940 à 1944*, Paris: De Fallois, 71, 89–90; E. Ehrlich, 1985, *Cinema of Paradox: French Filmmaking under the Occupation*, New York:

Columbia University Press, 107. The actor Jean Daurand had also starred in several 'vichyssois' features before *La Bataille du rail*.

15. O. Curchod, 2012, 'Avant La Bataille', *Positif* 612, 92. For Alekan's work see A. Weber, 2007, *La Bataille du film*, Paris: Ramsay, 192–94. This material is based on Alekan's own memoirs, 1999, *Le Vécu et l'imaginaire*, Paris: Sirène.

16. Ehrlich, *Cinema of Paradox*, 169, 221. Where Ehrlich explains: 'These and other claims of Resistance activity must be looked at with a certain amount of skepticism. After the Liberation nearly everyone in France claimed to have aided the Resistance in some way.'

17 W. Faulkner, 1984, *Faulkner, Brodsky Collection Volume Three: De Gaulle Story*, Jackson: University Press of Mississippi.

18. See Sand, *Le XXᵉ siècle*, 169.

19. Frodon, *L'Âge moderne*, 827.

20. See 'L'armée des ombres', 1969, *Journal du dimanche*, 28 September; R. Chazal, 1969, 'L'armée des ombres', *France Soir*, 13 September; A.Cervoni, 1969, 'L'armée des ombres', *France nouvelle*, 1 October; L. Chauvet, 1969, 'L'armée des ombres', *Le Figaro*, 15 September; M. Duran, 1969, 'L'armée des ombres (En pleine lumière)', *Le Canard enchaîné*, 17 September.

21. P. Labro, 1975, 'L'armée des ombres: de tous ses films, c'est celui que Melville préférait', *France Soir*, 21 June.

22. Untitled review, *La France catholique*, 1969, 3 October; M. Martin, 1969, 'Le point de la semaine', *Lettres françaises*, 17 September.

23. J-L. Comolli, 1969, 'L'armée des ombres', *Cahiers du cinéma* 216, 63.

24. T. Judt, 1992, *Past Imperfect: French Intellectuals 1944–1956*, Berkley: California UP, 47–48. It is worth adding here that Lindeperg's work particularly emphasizes the very nuanced and textured nature of early resistance cinema; noting too the disputes and debates that surrounded many films. Of course much depends on which films one emphasizes for one's research and the level of interpretation offered (scene by scene; or more general narrative patterns) as to what conclusion is drawn. One is left with the impression that cinema played a mythopeic function – celebrating history and social unity – but that works were far from straightforward and certainly not always consistent or unanimously well received. To exemplify the complexity both Lindeperg and I have read the same Clément-*Lui* interview (1966) that is discussed in this chapter, but we note different aspects of its content. See Lindeperg, *Les Écrans de l'ombre*, 347.

25. The film's release coincided with huge tensions within the provisional coalition government. General de Gaulle resigned from office on 20 January 1946, just days after the release of *La Bataille du rail*.

26. See O. Barrot, 1979. *L'Écran français 1943–1953, histoire d'un journal et d'un époque*, Paris: Les Éditeurs Français Réunis, 110–11; A. Spenle, 1946, 'La Bataille du rail', *La Revue de cinéma* 1.1, 73.

27. G. Vincendeau, 2003, *Jean-Pierre Melville: An American in Paris*, London: BFI, 51.

28. R. Chateau, 'Clément sur le gril', 1966, *Lui*, May, 105–6. See also note 24 above.
29. M. Duran, 1966, 'Paris brûle-t-il? Mais qui a tué Bidault?', *Le Canard enchaîné*, 2 November.
30. Press release biography – 'RENE CLEMENT', Paramount, London. (BFI Microfiche: R. Clément).
31. See Ory, *L'Anarchisme*.
32. K.H. Adler, 2011, 'Nation and Alienation: Retrievals of Home in Post-war French Film', *History*, 326–53.
33. Rousso, *Le Syndrome de Vichy*, 114–29.
34. D. Caute, 1994, *Joseph Losey: A Revenge on Life*, London: Faber, 410.
35. R. Darnton, 1990, *The Kiss of Lamourette*, London: Faber, 37–52.
36. 'Wajda interroge avant la première de Danton à Varsovie. En Pologne l'Histoire n'est jamais innocente..."', 1983, *Le Soir*, 8 February.
37. J-C. Carrière cited in P. Montaigne, 1982, 'Wajda commence "L'Affaire Danton"', *Le Figaro*, 21 April.
38. '"Danton" visionné par la Culture', 1983, *Le Matin*, 8 January.
39. P. Joxe, 1983, 'Les enfants ne sauront pas', *Le Monde*, 16 January; A. Chaussebourg, 1983, 'Un entretien avec M. Louis Mermaz', *Le Monde*, 16 January.
40. 'An embarrassing film show', 1983, *The Evening Standard*, 14 January; '...always boldness!', 1983, *The Sunday Telegraph*, 13 January. Paul Quilès wrote in 1985 that the Valence speech had been entirely misunderstood by the media. See Quilès, 1985, *La politique n'est pas ce que vous croyez*, Paris: Robert Laffont, 35–37.
41. G. Vaugeois, 1983, 'La Pologne hors ses murs', *L'Humanité*, 7 January.
42. M. Vovelle, 1983, 'La Révolution n'est pas un délire', *L'Humanité*, 7 January.
43. See M. Mondo, 1983, 'Danton', *L'Humanité*, 14 January; J. Marcenac, 1983, 'Trois roses rouges, s'il vous plaît', *L'Humanité*, 21 January.
44. E. Breton, 1983, 'Conformisme', *Révolution*, 28 January.
45. J-P. Domecq, 1983, 'Danton', *Positif* 264, 76–78.
46. T. Maulnier, 1983, 'Danton et Robespierre', *Le Figaro*, 22 January.
47. *Danton* was released in Poland in February 1983 where state reviewers were damning. In France a minority of liberal critics did support the work, notably the historian F. Furet.
48. 'Les Socialistes n'aiment pas "Danton"', 1983, *VSD*, 13 January.
49. 'Cinémathèque Française: Les Écrans de la Liberté', 1989, *Le Film français* 2244/2245, 5 May, 178. For an overview of the bicentenary see Stephen L. Kaplan, *Adieu 89*, Paris: Fayard.
50. See D. Wallon, 1989, 'Éditorial', *Le Film français* 2244/2245, 6. The theme of liberty was timely. In 1988 right-wing Catholic groups had protested against *The Last Temptation of Christ* (Scorsese – see chapter 7 herein) and the controversy around Rushdie's *The Satanic Verses* had started.
51. See *Première*, 1989, April, 145.
52. 'Tournage: La Révolution franglaise', 1989, *L'Express*, 24 March, 126.

53. Robert Enrico, BFI press files on Enrico/*La Révolution française*.

54. F. Reynaert, 1989, 'Sous les clichetons, la Révolution', *Libération*, 31 October.

55. M. Vovelle, 1989, 'C'est du bon Mallet-Isaac, et c'est plutôt positif', *Le Quotidien de Paris*, 25 October.

56. De Broca quoted in S. Molitor, 1988, 'Destins', *Première* 123, 78.

57. M. Rothberg, 2009, *Multidirectional Memory*, Stanford: Stanford University Press.

CHAPTER THREE

The Representation of a Modern Chic People

As Ferro's original definition of 'film event' implied, it is evident that individual landmark films and their reception do impact on society and contribute to changing attitudes and perceptions. This chapter proposes that Claude Lelouch's *Un homme et une femme* (1966) and its reception, including a controversial triumph at the Cannes Festival that year, worked in precisely this way as a vector for nationalism. Lelouch's seemingly neutral work perpetuated the myth that France was a united, economically thriving and morally upstanding community. The debates that developed around it in Paris are important too because they exemplify how discussing cinema can be a metaphorical means for speaking more generally on society and contemporary politics. As will be explained, that is a mode of reception that was very different from when, for example, Lelouch was reviewed in London.

It is also worth tracking how the political mythmaking evidenced in Lelouch's first successful film was influential on several of his contemporaries. Thereby, this chapter sheds new light on the politics of cinema made by Jacques Deray, Claude Sautet and Pascal Thomas. Discussing selected examples of their work allows one to see how imagining a (fantasy) chic and bourgeois nation was extended beyond the real crisis point of May 1968. As Alison Smith has analysed in her nuanced study, *French Cinema in the 1970s: The Echoes of May*, much of cinema in the 1970s was changed by those events; whereas, this chapter explores how the Lelouchean form for asserting national pride was meanwhile maintained.[1]

Un homme et une femme and the 'Get-away' Generation

For those unfamiliar with its relatively simple plot, Lelouch's *Un homme et une femme* is a love story about how a couple in their mid thirties meet, depart, and come together again. Jean-Louis (Jean-Louis Trintignant) first encounters Anne (Anouk Aimée) at the gates of the boarding school that their children attend in Normandy. They spend an afternoon together as if they were a family, taking a fishing boat for a short trip around the bay. While driving back to Paris they tell each other their life stories. She is a script girl who was married to a stuntman (Pierre Barouh). They had a wonderful marriage, working together on films, travelling to exotic foreign countries. However, he has died in a horrible accident. Jean-Louis knows about life's tragedies too: he is a racing-car driver and although he survived a serious accident, his partner committed suicide because she was so terrified he would never recover.

When Jean-Louis drives in the Le Mans–Monte Carlo Rally, Anne telegrams him: 'Bravo. I love you'. He returns north to tell her about his feelings for her. Taking his Ford Mustang up to the beach, he spies Anne and her daughter walking near the waves and he flashes his yellow racing lights at them. They run towards each other. Famously, Francis Lai composed the simple but catchy score to accompany these images: chabadabada chabadabada. It is a sequence that is frequently reshown and is one of the most famous from all of modern French cinema. In the final quarter of the film Lelouch explores whether the new relationship will work out. When they make love Anne's thoughts turn to her deceased husband. She tells Jean-Louis that she must return to Paris and would prefer to travel by train without him. Jean-Louis makes yet another car journey speeding to Paris to meet Anne. His car is quicker than the SNCF service from Deauville to the capital so when she walks along the platform he awaits her. They embrace. *Fin.*

The photography and fast editing greatly enhance *Un homme et une femme*. Similarly, the look of the film is modern because it combines sequences shot in colour with passages of black and white and sepia. This mixing was because Lelouch had not been able to afford sufficient colour film. In fact, the blending together of film stocks is a positive feature that provides some narrative interest beyond the very simple core plot I have just summarized in its entirety. Lelouch uses the colour film to emphasize two romantic sequences that take place between the couple. It is deployed for their first encounter, the afternoon fishing trip. Subsequently, it is used for Jean-Louis's return to Deauville. These sequences are neatly balanced with those other colour passages that depict Anne's memories of her late husband. There is therefore a loose visual correspondence that underlines how Anne is falling in love with Jean-Louis, just as previously with her deceased partner. These aesthetics make the film look modern, despite the very traditional plot, and they also keep the attention of an audience who might otherwise find it all a little clichéd.

Representing France in the twentieth Cannes Festival (May 1966), Lelouch was awarded the Palme d'Or, an honour that his film shared with *Signore e signori* (Pietro Germi). This triumph was followed by a double success at the Academy Awards of 1967 where *Un homme et une femme* took Oscars for Best Foreign Film and Best Screenplay. In the U.S.A. it ran for exceptionally long periods in theatres, apparently for 'more than two years in Los Angeles', which is quite remarkable.[2] Opening in Paris at the Biarritz, the Imperial, the Ursulines and the Dragon cinemas, there as well it obviously captured the zeitgeist of the mid 1960s, grossing the second-highest audience for a film that year, falling short of the super-hit historical comedy *La Grande vadrouille*.[3]

Lelouch recalls in his memoirs, *Itinéraire d'un enfant très gâté*, that before the Cannes Festival President de Gaulle and his wife Yvonne had invited him to view the film with them at a private screening. The President enjoyed it greatly, commenting favourably throughout. Lelouch remembers:

> *Pendant la projection, le Général, à chaque fois qu'une scène lui plait particulièrement, abat une main pesante sur mon genou et me dit: 'C'est bien ...' Ou alors: 'C'est un très beau film.' Je suis stupéfait par la candeur, pour ne pas dire la naïveté, dont il fait preuve en regardant mon film, me posant parfois des questions suprenantes, telles que: 'De quelle race est-il, ce chien?' (celui qu'on voit courir sur la plage).*

> [During the screening, each time that the General especially enjoyed a scene he placed a weighty hand on my knee and said 'It's good' or 'It's a very beautiful film'. I was stupefied by his candour, not to say naiveté, which he showed while watching my film, sometimes asking surprising questions such as 'what breed is that dog?' (the one that one sees running on the beach).]

Apparently, according to Lelouch, Madame Yvonne de Gaulle was moved to tears by his melodramatic film.[4]

What were the mythopeic qualities of the film and where is the nationalism in such a seemingly apolitical romance? The beginnings of an answer to that question lie in two quite distinct but interrelated aspects of the work. First, it is helpful to consider narrative and how the depiction of the central relationship is marked by ideological values and, next, to discuss the equally significant role of settings and landscapes. It is my hypothesis that it is the synthesis of the ideological values proposed in these combined aspects that make the film a powerful vector for political communication.

The narrative of relationships, male and female sexuality, in *Un homme et une femme* resolved a perplexing paradox of the New Wave. The arrival of the younger generation of cineastes circa 1959 had already suggested to the world that France was a lively and modern culture, capable of renewal, healthy and upwardly mobile. Minister of Culture Malraux sponsored the New Wave directors, seeing the value of them and their works for promoting an impression of national cultural superiority, offering the reassurance of cultural grandeur for the newly founded Fifth Republic (1958). The new cinema signified vibrancy, daring, intellectualism and sexual liberty. However, these images of France projected in the New Wave, and specifically around Brigitte Bardot, were also a cause of anxiety, even moral panic, among conservatives. After *Et Dieu créa la femme* (Vadim, 1956) Brigitte Bardot was the world's leading sex symbol. Her illustrious career and the other works of cinema that focused on younger women's independence, and freedom to take lovers, caused a public controversy over what was appropriate for the public. Intellectuals, commentators, guardians of national moral honour identified cinema as contributing to the moral decline of the nation. Grosso modo, *Bonjour tristesse* (Preminger, 1958), *Et Dieu créa la femme*, *Les Amants* (Malle, 1958) all indicated a version of female sexuality that broke down accepted norms of chasteness before marriage, orderly sexual reproduction and good motherhood in wedlock.[5] For conservatives it was wonderful that France was being recognized for its cultural achievement (in the 'new' cinema) but the content of the films being made was worrisome because they signalled the wrong idea of the morality of the country. For example, in a fascinating passage of *It's So French!*, Vanessa Schwartz underlines how the French Consul General in New York reported to his Ambassador that, although commercially successful, *Et Dieu créa la femme* was selling a disreputable image to audiences across America. He complained: 'I am sorry to say that it is "porno" that attracts the ingenuity of our producers who are cultivating the taste for it among Americans who are usually repressed and because of this always eager to see representations of a sexual nature'.[6]

The plotting used in *Un homme et une femme* resolved the moral concerns about the new cinema sketched out above. Lelouch's film looks fresh, he was young, original and his cinematography was close to that of Godard's and the other internationally hip French filmmakers. However, the narrative content of Lelouch's form was different from their more racy work. The lovers in *Un homme et une femme* were grown up, in their thirties, smartly dressed, holding down impressive careers. Anne (Aimée) is filmed wearing a warm sheepskin coat, wandering along beaches in mid winter, and there is not a bikini in sight on the wintery Normandy beach. Moreover, Lelouch's character Anne did not enjoy sex because she remained loyal to her deceased husband. Let me be a little bold and suggest that she is the anti-Bardot, the antithesis to Bardot's lithesome movements and her image of a more untamed sexuality.

Important works from the field of visual studies, such as W.J.T. Mitchell's *Landscape and Power*, Nicholas Mirzoeff's *The Right to Look* and Tom Conley's *Cartographic Cinema*, teach that spatiality, landscape, what we see and what is concealed from us are as important modes for political communication as narration and plot.[7] Employing such a critical perspective to *Un homme et une femme* reveals further how the work was again a repository of nationalist values. Indeed therein the portrayal of space, people and social context is quite as significant as the conservative narrative structure.

The landscape/setting imagined in the work allows one to fully recognize the subtle politics of this film. Throughout *Un homme et une femme* the France we are shown is a successful and modern nation, embracing modernity and at peace with itself. All of the main locations that feature and structure the film's plot are chic, upper bourgeois places, and it is through movement to and from these sites that the film develops. For example, there is the private boarding school near the Normandy resort town, Deauville itself, Paris and the glamorous Monte Carlo. Furthermore, the two main protagonists are employed in exciting, international careers, in the worlds of motor sport and the cinema. This internationalism of the French protagonists signifies their success in the world, and potentially by implication the rank of the nation that has trained them in their professions. We are even told that their children are learning Spanish and English, which is clever shorthand for both economic ambition and family values.

Banished from our purview is the chaotic if charming world of the cinema of Jacques Tati, where rural France is favourably contrasted with modern city life and there is a mock menace of Americanization (the disposition first revealed by biographer of Tati, David Bellos). In the Lelouch imagination, Tati's admiration for rustic traditional society as offered in for instance *Jour de fête*

(1949) evaporates, as does any other hostility towards the arrival of urban modernity. For Lelouch, the car and the road to and from chic places are the happy symbols of social change. Indeed, traditionally evocative images of rural landscapes, farming and peasant life – *la France profonde* – are absent in *Un homme et une femme*. Nonetheless, Lelouch signals that his protagonists respect the old ways, exemplified by their picturesque encounter with the fisherman and their trip on his boat. Fishing was a preferable image of France than that offered by the peasantry, with their farms, odd-looking tools and muddy livestock. That was far too passé for this film. Fishing also had no deep political connotations, whereas Vichy-era ideologues invested in folklore and the idea of the noble peasantry.[8] Like the sport of motor racing, sailing was cinematographic because it involved movement through space. This material was also a rich part of the popular literary imagination, established in Pierre Loti's *Pêcheur d'Islande*. It also corresponded to an aspect of de Gaulle's writings in his *War Memoirs* wherein metaphors of the nation as a ship at sea are recurrent. Incidentally, readers may be interested to learn that rumour has it that Anouk Aimée nearly quit the picture because of not wishing to film at sea (even the Normandy bay, near to shore).[9]

Moreover, it is important to underline next that Lelouch's film evidences peace and political stability and that what is not shown as backdrop to the film is significant. Throughout its ninety minutes the film glosses over any reference to Algerian nationalists or the anti-de Gaulle OAS (even though of course the legacies of the conflict burned on). Similarly Lelouch's camera does not show any of the graffiti inspired by the Algerian war, which lasted on walls long after its conclusion. Nor does he capture the café colour bars that prohibited Turks and North Africans from dining in white-only restaurants in the mid 1960s. The huge *bidonvilles* where migrant workers lived on the outskirts of the cities disappear from view, although Jean-Louis must have been regularly speeding around them in his rally car. One thinks for example of the sprawling and ramshackle huts and bungalows at Nanterre.[10] There are no conflicts (political or otherwise) at all on screen other than those to be resolved through the working out of the central relationship that concludes with the joyous reunion on the railway platform. In this context the casting of Trintignant is important. Until this film his star persona was associated with portraying extreme right-wing military figures, characters that were linked to the OAS (see Cavalier's *Le Combat dans l'île* [1961] and *L'Insoumis* [1964]).[11] Now, through the Lelouch film his public identity is converted into the successful, romantic racing driver, without any dubious political connections.

In its setting, use of landscape and character back stories, *Un homme et une femme* normalized and exaggerated the idea of France being a modern, successful society. The people were still sensitive and passionate, but they owned sports cars, worked abroad for extended periods and sent their children to private schools. The nation was at peace; its citizens could engage in leisure-type professions but not immoral affairs. The film's depictions also achieve what I will identify as a zero-mirroring effect. That is to say the film closes off multidirectional meaning; it does not speak to any complex past from French history nor does it invite an awareness of postcolonial context, other than through Trintignant's prior casting in preceding works. Therefore, neither plot nor setting raised an explicitly political subject matter, yet they combined to offer a very conservative and reassuring image of the nation.

The reception of the film in Paris illustrates how the combined mythopeic aspects of the work (moralizing plot; the backdrop of a happy chic France) attracted and divided reviewers along traditional party-political lines. Firstly, that Lelouch had won the Palme d'Or in Cannes in the same year that Alain Resnais's work on the Spanish civil war, *La Guerre est finie* (1966), was dropped from the competition because its organizers feared angering General Franco's government, was unfortunate for Lelouch and gained him few friends on the left. It seemed for some critics that *Un homme et une femme* had won at Cannes at the expense of the poor treatment of Resnais. In the pages of *Cahiers du cinéma*, Jean-Louis Comolli attacked Lelouch. He explained that it was not surprising that the upper-middle class, the Champs-Elysées strollers, enjoyed the work. *Un homme et une femme* was reassuring for them – it was a relief from the radicalism of Godard, whose recent films had questioned their value system. According to Comolli, Lelouch's work looked modern, like Godard's (the quick editing, the colour/sepia exchanges), but it removed all criticism of the status quo. It was easy to understand because according to Comolli it offered nothing to think about.[12]

There is further contextual detail that explains the quite intensive left-wing criticism of *Un homme et une femme* in 1966 in France. According to Lelouch, the screening of his work for the President had already jeopardized his chances of the Palme d'Or because it meant the left-leaning clans in the world of cinema viewed him as a Gaullist. Historians will also appreciate that it was at precisely this same time, while the General was courting Lelouch, that his government were censoring Jacques Rivette's interpretation of Diderot's *La Religieuse*. Remember the film periodical *Positif* considered the banning of Rivette's work tantamount to a declaration of war against them. 'Le Manifeste de 1789' petition was drawn up to support Rivette, including signatures from all of the major figures working in film and theatre.[13] In addition, Godard wrote a biting public letter to Minister of Culture Malraux and *L'Express* magazine dedicated an issue to the affair, devoting its powerful cover to the scandal. In this context de Gaulle's invite to Lelouch to watch *Un homme et une femme* with him was significant for it divided the film milieu against itself, even though Lelouch was no supporter of the censorship.

In contrast to the above negative reactions, it was a group of rightist intellectuals that quite extensively promoted Lelouch and his work. Claude Mauriac, writing for *Figaro littéraire*, claimed that other critics had too quickly turned against him and that this great young talent would be destroyed by pointless intellectual terrorism. Michel Cournot asserted in *Le Nouvel observateur* that Lelouch was a victim of a cynical left-wing press that was intimidated by his stylishly shot conventional love story.[14] The conservative film critics lapped up Lelouch's sweet, anxious, older couple. At the Catholic *La Croix* Jean Rabine was a dedicated supporter of the work. He told his readers that he enjoyed how the film offered a naturalistic portrait of a couple falling in love. These protagonists did not simply jump into bed with each other in the casual style. He explained:

> *Au debut, ce n'est rien qu'une amitié, que Deauville le dimanche et la joie des enfants, qui se transforme imperceptiblement en un sentiment plus tendre, qu'aucun d'eux n'exprime pourtant le mari d'Anne habite encore trop manifestement ce coeur délicat, tant et tant qu'il n'y a sans doute de place en lui pour personne d'autre.*

> *[At the beginning it is only a friendship, only a Sunday afternoon in Deauville and the enjoyment of the children, that imperceptibly transforms into a more tender feeling, that neither of them yet express, Anne's husband still clearly living in her delicate heart, so that there is no doubt no room for anyone but him.]*

Lelouch had made a 'belle histoire d'amour', and what was refreshing was that it was French, a national triumph according to Rabine.[15] Michel Cournot expressed delight, describing it a masterpiece because it integrated the story of the relationship into a solid depiction of the world of work.[16] *Le Figaro*'s Françoise Parturier went as far as to claim that a quiet revolution was underway. *Un homme et une femme*, as well as Jacques Demy's *Les Parapluies de Cherbourg* (1964), the romantic novel by Delly, *L'Infidèle*, the restoration of the Trianon at Versailles, all signalled an end of 'sécheresse sartrienne' ['Sartrean dryness']. Spring 1966 was a positive rejection of angst, casual sex and leftist nihilism – all of which was a sophisticated way of suggesting that good it was to be alive in de Gaulle's Fifth Republic![17]

To provide further context to the right-wing appreciation of the work and especially its handling of romance, it is important to underline again that from the nineteenth century onwards it was bourgeois European nationalists like the modern Gaullists who imagined relations between sexes required control and purity. Liberal conduct, homosexuality, female promiscuity were imagined threats to national success and stability. George L. Mosse underlines, 'Nationalism and respectability assigned everyone his place in life, man and woman, normal and abnormal, native and foreigner, and any confusion between these categories threatened chaos and loss of control'.[18] The New Wave cinema had disturbed this pre-existing moral-sexual order, even though some of its representations were themselves sexist. Now, Lelouch was an exciting figure for conservatives because his filmic imagination continued the aesthetic spirit of the young cinema but glossed over its sexual provocations. His work revised Sagan, Godard, Vadim and Malle; also it negated that social-sexual chaos imagined in Renoir's *La Règle du jeu*. It brought back respectability and then sold it as an image of France around the world. De Gaulle had held the presidency at the elections in 1965 and the moral rot had been halted. Lelouch's thoroughly decent image of intimacy between the widow and widower confirmed the victory. The film even implicitly supported official government statements about national success and stability. Just three years before May 1968, these government documents were proudly asserting that the youth were a success story, owning their own cars, studying in high numbers at university and working to pay their way.[19] (It is worth noting quickly here that the fictional characters' conservative conduct in *Un homme et une femme* that was so appreciated and almost taken as 'real' contrasted to that of the stars themselves. For instance, in 1956, Trintignant had started an affair with Bardot when filming *Et Dieu créa la femme* for her then husband, Vadim.)

The disputes charted above show how a seemingly commercial work, a pure entertainment, did impact on the conventional realm of politics, with attitudes towards the film becoming markers of a Parisian intellectual's or film critic's relationship to the sitting government. The material analysed also indicates how film reviewers do form coherent groups of opinion, and that the traditional 'political families' do become aligned 'for and against' important examples of film, especially if one side starts to recuperate a film as its own (as de Gaulle and the right clearly did with *Un homme et une femme*). To be clear: obviously the debate in France around *Un homme et une femme* was more subtle than many other better-known film events, and it was far more low key than the classic examples such as the *Danton* affair of the early 1980s or the fight against the censorship of *Le Chagrin et la pitié*. Nonetheless, the film functioned to create a space for divergent attitudes on de Gaulle's France to be expressed. It gave journalists and intellectuals a means to comment on society without becoming explicit or overt: taking a stance on the film was an elegant form of making a political judgement. This type of film event is distinct from the more common examples where a work is literally shaking things up in society because of its explicit politics or highly original visual or dramatic content. This example is a different case because the reviewers are using their writing on the film to metaphorically speak about society at large through their reaction to Lelouch. Of course they had watched Lelouch's work, but they were never only writing about it as simply a work of cinema.

One can identify that this film event was localized and about domestic politics. In other words, outside France the work was not subject to dispute or division. Instead it exemplified French chic and little if any note was given to the controversial polemics surrounding the film in Paris, with Peter Lennon's fascinating article for *The Guardian* being an unusual exception in British reportage. In London the critics identified the film as a projection of France as a modern and successful place and relayed this interpretation to their readers. Casting an eye over the British reviews of the film, it is clear that the positive images of France found in the work provoked some envy, and a slightly grudging and satirical undertone marks a lot of the coverage the film received. For example, Alexander Walker, for *The Evening Standard*, stated it was an 'ultra-chic romance' with main characters that are 'getaway people' but that, 'one is slowly asphyxiated between the pages of a weekend colour magazine'. *The Guardian* film critic Richard Roud described it as a film for the middle-class, 'Nescafé people'.[20] Penelope Houston, editor of the British Film Institute's *Sight and Sound* film magazine, but here writing for the right-wing weekly *The Spectator*, explained:

> *Back from the beaches it's more Sunday supplement, in the not un-engaging area where the advertisements and the editorial comment meet. Jean-Louis Trintignant zigzags his car in exuberant circles: a Ford Mustang for the getaway people. Anouk Aimée, on her film set, peers over the collar of a sheep-skin coat at a property camel. He reads* Time *and* Nouvel Observateur; *she reads those luxuriously printed French editions of comic strips.*[21]

As one can read in several publications, the British reviewers linked the slickness of Lelouch's work to the world of advertising. The repeated term they used, 'getaway people', was a direct reference to a recent advertising campaign for Benzol Super National. That petrol company had used the slogan to promote their fuel to younger drivers. The campaign had implied the middle-class kids, who could now afford to own cars and spend their weekends away at the beach, should fill up with Super National. When they were thus empowered they were the 'getaway people'. Viewing the original advertising posters one can see why Alexander Walker and Penelope Houston associated the campaign with *Un homme et une femme*. The photographic stills that were used by Benzol employ very similar aesthetics to those in Lelouch's film. Created by the photographer Norman Parkinson in 1963, they feature happy, sexy, young couples and their cars. In one shot for the campaign the world of cinema is even evoked: a young couple are lying on top of their vehicle, the topless male shooting film with his cine-camera.[22] Of course not all these images were actually shot in very glamorous locations, sometimes beaches in south Wales were used to evoke France or Spain. By the way, the London reviewers were on to something. It was true that Lelouch had worked in advertising and that in the early 1960s he had made short promotional films for francophone rock and roll stars using the now defunct video-like technology, Scopitone.[23] There was also a strong hint of product placement in *Un homme et une femme*: for example, Ford France had provided the director with seven vehicles.[24] Furthermore, shortly after his breakthrough Lelouch contributed the official film for the Winter Olympics that were hosted in France in 1967, *Treize jours en France*. Therein he showcased the national downhill ski champion Jean-Claude Killy, and again employed a catchy Francis Lai soundtrack.

In summary, Lelouch pictured modern France as a society at peace with itself. His film achieved this implication through using chic settings and glamorous-looking people. The conservative sexual politics of the film's plot brought a new demureness to the screen that was much appreciated in the right-wing and Catholic press. When one moves from the film itself to the history of its reception, one can see that it was read in Paris as having significant political subtext and that there was a quite full debate around the rise of Lelouch. Fascinatingly, the right wing (from President de Gaulle down) encouraged, celebrated and recuperated Lelouch, while on the left there was rejection and considerable hostility. The right pushed the value of the film because it seemed to confirm their broad contentment, as well as social attitudes towards gender and sexuality. For the left, the film's content and timing were subject for much complaint. One can conclude by underlining that it was the case that liking or disliking Lelouch was a mode of expressing a more general view on the state of the Gaullist-run nation. In New York or London these localized political melees mostly disappeared. Outside France the film functioned more or less just as de Gaulle would have wanted: as a signifier of national achievement, filtered through stylish if conventional bourgeois romance.

Normality restored...

Through the late spring of 1968, students in Paris and the provincial university towns protested against conditions on campus, the conservatism of de Gaulle's regime, and the U.S.A.'s war in Vietnam. By the week of 23 May 1968, there were barricades in Paris, a general strike and what one recent historian neatly calls a 'celebratory defiance' stopped the normal running of the state.[25] For twenty-four hours de Gaulle fled from Paris by helicopter to an army base in West Germany (29 May 1968). In the streets rumours ran wild as to where he had gone: consulting a fortune teller, searching out cycle champion Jacques Anquetil's masseur, preparing an atom-bomb attack on the Sorbonne, anything was possible.[26] The world of cinema was an influential player in an event more dramatic than any film. Protests at the firing of Henri Langlois at the Cinémathèque had been part of unrest in the early spring of 1968. In May, the New Wave cineastes in Cannes closed down the Festival in support of the revolt. Returning to Paris, some directors, actors and technicians were active supporters of the students and workers. An États Généraux du Cinéma [Estates General of Cinema] was established as a meeting place to debate the future of cinema for the post–May world. Complex organigrams that offered utopian maps of how a film industry could work better were drawn up. Free speech, the end to commercialism, everything seemed possible for a while. The famous scriptwriter Jean-Claude Carrière recalls colourful details from the tumultuous period in his memoirs: marching with the students, standing with Louis Malle humming the 'Internationale' because they did not know the words, Delphine Seyrig abandoning film work to drive to the Renault factory to support its workers, but uncertain which of her cars to take.[27]

Despite the brevity of the revolt (de Gaulle had reasserted control by the end of June), the landscape of cinema had to some extent changed. Films on the protest movement came out quickly, such as the international cooperation featuring a Godard short, La Contestation (1969). Godard's own credibility was itself greatly enhanced for having made a work on student protests two years before they occurred in his La Chinoise (1967). Voices from different strata in society, previously ignored in film, were heard for the first time too, a post-1968 trend that chimed with the new cultural history developing out of the Annales school of historiography. For example, René Allio's adaptation of Michel Foucault's Moi, Pierre Rivière is a radical work, as is René Vautier's oral history style treatment of military service during the Algerian war, Avoir vingt ans dans les Aurès. Provocations around sexually explicit themes were popular too, notably Louis Malle's witty film on incest, Le Souffle au coeur (1971), and Bernardo Bertolucci's Dernier tango à Paris (1972).[28] In a different genre, Costa-Gavras's Z (1969) inspired a series of French-set political thrillers that echoed May 1968.[29] Maybe less familiar is the history of how commercially and critically successful directors quickly made works that denied the significance of May 1968 altogether. The mythology set up in Un homme et une femme, the Lelouchean mode vintage 1966, returned with a vengeance, taken forward in subtly different directions by directors Claude Sautet, Jacques Deray, Eric Rohmer and, in a new variant, Pascal Thomas. Lelouch himself preferred to address May 1968 in a rather silly comedy that undermined the significance of the events by making fun of them (see his in fact very boring action-comedy caper *L'Aventure c'est l'aventure* [1972]).

To repeat, the general ideological themes established by Lelouch in *Un homme et une femme* were restaged in several popular melodramas, thrillers and romances post–May 1968. Chic France, luxury cars and cool polo shirts remained in the cinemas, an imagery that was ignoring the social uprising and offering a different cinema to the works from Godard or even the upper-middle-class Malle.

For example, Jacques Deray's *La Piscine* (1969), a thriller, replays and slightly exaggerates many of the ideological elements of Lelouch's better-known earlier work. Again the setting is haut bourgeois, the mansion house Loumède in Ramatuelle village, overlooking St Tropez, complete with maidservant, and it is here one finds the pool of the film's title. In 1969 a swimming pool was a luxury, unusual even for the south of France. The characters sport designer clothes and have affluent and successful lives. Like in *Un homme et une femme*, sports cars are shown off when Harry (Maurice Ronet) drives his soft-top up and down the coast road to St Tropez. Writing for *Le Nouvel Observateur* Jean-Louis Bory commented on the luxury, 'un décor tout désigné pour figurer dans un reportage "Maisons et Jardins" consacré aux résidences luxueuses de la Côte, ou dans le numéro special sur les piscines privées' ['A decor designed to feature in a report in *Homes and Gardens* about luxury properties in the south of France, or in a special issue on private swimming pools'].[30] Like Lelouch before him, Deray films the protagonists as ultra healthy and beautiful. The opening sequence of the film sets the tone for this aesthetic. Therein Jean-Paul (Delon) is framed wearing no more than his swimming trunks, lying poolside. The camera pans in to luxuriate on his tanned and muscular body. Marianne (Romy Schneider) runs past him in a black bikini. They start a clinch together, interrupted only by the telephone. *Cinémonde*'s promotional write up called them 'the apparently ideal couple'.[31] They were more eroticized than in Lelouch but the landscape, decor and setting remained the same, if not further exaggerated.

As in *Un homme et une femme* the French protagonists in this film are linked consistently to other Western Europeans, notably the international jet set. Thus, Jean Paul's (Delon) partner is the Austrian Marianne (Romy Schneider), while his best friend Harry's daughter is played by English-accented Jane Birkin. The impressive soundtrack includes songs performed in English language, upbeat numbers, 'Ask Yourself Why' and 'Run, Brother Rabbit, Run'.

In this way, France's Western European connections are implicitly underlined. These allusions to internationalism again project France as an important place in the Western world where affluent people can feel at home and achieve success. The same images also again gloss over France's history as a colonial world power and, despite the glittering sun shining on the pool, there is a zero presence of the non-Western world in this film.

Jacques Deray had wanted to make *La Piscine* in 1968 but the *événéments* had halted his production schedule. As one can see in the finished work, this was only a practical inconvenience and not a moment for a political conversion. In his memoirs Deray remembers that the political crisis didn't change a thing for him and he explains that he was in Paris quite a lot that summer only because he was in love with a woman who lived near the Sorbonne.[32] Onscreen in the completed *La Piscine* it was almost as if no social protests had ever occurred. No mention of the contemporary rioting is made, and not a single countercultural figure – a student, let alone a hippy – is to be found, mocked or recuperated. The casting of Jane Birkin is a nod to the fashion and music industries, nothing more. Deray's France is just a little richer, more sexy and decadent than Lelouch's, but otherwise it repeats the advertisement for economic success, romantic pleasure and exciting lifestyle choices for the affluent. France is still the chic nation for the getaway people. The coded political myth was that France could rival any other country for vitality and success. Indeed, for at least three quarters of the film the decor outshines the plot and the police investigation that closes the work is completed in less than a quarter of the running time.

Claude Sautet, who knew Jacques Deray, visited his studios when he was completing *La Piscine* and was so impressed with the rushes he was shown that he cast Schneider in *Les Choses de la vie* (1970). That is another important film where one can identify traces of the format first found in Lelouch's debut feature film. *Les Choses de la vie* is another neat and effective love story set among middle-class citizens, cleverly recounted entirely through flashbacks. Michel Piccoli was cast as Pierre, a forty-something architect who has started a new life with his lover, a German journalist played by Schneider. He continues to have reasonably positive relations with his ex-wife (played by Italian actress Lea Massari). The decor of the film again highlights a world of affluence and social ease. Pierre (Piccoli) runs his own business with the help of his ex-wife; he is financially successful, maintains his company, his family apartment and also lives with his new partner. He takes holidays by the seaside, on the west coast, where he owns a sailing boat and it is here on holiday in La Rochelle, at an antiques auction, that he first meets his lover (Schneider).

As well as the similar middle-class decor and setting (sailing boat; a smart car; fresh air and sunshine; antiques), Sautet's treatment of relationships repeats the conservatism of Lelouch's plotting in *Un homme et une femme*. Pierre (Piccoli) cannot decide whether to stay with his new partner or return to his wife. There is a moralizing tone to the treatment of this dilemma. At the beginning of the film Pierre is speeding through the French countryside having finally selected his mistress. However, he has in his pocket a letter to her with contradictory information. No doubt distracted, he crashes his car in a fatal accident. The middle-aged, successful Frenchman is the dominant figure in the love triangle, perplexed about which woman to choose to spend his life with. Until his car crash it is Pierre who is empowered to decide which woman to prefer to build his life with (albeit a difficult and irksome decision that distracts him from driving carefully). Moreover, the film asserts that both his women are loyal to him whatever he decides. This structuring of the interactions is a male fantasy of a ménage à trois. Indeed, Sautet played with it again in his later work *César et Rosalie* (1972): there César loves his wife Rosalie, while she prefers a previous lover. In the end Rosalie returns to the two men, which is another male fantasy of a harmonious reconciliation.

Sautet's melodramas – notably *Les Choses de la vie* – are to some extent structural reiterations of the political communication identified in *Un homme et une femme*. Again, the works display a coherent and consistent combination of an uncritically depicted middle-class milieu and a masculinist conservative love triangle. To be a little flippant, if I may, one main difference is that in Lelouch's film that same love triangle included a deceased husband and not a living person.

It is widely recognized among film-studies scholars that Eric Rohmer established his own more austere means than Deray or Sautet to implicitly counter the carnival atmosphere of May 1968. *Ma Nuit chez Maud* (1969) was viewed by over a million people in France and was garlanded with prizes, Trintignant winning the best actor award at Cannes 1969 for his performance (a small link in casting to *Un homme et une femme*; and in both films he portrays his namesake, 'Jean-Louis'). It is historically important because of how it too so adroitly represented modern France just months after the crisis of May 1968.

Rightly, Norman King has explained that in Rohmer's imagination, 'It was as if May '68 had not existed, or at least as though audiences could simply overlook it in a nostalgic glance back towards less troubled times'.[33] Furthermore, King revealed that conservative critics welcomed the film because it seemed so reassuring, a superficially apolitical depiction of the young. For example, Pierre Billard praised it for having found the real youth of France, the implication being that those who had gathered at the Sorbonne in May of the previous year were not the nation's true offspring.[34] The work evoked nineteenth-century literature more than anything crude from the twentieth century. Its opening depiction of Catholic mass in Clermont-Ferrand adds to its implicit conservatism. Here Rohmer's filming of Christian worshippers attending service is a powerful if not triumphant scene, which can be interpreted as a bold opening statement that Catholic France is unperturbed by any socialist revolt. As his camera roams through the congregation, one sees that Rohmer's good provincial Christians dress conventionally, the men have their hair cut very short and the women look demure in their winter coats. Everything is as it should be, conservative order fully underlined by Rohmer's black and white photography, which freezes French society in a world before colour.

Lelouch is not Rohmer and Rohmer is not Lelouch, quite obviously. The perhaps crude analytical suggestion I am making, however, is that both directors were making conservative cinema about youth and love and France. It is also the case that their works stand out as the most significant positive depictions of a chic middle class – the landscape they inhabit and the dress they wear. Here they contrast boldly with the work of Claude Chabrol, the one-time co-author with Rohmer on a book on Hitchcock. As readers will appreciate, Chabrol's works, *La Femme infidèle* (1968), *Les Biches* (1969), *Le Boucher* (1970), *Les Noces rouges* (1973) and much later *La Cérémonie* (1995) and *Au coeur du mensonge* (1999), similarly provide detailed and thorough depictions of the bourgeoisie. In these films Chabrol's settings or landscapes are again country houses, Mediterranean villas and Normandy mansions. However, Chabrol's portrayal of the bourgeoisie is a consistently violent one, the very antithesis of *Un homme et une femme*. Rather than representing the young and rich as the happy face of a modernizing France, he picked at their psychological torments, detailed their hypocrisies and filmed them destroying each other. His cinema put on to screen dynamics of class power and hatred, and in the 1990s he was describing himself as being the last Marxist filmmaker working in France. As André Bessèges wrote when reviewing *La Femme infidèle* in 1968, Chabrol's world is 'le *sordide* riche et demi-luxe'.[35] His specialism was the decomposition of middle-class society, and that was a genuinely radical contribution. Viewers on the political left wing who dislike Chabrol's political imaginary do so because they are alienated by the settings; which can of course be overwhelmingly elitist, and actually far exaggerated when compared to Lelouch's or Sautet's much less gothic depictions of the high life. Nevertheless, it is usually only a matter of time before Chabrol makes sure that the expensive carpets are splattered in blood. One could say that for him every heavy bourgeois antique is as much a potential murder weapon as a signifier of a luxury lifestyle. Indeed, when one compares Chabrol with Lelouch or Sautet, one begins to see his upper bourgeois mise en scène as a very sharp satire. For what it's worth, much of course could be said too of Chabrol's deconstruction of the myth of fast cars in the brutal first five minutes of *Que la bête meure* (1971), for if ever there were a counter-film to *Un homme et une femme* then this is a primary example.

It is also important to underline before concluding this chapter that very different aesthetic modes of cinema came to the forefront in the 1970s and that in this 'new naturalism' one can identify another conservative and nationalist perspective of relevance. Relatively undiscovered outside of France, the director Pascal Thomas contributed a series of melodramas that were far subtler than the Lelouch–Deray–Sautet line of representation. Nonetheless, his cinema perpetuated a rejection of May 1968 and proposed original and positive images of being French.

Pascal Thomas's treatment of youth in his debut work, *Les Zozos* (1972), is a reassuring and nostalgic depiction. The film narrates the lives and loves of a group of adolescents, exploring how the boys and girls from two neighbouring schools socialize with each other out of class. Thomas's male teenagers, Frédéric (Frédéric Duru) and François (Edmond Raillard), are obsessed with making their first sexual conquests, whereas politics and ideology are not significant at all. Their minds are on summer hiking holidays to Sweden to meet exotic penfriends to 'get off with', not reading Marx or Mao, let alone protesting against anything or anyone. When the boys from *Les Zozos* reach Sweden they are shown to be out of their depth. One of them spends most of the trip throwing up outside his tent. Towards the end of the film, a Swedish girl takes the other lad to bed but he is too nervous to achieve an erection, waiting all night to see what might transpire. It is a gentle comedy that shows teenagers to be anything other than anarchic rebels or sexual delinquents tearing up the nation. They have normal desires and experience all the usual trials and tribulations of growing up. The director treats the material with nostalgia and sympathy, laughing with the characters and implicitly celebrating everyday life in a small-town rural community. As the story of youthful misadventure concludes, Thomas inserts the text: 'Frédéric et François qu'avez vous fait de votre jeunesse? – Rien de particulier ... nous l'avons paisiblement gachée entre les murs d'un lycée ou dilapidée auprès des filles qui voulaient bien de nous ... Pas de quoi se vanter ... non rien à regretter.' ['Frédéric and François what did you do with your youth? Nothing special ... we wasted it peacefully between the walls of grammar school or squandered it with girls who wanted us ... little to show off about ... nothing to regret.'] As one reads these words, the camera focuses on a school map of France, implying that such an ordinary life was the collective national experience.[36] Thomas is also implying that there will always be a corner of France where the young find innocent fun to be had. It is a good example of cartography's importance in film and a far less sophisticated one than the many examples so well discussed in Conley's academic study, *Cartographic Cinema.*

Generally speaking, the attack on May 1968 articulated in *Les Zozos* was a profoundly nationalistic and conservative move. It asserted a stable and traditional vision of French life, while sweeping aside the different new thinking of the young. It denied generational division as a breach in the national fabric (once again, cinema operating as a search for collective unity). The nostalgic feel, the countryside setting, imagined a timeless France untroubled by radicalism. These themes are commonly associated with heritage film of the 1980s and 1990s but it was probably Thomas who invented this ideological subtext through his realist comedies. Through these images and narrative devices *Les Zozos* displaces May 1968 from the public imagination. The film replaces the radical uprising with the conservatism of bucolic good old days, the young men interested in girls and not politics. The clever trick was that Thomas used a realist, naturalist style to appear to be capturing reality, which is subtly different from, for instance, Lelouch's far more glossy and self-conscious aesthetic. Setting the work in 1958 was similarly deceptive. The youths look and speak as if they were of the 1970s but the story can be told without any reference to May 1968, since it is yet to occur. Speaking in interview for the newspaper *Combat*, Thomas noted that the young actors he had worked with in 1972 were no different to how he remembered being a teenager just a few years earlier. For him this was a good thing: his implication was that May 1968 might as well never have happened. When René Quinson asked him if May 1968 had altered youth culture, Thomas was explicit that in fact nothing had changed.[37]

Thomas was widely praised for *Les Zozos* and he was quickly identified as the bright new hope for French cinema. Critics touted *Les Zozos* as evidence of the birth of a new New Wave. Repeatedly, it was compared with Truffaut's first short film, which was also about growing up in the provinces, *Les Mistons* (1958).[38] Like the *Cahiers du Cinéma* gang, Thomas had also been a journalist and film critic: he had worked for *Elle* magazine and with his scriptwriter Roland Duval on regional film periodical *V.O.* He socialized with hard-drinking actors such as Maurice Ronet and had worked in the increasingly trendy field of adult comic strips. Like Lelouch he was fashionable and chic but also conservative. For instance, in 1967, he co-wrote a satirical manual on how to be a success, *Comment briller en société*.[39] Coauthor of that work, Xavier Antomarchi, was the brain behind a propagandistic children's book dedicated to the life of de Gaulle, *Le Général raconté aux enfants*.[40]

One can add that through the 1970s Thomas was highly adept at advocating his conservative patriotic political philosophy through interviews and promotional events at the time of new works of cinema. For example, when asked if his admiration for the countryside was reactionary the director was happy to oblige his interviewer. He explained that yes he did find modern city architecture ugly, and that he doubted whether the architects of the Montparnasse tower were motivated by the spirit that inspired the great cathedrals of France. He added: 'Que voulez-vous, je crois à la maison avec un toit, un grenier, et une cave! C'est ça être réactionnaire?' ['What do you want, yes I believe in a house with a roof, attic and a cellar! Is that being reactionary?'][41] In 1979, he went further claiming he was the only director interested in the real France and that he considered his nationality a disadvantage since he felt foreign directors were overvalued in Paris and Cannes. He told Alain Riou: 'Je voudrais m'appeler Bob, comme Altman, ou mieux Dino, comme, Risi. Voila. Désormais je signerais Dino Thomasi, et l'on m'accusera plus d'être un Français en France qui, voyez-vous, est une grave péché' ['I would like to be called Bob, like Altman, or Dino, like Risi, I'll call myself Dino Thomasi and then no one can accuse me any longer of being a Frenchman in France, which you see is a terrible sin'].[42]

One should underline too that Thomas's successes contributed to the creation of a new comedy star: Bernard Menez. Menez features in Thomas's second and third films *Pleure pas la bouche pleine* (1973) and *Le Chaud lapin* (1974). He contributed memorably comic turns, notably as a provincial Romeo in *Pleure pas*. These performances led to an earlier, important Menez film reaching cinemas. In 1968 Jacques Rozier had cast him in another naturalistic comedy, *Du côté d'Orouët*. In 1974 it found distribution in light of Thomas's success. Years later the two worked together again on *Maine Océan* (1986). Through these and other films, Menez developed and rounded out the role of the ordinary, lower-middle-class French male. Deliberately not Trintignant, Belmondo or Delon, he is the type of man who admires these action heroes but who cannot look or be like them. The contribution to *Du côté d'Orouët* is especially memorable for the scenes where he plays a young Parisian office worker who holidays with his three pretty female workmates. In an extended sequence he attempts to seduce one of them, culminating in him cooking dinner but he drinks too much and his seafood speciality is a disaster. The stereotype being modelled by Thomas, Rozier and Menez is of a lovable ordinary Frenchman: he is not interested in politics, slightly inept, but holding good conservative values, he believes in French traditions and enjoys living life. Note, he is not a student, nor is he connected to anything political. Let us note too that Truffaut added to this mythology when casting Menez as the funny but skilled prop man in *La Nuit américaine* (see chapter 1). These roles evoke Jacques Tati, as well as some of the cinema of Marcel Pagnol from the 1930s. Certainly, in *Maine Océan*, where Menez is cast as an SNCF ticket guard, there is more than a touch of Pagnol at play when there is a direct reworking of his use of Fernandel in *Le Schpountz*.[43]

Finally, there are two further distinctive and explicit modes through which a conservative cinema emerged post–May 1968: (1) through popular comedy, the countercultural figure par excellence, the hippy, was satirized; (2) in the recuperation of countercultural products for commercial gain. Let us briefly explore the core aspects of each in turn, as they are often overlooked in more general histories.

(1) The action filmmaker Georges Lautner's *Quelques Messieurs trop tranquilles* (1973) offers us the definitive example of the portrayal of hippies in

French film. It is a conservative sexist fantasy in which the dropouts indulge in eastern philosophy and are shown in states of undress indulging in free love. Local Frenchmen watch them astounded and are understandably keen to discover more. In the end the French rustics and Americanophile hippies, who are straight out of *Easy Rider* (1969), form an alliance against evil Parisian gangsters. American actor Charles Southwood played their leader and made a short career in France playing this kind of stereotypical role: after his contribution to *Quelques Messieurs trop tranquilles*, Michel Audiard cast him in *Elle cause plus elle flingue* (1973) in which he pastiches *Jesus Christ Superstar*. Despite the sympathetic plot of Lautner's film, the representational mode served to exaggerate and to mock the countercultural lifestyle.

(2) A different approach to controlling the legacy of May 1968 was to recuperate the younger generation and start to commercialize their subculture. Contemporary film critics identified this process taking place when *Woodstock*, the movie of the festival, was released across France by Warner Brothers (1970). Director Michael Wadleigh, alongside the Beatles, travelled to be in Cannes for the Festival premiere to promote the work. Before the film Wadleigh made a short speech, dedicating his film to the victims of the war in Vietnam, and expressing his sympathy for the American students recently killed in the Kent State riots. After the three-hour film, black armbands made by fashion designer Jean Bouquin were distributed, eagerly snapped up by the crowd and worn by, among others, Yves Montand and Michel Audiard. Reports state that in the run-up to the screening the couturier had sold out of garments to wear for the premiere evening, selling two hundred and fifty dresses and five hundred shawls. Warner brothers were marketing *Woodstock* across Europe and in Paris the cinemas suspended student discounts on tickets for the film.[44]

Conclusion

Important melodramas made from the mid 1960s to the turn of the 1980s offered conservative, nationalist subtexts. For me, Lelouch's *Un homme et une femme* represents the most influential work of its type and an instigator of a patchily recurrent format. Conservative in its depictions of sexuality, it mapped out symbolic territory that was repeated by several other directors in the years that followed. It continued New Wave aesthetic modernism but by now aligning it with Gaullist capitalist Catholicism. Working after May 1968, Rohmer, Deray and Sautet continued aspects of this symbolism in the films discussed in detail above. They offered encouraging images of bourgeois success, a mark of esteem for France. They shot morally acceptable images of heterosexual relationships, which contained and replaced the more libertarian New Wave depictions. The French men in these films were perplexed by their relationships with women but were shown to be still dominant. This was a further reassuring subtext for nationalists who did not want any change to disrupt French society, not least in classic gender relations.

Pascal Thomas is important for this book because he provided new forms of intimate cinema with sharp patriotic purpose, which until now have been largely unrecognized by scholars. His rustic comedies about teenage boys and girls swept aside ideas of socialist revolution. These were replaced with nostalgia for the innocence of young love and sexual initiation. For a period of time he wore his colours proudly: attacking modern architecture (the Montparnasse Tower), accepting the epithet 'reactionary' and challenging leftist hostility to his praise of rustic France. Jacques Rozier's career was also assisted by the success of Thomas's early films. In his work he developed new light comedy about everyday life, to some extent updating the tradition of Tati and the earlier Pagnol. Together Thomas and Rozier helped invent the star persona of Bernard Menez, patriotic everyman for the 1970s and 1980s: a decent funny fellow, rooted in France, clumsy but admirable, the new Tati and the refreshing antithesis to Delon's machismo.

In fact Thomas referenced Lelouch's work in his own *Confidences pour confidences* (1979). This is a melodrama about a lower-middle-class Parisian family, following them through their lives from 1945 to the present. In a neat and amusing touch the Parisians take a short holiday in Deauville. It is 1966 and they arrive precisely to find Lelouch filming his famous work on the beach. In this sequence Thomas suggests that the dog belonging to the family in his film runs in front of Lelouch's cameras and it is shown that this is the canine seen very briefly on the beach in the completed *Un homme et une femme*. When Lelouch's film hits the Parisian cinemas, the fictional family and their 'star', the pet dog 'Popeye', all go to watch his screen debut. Here I would suggest that Thomas is making a neat and knowing nod to Lelouch. The director was not remaking the elder statesman's earlier film, for he had his own style, yet he did decide to cite Lelouch and not anything more avant-garde (Godard; Chabrol;

Buñuel). The sequence is therefore a very discreet if self-aware way for Thomas to appreciate Lelouch's film and to celebrate its long-term significance.

The chapter has also taken *Un homme et une femme* and analysed it as a detailed case study of another kind of subtly different film event. Among film reviewers on the different newspapers (ranging from *La Croix* to *L'Humanité*) the seemingly apolitical film was championed or critiqued because it did have an implied political subtext and that was made public and widely recognized. Just as importantly, one can also see that writing about the work was also a way to make value judgements on the Gaullist government, without slipping into polemic. De Gaulle's explicit support for the film, simultaneous with censorship of Rivette and Resnais (at Cannes), played a role too, making Lelouch look like a state-approved filmmaker when he was more independent. One should add that the case is fascinating because this Parisian reception was different from outside France where the film was critiqued for being almost too stylish, too close to an advertising campaign. To this day, in London *Un homme et une femme* is screened as a classic Valentine's Day movie and it works quite efficiently as that. In its own time and place it was a more complex and disputed work that recruited loyal supporters as well as virulent opponents.

Notes

1. A. Smith, 2005, *French Cinema in the 1970s: The Echoes of May*, Manchester: Manchester University Press.
2. P. Lev, 1983, *Claude Lelouch, Film Director*, London: Fairleigh Dickinson UP, 39.
3. Lelouch's film won an audience of 708,000 viewers.
4. C. Lelouch, 2000, *Journal d'un enfant très gâté*, Paris: Pocket, 129.
5. See also R.I. Jobs, 2007, *Riding the New Wave: Youth and the Rejuvenation of France after the Second World War*, Stanford: Stanford University Press, 229–30.
6. Schwartz, *It's so French!*, 143.
7. W.J.T. Mitchell, (ed.), 2002, *Landscape and Power*, Chicago: University of Chicago Press; T. Conley, 2007, *Cartographic Cinema*, Minneapolis University of Minnesota Press; N. Mirzoeff, 2011, *The Right to Look. A Counterhistory of Visuality*, Durham: Duke University Press.
8. See S. Peer, 1998, *France on Display: Peasants, Provincials and Folklore in the 1937 Paris World's Fair*, Albany: State University of New York Press.
9. See P. Loti, 1886, *Pêcheur d'Islande*, Paris: Calmann-Lévy (republished in numerous postwar editions including from Calmann-Lévy, Gallimard and France-Loisir). C. de Gaulle, 1954, *Mémoires de guerre*, Paris: Plon.

10. For more on the shantytowns see R. Kedward, 2005, *La Vie en bleu: France and the French since 1900*, London: Allen Lane, 409–11. See also W. Walton, 2010, *Internationalism, National Identities and Study Abroad: France and the United States, 1890–1970*, Stanford: Stanford UP, 157. U.S. exchange students to France were surprised at reading signs 'No Turkish people allowed' and 'No Africans here'.

11. See D. Joseph, 1972, *Guerre et cinéma. Grandes illusions et petits soldats, 1895–1971*, Paris: Armand Colin, 402.

12. See J-L. Comolli, 1966, 'Lelouch, ou la bonne conscience retrouvée', *Cahiers du cinéma* July, no. 180, 67–68; E. Bickerton, 2009, *A Short History of the Cahiers du Cinéma*, London: Verso, 55–59.

13. See 'Nouvelle vague de protestation', *Combat* 13 April 1966. See also Garreau, *Archives secrètes*, 216–29; V. Vignaux, 2005, *Suzanne Simonin ou La Religieuse de Jacques Rivette*, Liège: Editions du Céfal.

14. These quite intense disputes were neatly summarized in P. Lennon, 1966, 'A Man and a Woman', *The Guardian*, 9 July. It is interesting to note further here (and not directly related to Lelouch's film) that Gaullist policy directly used the motor car to promote itself: thus, prior to the 1965 presidential election, and for a limited period, de Gaulle offered amnesties for driving offences.

15. H. Rabine, 1966, '*Un homme et une femme*', *La Croix*, 12 May.

16. M. Cournot, 1966, 'Plus fort', *Le Nouvel Observateur*, 15 May.

17. F. Parturier, 1966, 'La petite fleur bleue', *Le Figaro*, 15 June.

18. G.L. Mosse, 1985, *Nationalism and Sexuality: Respectability and Abnormal Sexuality in Modern Europe*, New York: H. Feritg, 16.

19. Ambassade de France, New York, 1965, *France and the Rising Generation*, cited in Kedward, *La Vie*, 414.

20. See A. Walker, 1967, '*Un homme et une femme*', *The Evening Standard*, 19 January; R. Roud, 1967, '*Un homme et une femme*', *The Guardian*, 20 January.

21. P. Houston, 1967, '*Un homme et une femme*', *The Spectator*, 20 January.

22. The 'Getaway People Get Super National' campaign included magazine adverts, a special issue of *Queen* magazine and a short film.

23. Lev, *Lelouch*, 24, 29.

24. Lev, *Lelouch*, 31.

25. Kedward, *La Vie*, 416–31.

26. J-C. Carrière, 2003, *Les Années d'utopies, 1968–1969*, Paris: Plon, 58–92.

27. Carrière, *Les Années*, 62, 67.

28. H. Frey, 2004, *Louis Malle*, Manchester: Manchester University Press, 15–17.

29. Smith, *French Cinema*, 35–73.

30. J-L. Bory, 1969, 'La Piscine', *Le Nouvel Observateur*, 10 February.

31. GD, 1968, 'A St Tropez, Jacques Deray réunit Romy et Delon', *Cinémonde* 175, 26–27.

32. J. Deray, 2003, *J'ai connu une belle époque*, Paris: Christian Pirot, 89.

33. N. King, 2000, 'Eye for Irony: Eric Rohmer's *Ma nuit chez Maud* (1969)', in S. Hayward and G. Vincendeau (eds), *French Film: Texts and Contexts*, London: Routledge, 202.

34. Cited in King, 'Eye', 202.

35. A. Besseges, 1969, 'La Femme infidèle', *La France Catholique*, 21 February.

36. It is also an image that refers back to Truffaut's depictions of school life in *Les 400 coups* (1959).

37. R. Quinson and P. Thomas, 1972, 'Dans son premier film, Pascal Thomas raconte l'aventure de quelques lycéens', *Combat*, 22 June.

38. Enthusiastic reviews include: J. de Baroncelli, 1973, 'Les Zozos', *Le Monde*, 17 January; R. Chazal, 1973, 'Les Zozos. Drôlement sympa', *France Soir*, 15 January; J. Doniol-Valcroze, 1973, 'Les mistons dans le Poitou', *L'Express*, 15 January; M. Flacon, 1973, 'Nous sommes tous des zozos', *Le Point*, 15 January.

39. X. Antomarchi and P. Thomas, 1967, *Comment briller en société*, Paris: Robert Laffont.

40. X. Antomarchi and J. Schoumann, 1968, *Le Général raconté aux enfants*, Paris: Julliard.

41. Cited in M. Lengliney, 1974, 'Pascal Thomas', *Télérama*, 23 March.

42. Cited in A. Riou, 1979, 'Pascal Thomas: le péché d'être français en France', *Le Matin*, 5 January.

43. See also chapter 6 herein.

44. J.F. Launay, 1970, 'Tenues hippies et brassards noirs pour les invités de la soirée pop du Festival', *France Soir*, 12 May; M. Mardore, 1970, 'La révolution en musique', *Le Nouvel observateur*, 27 July.

CHAPTER FOUR

A Paradox in Anti-Americanism
Public Protest and Visual Ambiguity

One of the most memorable scenes from Jean-Pierre Melville's resistance epic, *L'Armée des ombres*, which I discussed at some length in chapter 2, follows its central protagonists in their escape from occupied France to freedom in London. The sequence offers an audience significant repose from the violence and tensions of the preceding acts and makes a powerful tribute to the British war effort. It also includes for me one of the most touching and effective passages from any work of cinema ever made. Cutting quickly from a solemn ceremonial meeting with de Gaulle, Melville shows how the resisters spend an afternoon at the cinema watching *Gone with the Wind* (Fleming, 1939). The heroes stare in awe and fascination at the screen and when returning to the streets of London assure each other that France will only be free when such films can be watched there again. Melville pictures Hollywood cinema as freedom and hope, a brilliant contrast to the sobriety of the French war experience.

I highlight very quickly the passage from Melville's work because it is so powerful and also to underline that French film has had a highly complex and contradictory relationship when encountering Hollywood. What I will examine in the next pages adds just one small piece to a labyrinthine puzzle that extends beyond the parameters of this study. The issue in question is one significant paradox among the many that make up Franco-American friendships and enmities: the substantial differences in tone and style that occur offscreen in relevant film events when compared with content of works themselves. On the one hand, film events, debates, discussions and critiques of Hollywood cinema show a rich and quite polemic sense of nationalism. On the other hand, in a sample of contemporary films this is a relatively watered down element.

Protesting the Enemy Invasion: Anti-Americanism on the Streets of Paris

On 4 January 1948 the film industry took to the streets to attack Franco-American trade agreements of 1946 (the Blum–Byrnes accords), which they perceived to be destroying cinema. Records indicate that ten thousand people marched through central Paris, from the Madeleine to Place de la République, and as they went they shouted 'Cinéma français! Cinéma français!' Parisians lined the streets competing with each other for autographs from the stars who mingled among the protesters.

Weeks earlier the demonstrations had been organized by a committee established to defend cinema from U.S. imports. Meeting at the national film school, the IDHEC, on 17 December 1947, most of the significant directors, actors and technicians of the day constituted a Comité de Défense du Cinéma Français. Instrumental in its creation were the director of IDHEC, Marcel L'Herbier, and his protégée, director Autant-Lara, who was also serving president of the film technicians' trade union. The committee agreed that the socialist minister Léon Blum had failed to defend film industry interests when negotiating U.S. aid, debt rebates and free trade. In their opinion Blum had sold out cinema by conceding too high a quota for the display of Hollywood films in France.[1] The Comité established regional branches and organized a petition to revise the accords. Throughout spring 1948 the film magazine L'Écran français provided its readers with a form that they could sign to then submit to the Ministry of Industry calling for a revision of the trade arrangements. Before films were shown, directors, actors and actresses offered lectures on the crisis. They informed audiences about the foreign threat and gathered signatures for a petition to revise Blum–Byrnes. For example, Henri-Georges Clouzot and Henri Diament-Berger spoke to an audience at the Saint-Michel, Paris, where they gained 290 new pledges from the public. Henri Decoin, Simone Signoret (on three different occasions), Paulette Dubost and Claude Renoir, Jacques Becker, René Clément and Gaston Modot contributed too.[2] An anti-Blum–Byrnes propaganda film was made that presented scenes from the aforementioned Paris demonstration and included a voiceover by the director Pierre Le Chanois. On the radio, Claude Autant-Lara delivered a broadcast to campaign further.[3]

In Hollywood itself, Charles Boyer lobbied for the French industry to attempt to gain some traction there. Jean Renoir, also then living in California, wrote to his brother Claude saying that he was trying to influence Hollywood studios, 'to make them less demanding'. However, in private he was pessimistic of his chances and told Claude: 'Once again our government has sacrificed an industry that it has always despised, that it still despises and will always despise.

This makes me want to stay here more and more.' He inquired after his brother's cinema in Antibes, The Antipolis. In this context, he suggested to his brother that since Blum–Byrnes would destroy film production then distribution was the preferable sector for him to invest in.[4]

The campaign continued apace and on 13 and 14 July 1948 the committee used the National Day to campaign for a second time around Paris. On 13 July, a cortege of cars met at the Place de la Concorde and formed a cavalcade, including lorries and other vehicles. Stars stood on the trucks and waved to Parisians as they drove around the city. This publicity stunt climaxed with a tango party back at Place de la Concorde where the happy participants jived to a new song, 'Le Cinéma Français a le Droit de Vivre' ['French Cinema has the Right to Live']. On 14 July 1948, IDHEC hosted a rally-cum-party that was attended by Autant-Lara, Pierre Blancha, Jean Delannoy and Michèle Morgan.[5]

The autobiographical writings of the director René Vautier provide further historical details that shed some new light on the above events. Vautier underlines that it was IDHEC Directeur D'études, the documentary filmmaker Jean Lods, and Léopold Schlonberg who had explained to students that because of the accords they should plan new careers. After these pessimistic lectures the students debated among themselves how to stop Blum–Byrnes. According to Vautier, it was the IDHEC students who first decided to encourage a unified national opposition: together they formed a Comité Étudiant de Défense du Cinéma Français. Moreover, fifty students interrupted a visit from Blum and the President of the Republic, Vincent Auriol, to the Sorbonne. The politicians were speaking there to commemorate the revolution of 1848 and the evening was broadcast live on national radio, including the students shouting their complaints. According to Vautier, writing in his memoirs Caméra citoyenne, it was this dramatic, nationally disseminated radio protest that next inspired a wider public debate at the Cluny, a Latin Quarter cinema. Vautier remembers that the students invited every significant figure from the cinema to attend. If one follows Vautier, it was only after this soirée that the senior filmmakers formed their own national committee.[6]

The French Communist Party (PCF) supported the film industry's campaign and maximized it for their own purposes. Leader Maurice Thorez rounded on U.S. imperialism in speeches and press articles, citing the U.S. threat to film production as a key battleground in defence of national independence. Thorez declared to massed ranks of supporters at the Buffalo sports stadium, Paris, that U.S.-American cinema was poisoning the souls of children. American films were invading France, bringing with them decadence and the values of gangsters. Fellow communist Georges Soria published *La France deviendra-t-elle une colonie Américaine?* (1948, preface by Frédéric Joliot-Curie). It is an early work that imagined the nation as a victim of American colonization. In addition, the film historian Georges Sadoul tirelessly attacked Hollywood and Blum. Teaching at IDHEC, and co-director of the Cinémathèque, Sadoul's rhetoric was often as colourful as that of Thorez. For instance, writing for the communist newspaper *L'Humanité* he accused Blum of treason. The minister had sold out French cinema for U.S. grain so rotten that it was not good enough to feed a pig in Minnesota.[7] For what it is worth, Georges Sadoul was well practised in making attacks on American popular culture. Already, in 1934, he had denounced the invasion of foreign comic strips, notably Walt Disney and the syndicated magazine, *Journal de Mickey*. In all seriousness, back then he had claimed that Disney was a front organization for William Randolph Hearst and Adolf Hitler.[8]

The PCF manipulated anti-Blum–Byrnes sentiment to chastise two fundamental ideological enemies: socialism, Blum; and capitalism, Hollywood. Attacking the accords allowed the PCF to continue the patriotic image the party had won from anti-Nazi resistance, precisely when this was challenged by General de Gaulle's Rassemblement political movement. The future of cinema was a distraction from his attacks and it also turned attention away from anti-Soviet defector Victor Kravchenko, whose book, *J'ai choisi la liberté!*, was a bestseller at around the same time.[9]

Conservative members of the Académie française, Etienne Gilson and Pagnol, supported the struggle of the Comité de Défense du Cinéma Français, as did right-wing politician Roger Duchet. Unity among the different factions was fragile because of other obvious ideological tensions that existed between them. Gilson, academician, historian and theologian, made jibes against American popular culture but also mocked the hypocrisy of the communists. Writing in *Le Monde* he explained that American comic strips represented as dangerous a threat to the nation as film, yet he noted that the PCF's *L'Humanité* had reprinted *Felix the Cat*. Gilson suggested that this syndicated comic would earn American business conglomerates increased monies and so he feared that the communists were unable to see the wood for the trees. The Comité de Défense du Cinéma knew of the communists' outspoken support for their cause and were sometimes uncomfortable about it, and in time-honoured fashion they underlined that they were a non-political organization.[10]

Grosso modo, the common refrain throughout the protests was that France was being invaded by U.S. films, to the cultural detriment of the nation, even its death. American imports also meant more than the decline of French film. The arrival in France of Hollywood-fare was interpreted as a force for deep cultural change, a loss of perceived true qualities of Frenchness, a national de-culturation and a more general contamination of the national identity. This language of invasion borrows an essentially military-political term and then applies it to the field of cinema. The implication of the metaphor is that U.S. products are not only single works of art or entertainment but are part of a chain in an intended and aggressive U.S. strategy to stop French filmmaking and consequently remove the traditional French way of life. Such a rhetorical move dramatized and polarized cultural difference between the French and the citizens of the United States. It negated positive interactions between French and American film communities and it imagined a military conflict where one did not exist. Importantly it also positioned France and the French film industry as a 'plucky' site of resistance. Here the nation was aligned with its filmmakers and they encouraged anyone and everyone to see this link as vital. They also implicitly positioned France as the underdog, the left-wing European nation capable of some kind of independent resistance despite the strength of the superpower and its film industry. One might add here that this was the discourse that in 1969 Melville challenged implicitly in *L'Armée des ombres*. As Ginette Vincendeau highlights, the premise of the scene discussed in the introduction to this chapter was, 'American cinema is resistance, in the context of the German ban'.[11]

The anti-Americanism of the anti-Blum–Byrnes protests was also a fantasy of national cultural purity, wherein no international cross-cultural sharing was perceived as at all possible. It rests on the presumption that the national tradition is always preferable to any change that brings about impurity. Filmmakers who saw themselves as socialists, anarchists, communists and conservatives expressed views that were essentially variations on forms of organic nationalism. For all of them in the midst of the Blum–Byrnes crisis, national identity is based on cultural-ethnographic definition rather than legal citizenship. Little if any space is left for multiculturalism, although there is a fascination with the menace of U.S. power and whether the French can pit themselves against it despite the odds. As is discussed later in this book (see chapter 6), the same period also witnessed a return of implicitly anti-Semitic rhetoric, notably in the personal attacks that were hurled at Blum.

There are nuances and variations in tone that are worth expanding on. For example, some anti-Blum–Byrnesers worried about confronting the U.S.A. so soon after the Liberation (1944). Scriptwriter Pierre Laroche offered a public statement dedicated to the memory of the GIs, but that also maintained an argument against the hated accords. Laroche made it clear that he preferred America and Hollywood to the German Continental films and its Nazi chief, Alfred Greven. However, Blum's trade arrangement had placed French film in peril. Laroche argued that the GIs fighting on 6 June 1944 had not sacrificed themselves with this in mind. By defending French film, the art of Meliès, the Lumières brothers and others, it was the French who were truly upholding the memory of the fallen GIs. Similarly, Pagnol made it public that he understood the sacrifice of U.S. Americans during the Liberation. However, he insisted that this did not mean the French wished to now become Americans.[12]

The intensification of the Cold War heightened the anti-American mood that gained so much influence in public debates around the future of the cinema in the early years of the Fourth Republic. For example, communists chided the former ally (the U.S.A.) for assisting in the rehabilitation and rearmament of the old enemy (Germany), and the reaction against the U.S. war film *The Desert Fox* (1952) was especially extreme on precisely these grounds. This picture was one of the first postwar films to narrate a war story from the perspective of a German – Rommel (James Mason). Leftists in France, and across Europe, believed it to be a U.S. propaganda tool to legitimate West German rearmament and therefore they attempted to block it. For example, when Fox Studios Europe filmed outside locations for it in France, the local crew refused to fulfil their duties because the film was a rehabilitation of a Nazi. A further boycott occurred when Fox tried to recruit French actors for dubbing purposes and the National Trade Union of Actors and Technicians called on its members to refuse the work.[13] None of this was unique to France. The original press coverage held at the BFI London illustrates how left-wing groups mobilized against *The Desert Fox* across Western Europe and around the world.[14]

The Korean War (1950–1953) further accentuated the film community's critiques of U.S. foreign policy and added a new set of tensions specific to that conflict. Rumour had it that a U.S. propaganda film in favour of the war was being prepared and that French crew were being recruited for it. Without naming names, the director Louis Daquin addressed the industry in the pages of its leading periodical, stating that he knew someone was on the brink of working on the Korean War picture. He urged him to take no part in the venture, highlighting that several other workers had already boycotted the planned propaganda film.[15] For Daquin, anyone employed on the work would simply be legitimating the war and he explained that filmmakers were pacifists who had only ever made films that were opposed to war. By March 1952 it became public knowledge that it was the cameraman Henri Decaë who had accepted a contract to film for U.S.–U.N. forces in Korea. In riposte, Henri Alekan, Jean Leherissey, Henri Tiquet and others attacked him for this decision.[16] Decaë was unmoved. He argued he had every right to take on work of his choice. He explained that working on a feature length colour film was a relatively rare opportunity and the new international project was a fine chance for him to develop his knowledge.[17] After completing *Crève-coeur* (*Heartbreak Ridge*) with fellow Frenchman, director Jacques Dupont, he did not find work again for about two years, when Jean-Pierre Melville brought him back into the fold by employing him on *Bob le Flambeur* (1955). Shortly afterwards Louis Malle also contracted him, for work on his debut thriller *Ascenseur pour l'échafaud* (1956), the film we might recall that Raymond Borde, writing for *Les Temps Modernes*, stigmatized as fascist because of its celebration of a paratrooper (played by Maurice Ronet) who had served in the war in Indochina. Meanwhile, in Hollywood, Dupont and Decae's *Crève-Coeur* won an Academy Award nomination for best documentary feature. However, the director Dupont did not seem to make much of a career for himself compared with Decaë. After working briefly with Pierre Schoendoerffer and Raoul Coutard, by the early 1960s his associations with the OAS terrorist group led to his arrest.

Even after the quota war was won with revisions granted in favour of protectionism agreed in 1950, Georges Sadoul repeatedly attacked the Blum–Byrnes deal as a hostile American offensive against France. Insider accounts were published years later that offered new insights into the murky world of international relations (for example, in 1954 the AFP journalist Jean Davidson published *Correspondant à Washington, 1945–53*). Modern history textbooks repeat the same version of events when accounting for the 'film invasion' and the French riposte. Notably, Jean-Pierre Rioux's standard history of the Fourth Republic records that the Blum–Byrnes agreement had genuinely jeopardized cinema and that there had been an 'invasion of American films'. Detailed revisionist histories that have suggested that the agreements were the best available to Blum and that they had assisted in the modernization of the industry after 1945 find little if any public recognition.[18] In their place there is the more or less hegemonic view of American industrial might and the brave French resistance.

In hindsight, what is important to underline about the Blum–Byrnes controversy is that it was a film event par excellence and that it established a ready-made template for future Franco-American film rivalries around issues of trade. The invasion and counter-attack story that frames much of Franco-American film relations has been readily reused on more than one occasion in the decades that have followed. For instance, it featured again in 1972 when the Association Française des Producteurs de Films demanded new quotas in favour of French film in cinemas and on television screens. Its ghost was there too when in 1985 Robert Bresson, Michel Deville, Eric Rohmer, as well as actors Arletty, Michel Bouquet, Raymond Devos, Michael Lonsdale and Philippe Noiret, petitioned to restrict U.S. imports on television screens.[19] This is not to mention its re-deployment in some of the media furore that greeted the planned construction of a Disney theme park near Paris, a project one intellectual decried as being a 'cultural Chernobyl'.

Threats of invasion warrant a policy of pre-emptive strike, so to speak. Just such a rhetorically assertive approach marked phases of the Mitterrand presidency (1981–1994) and it was at key points in this period that filmworkers and politicians underlined again how France was a great nation because it resisted perceived cultural imperialism. It was in this period therefore that echoes of Blum–Byrnes were most significantly heard and that a series of new film events of similar tone developed, in several cases being loosely associated with the Deauville Film Festival (founded in 1975), which celebrated American cinema. These events will be discussed next to further build up a picture of the nuances of anti-Americanism in cinema debates.

For a relatively short time after Mitterrand took office in 1981, the battle around cinema and identity was taken to the Americans. Thus, when a journalist asked newly appointed Minister of Culture Jack Lang if he would attend the eighth American film festival in Deauville, Normandy in September 1981, Lang replied that to do so would be an anomaly.[20] He proclaimed that he would prioritize 'la culture française et les artistes français'. Pointedly, it was during the days of the Deauville festival that Lang travelled to Rome, with Madame Mitterrand, to the open-air screening of a restored print of Abel Gance's *Napoléon* and to hold meetings with Italian ministers to discuss the founding of a Mediterranean cultural community.[21] Lang considered using shared linguistic structures of the Latin-language-speaking peoples to create an international cultural grouping. In his first major interview after taking the post of minister of culture, he announced the appointment of Gabriel Garcia Marquez to chair a working party on the 'création d'un future rassemblement des peuples d'expression latine' [creation of a future collective grouping of 'Latin' speaking peoples]. In the same interview he suggested that a 'Mediterranean space' could be quickly created. These initiatives chimed with the film industry's FERA group (Fédération Européenne des Réalisateurs de l'Audiovisuel), founded in 1981 to establish a European cinema organization to defend cultural distinctiveness, stop standardization of products and support filmmakers' copyrights.[22]

President Mitterrand continued the proactive strategy in Yorktown, U.S.A., where alongside President Reagan he attended an anniversary celebration of General Lafayette's victory against the British. Here, Mitterrand compared the history of American independence from Great Britain with the resistance groups who were opposing U.S. policy around the globe. Mitterrand and Lang had invited Truffaut to this event, hoping to surround the president with icons of French culture (he did not attend, staying in New York with Fanny Ardant).[23] Flying from U.S.A. to Cancun, Mexico, next Mitterrand delivered a speech (drafted by Régis Debray) in which he supported Mexico's independence from the U.S.A. and declared France's understanding for all who stood for liberty and freedom from oppression, by implication including opponents of U.S. power.[24] Ten months later, back in Mexico, Lang returned to the same arguments when addressing UNESCO. He denounced the motivation of pure financial profit in cultural life, a tendency he implicitly linked to the U.S.A. In the same speech he defended Fidel Castro's Cuba, and suggested that the U.S. was imposing a single standardized culture across the planet.[25]

The socialist campaigns coincided with and legitimated renewed right-wing lobbying against Hollywood. For example, in May 1981 a Comité pour l'Identité Nationale appealed for national independence from what they described as the American colonization of France. They called on Lang to fight against the Motion Picture Association of America (MPAA), which they defined as a powerful lobby for U.S. cultural imperialism. According to the group, the MPAA's objective was to monopolize cinema in the Western world. The new Comité asserted that the cinema, including film distribution via television, was a core medium for the promotion of cultural values. To continue to paraphrase, U.S. dominance of television and cinema screens was negatively impacting on the young, and French youth knew more about the American Civil War than they did about the Revolution. The Comité called for a reduction in quotas of U.S. imports, so that only twenty per cent of U.S. films could be shown and preferably these were to come from independent distributors. In addition, they protested against the rise of the usage of English language over French and identified the dominance of English-language film and music as the means by which this was occurring.[26]

Fifty founding members of the Comité attached their names to its petition. Among them there were the veteran actor Jean-Louis Barrault and the playwright Eugène Ionesco. Several professional writers on the perceived U.S.-American menace to France were understandable supporters, including Henri Gobard, a professor of English at University of Paris VIII who was the author of two works that attacked a perceived Americanization of France, *L'Aliénation linguistique* (1976, preface by Gilles Deleuze) and *La Guerre culturelle* (1979). Jacques Thibau, a retired Gaullist diplomat and former director of the Antenne 2 television channel who had authored *La France colonisée* (1979), was another name on the list.[27] Another former Gaullist politician, Louis Terrenoire, was also a signatory, as was the onetime secretary to General de Gaulle, Claude Mauriac. Other right wingers featured, notably the maverick journalist Gabriel Matzneff and the royalist historian Philippe Ariès. Another conservative journalist and writer, Philippe de Saint Robert, supported the cause. Earlier that year it was the same de Saint Robert who had attacked an academic work that had praised cosmopolitan culture by describing its author Guy Scarpetta as suffering from 'Francophobie'.[28]

Five weeks after the original petition, again in *Le Monde*, a list of new adherents was circulated. The significant additional associate was Marguerite Duras, and she was listed next to the historians Marc Ferro and Jean Mitry, as well as alongside film scholar Guy Hennebelle. In addition, the outspoken actor-turned-filmmaker Gérard Blain and the film critic Michel Marmin were now supporters. In an additional column for *Le Monde* titled 'Le poison americain', Blain taunted the Americans by calling them zombies and underlining that Lang was a better socialist than Blum.[29]

Michel Marmin's turn to anti-Americanism was intriguing and unusual. During the Vietnam War he had supported U.S. anticommunist military action and had dedicated his published study of director of westerns and war films Raoul Walsh to serving GIs.[30] During the Vietnam War some on the extreme right wing, like Marmin, adopted a pro-U.S. position. *The Times* of London reported on 22 December 1967 that thirty right-wing Parisian youths attacked a showing of the anti-Vietnam war film, *Loin du Vietnam*. Nonetheless, the extreme right-wing political think tank where Marmin was a leading protagonist, Groupement de Recherche et d'Études pour la Civilisation Européenne (GRECE), made 1981 the year of a cultural war against the U.S.A. Marmin did not disappoint his colleagues, who were riding high in the early 1980s when the *nouvelle droite* was relatively influential in mainstream media, notably at *Le Figaro magazine*.[31]

However, one should be cautious about the status of this kind of evidence, as it is hard to assess whether consent was fully given by supposed signatories. André Halimi, co-director of the Deauville festival, explains that people informed him that they had neither read nor signed the petition even though their names had featured on it (notably: Claude Mauriac, Philippe Ariès, Jean-Louis Barrault, Yves Berger and Jean-Marie Domenach). Further evidence lends weight to these suspicions. Thus, Jean-Patrick Manchette learned that his friend and fellow crime writer Pierre Siniac, who had been listed as a supporter, neither signed any formal declaration nor followed the movement's thinking but nonetheless found his name on the petition.[32] Richard Kuisel, who recently wrote on this same lobby group, notes too that its campaign prompted intellectual counter-responses in periodicals such as *Esprit*, although he overlooks the suspicion that its very supporters were thinner on the ground than the published petition indicated.[33]

The devil can be in the detail and it is worth noting that Lang's hostility towards the Deauville festival was also an act of domestic political theatre. Halimi and Lionel Chouchan had founded the festival in 1975 with the support of then President D'Estaing's Minister of Industry and Research, Michel d'Ornano, the mayor of Deauville. D'Ornano had promoted the festival in its first year and had stated that it was an exceptionally positive way to encourage tourism. Hence, Lang was not obliged to attend an event that was linked to the previous rival political administration. Furthermore, Lang's career as the director of the Théâtre National de Chaillot had been abruptly terminated in

1974 by a colleague of d'Ornano, Michel Guy, then serving minister of culture. One should add that Mitterrand and Lang were also appreciative of the film people who had favoured the socialists in the elections of 1981 and maybe felt honoured to speak up for their profession in a very public manner quickly after the ballot. Named supporters of Mitterrand had included Chabrol, Demy, Depardieu, Sami Frey, Kast, Piccoli and Truffaut.

In the second *septennat* of the Mitterrand presidency, the Deauville festival sparked a new phase of anti-Americanism. In 1993, Minister of Culture Jacques Toubon, serving under conservative Prime Minister Balladur, with a now aging President Mitterrand watching them carefully, attended the festival. After the premiere of Steven Spielberg's *Jurassic Park*, he asserted that it was very impressive but not moving or humane because of its special effects.[34] He also stated that it was a threat to 'l'identité nationale' because in a world of post-GATT (General Agreement on Tariffs and Trade) reform free trade it would take over more screens than any other film. Journalists paid attention to Toubon's reaction and in a series of articles reported his concerns and offered extensive details on the massive budget that Spielberg had used for *Jurassic Park*, as well as the marketing campaigns that companies employed to stimulate dinosaur-mania among consumers. Reviewing the press from the period, one finds militaristic maps and diagrams describing Spielberg's plans to distribute *Jurassic Park* across the world.[35] There, the capitalist profit motive of a U.S. studio is reinterpreted through war metaphors similar to those voiced in the 1946–1948 protest campaigns against Blum–Byrnes.

Antipathy towards Spielberg's film was part of an ongoing discussion in France about the liberalization of the international film trade. Since the late 1980s, the French had been defending a protectionist position and now world trade discussions under the GATT meant that a new agreement had to be thrashed out. The GATT was established in 1947 to assist in postwar economic recovery and, through many rounds of revision and negotiation, nation-states from around the world had accepted the expansion of free trade across a range of sectors within the economy. By the 1990s, the U.S. was pushing for cinema as a new field for liberalization. The French government considered that such a situation would inevitably lead to domination by Hollywood. Therefore, *Jurassic Park* stood for far more than a big-budget film because in the minds of the French it represented the cinema that would dictate film culture in general if they were unable to maintain protectionism. In a speech made in the newly democratic Poland, Mitterrand marked out the fundamental issues:

> What is at stake is the cultural identity of all of our nations. It is the right of all peoples to their own culture. It is the freedom to create and choose our own images. A society which abandons to others the way of showing itself, that is to say the way of presenting itself to itself, is a society enslaved.[36]

Behind the scenes he encouraged Prime Minister Balladur to win German support in the GATT reform debate in exchange for conceding that the European Monetary Institute be located in Frankfurt.[37] Filmmakers supported their president, even if unaware of his wheeling and dealing around European fiscal matters. For example, director and novelist Pierre Schoendoerffer, who had recently completed his epic on colonial warfare *Dien Bien Phu* (1992), exclaimed: 'We French are rooted in our land; our culture and our agriculture are connected. America is not a melting pot but a series of lobbies'. In a similar tone, Claude Berri expressed the fact that he no longer wanted to be treated as if he were a 'redskin'. When an earthquake hit California, the former director of Gaumont, Toscan du Plantier, declared that God had chosen sides in the GATT feud (for which he later apologized).[38]

More positively, government and press championed Claude Berri's adaptation of Émile Zola's *Germinal* as evidence of the national cinema to be protected from predicted elimination by free trade. To such an end, on 26 September 1993, 350 honoured guests from the press and the arts were transported by Eurostar train from Paris to Lille for a premiere gala of *Germinal*. In the company of President Mitterrand, Claude Berri, the stars Gérard Depardieu and Miou Miou, they were the first audience to enjoy the new movie. A second event, less grand than the first, was organized for Minister of Culture Toubon. At Val-de-Marne, situated near the Eurodisney park, Toubon attended another gala showing to open a new Pathé Multiplex. Historian Rod Kedward describes these events most astutely: 'Mitterrand's personal journey to attend the Lille opening ... was interpreted as a part-socialist, part-romantic, but mostly national gesture'.[39] Again one can underline that there were always also dissenting voices and subtle variations beneath a general consensus. For example, taking a right-wing counterposition, Louis Pauwels, for *Le Figaro*, accepted the need for a national triumph in filmmaking at a time when

American cinema threatened to annihilate French cinema. However, for him *Germinal* was unconvincing for the task at hand and he protested that the Ministry of Education was funding thousands of cinema tickets for schoolchildren to watch a socialist work. He wondered what kind of history lesson that really was. In more marginal right-wing publications than *Le Figaro*, the sometime scriptwriter A.D.G. ranted about the absurdity of it all: 'On parle plus que de ça. C'est épatant, ça fait peur aux dinosaures de Jurassic Park, tout cet anthracite, c'est même plus noir que Malcolm X' ['We are only ever talking about this. It's amazing, all this coal is frightening the dinosaurs from Jurassic Park, it's even blacker than Malcolm X'].[40] Far more balanced views were expressed in *Cahiers du cinéma* where Thierry Jousse noted for his readers that no one in France was opposed to protecting 'l'identité cinématographique française', but that the cinema was also a 'territoire très personnel' without any sovereignty.[41]

It was also the case that the film prompted new 'making of' publications, thereby continuing a relatively impartial cinephile tradition discussed earlier in this book. Now, literary journalist Pierre Assouline had been given full access to Berri's filming and published in time for the film's completion his diary-like account, *Germinal: l'aventure d'un film*.[42] It is a sample of the type of enthusiastic publication that enriches a culture of cinephilia, although the marketing was no doubt swept up into the wider rivalry with *Jurassic Park*. Encouraged by the government, many French men and women considered it a patriotic duty to watch *Germinal*. Ticket sales for the film suggest that they were keen to play their part, with Berri's work gaining a good market share against *Jurassic Park*. Mitterrand, Balladur and Toubon's position of defending cinema from the liberalization of markets was equally successful. France, in tense cooperation with the European Union, asserted a clause in the GATT round that maintained limitation of free trade in film. This famous *exception culturelle* was a significant victory for the Mitterrand presidency.

Writing in his memoirs, the producer Toscan du Plantier compared Mitterrand's and France's GATT victory with General de Gaulle's wartime heroism of the 1940s. He writes: 'C'était une bonne idée! Métaphoriquement, "l'exception culturelle", c'est Londres, c'est le 18-juin. Un jour on pense "non", et l'on s'aperçoit qu'on n'est pas seul. Cela aura été mon honneur de faire partie de cette poignée de "non" au GATT' ['It's a good idea. Metaphorically, the "exception culturelle", is London, the 18 June 1940. One day one thinks "no" and one discovers that one is not alone. It would have been my honour to be a part of the handful of politicians who said "No" to GATT'].[43] This variation of anti-American discourse is especially telling. Both at the time of GATT and in several of the other film events noted in this chapter, the French describe themselves as fighting a campaign of resistance. The central trope of France as a threatened nation repelling an invader chimed with the classic historical image of the resistance as a militarily inferior force that was nonetheless able to repel Nazism and recover an honourable victory after humiliation. This mythology means that the French identify themselves and their compatriots as the plucky underdogs who are able, through ingenuity, community self-support and artisanship, to stand firm against a Goliath. The imagined Frenchness of the late 1940s, the early 1980s and the 1990s is that of a noble and united people who are threatened but who can nonetheless continue to achieve greatness against the odds.

Let us note too that language was an important issue in the 1993 dispute. French directors who were making films in the English language to expand their world market share were singled out as traitors by some of their fellow professionals. At the 1993 national film award, the Césars, these works were banned from the competition. President of Honour of the Competition, the filmmaker Roberto Enrico, justified the exclusions thus:

A l'heure où l'industrie audiovisuelle des États-Unis est omniprésente sur tous les marchés, à l'heure où le cinéma européen, reflet de nos cultures et de nos differences, est en danger, à l'heure où malgré son état de crise, le cinéma français est l'un des dernièrs à survivre, il nous est apparu nécessaire de redéfinir la notion de film 'français' dans le seul dessein de promouvoir des films d'expression originale française.[44]

[At a time when the American audiovisual industry is omnipresent in all markets, when European cinema, the reflection of our cultures and our differences, is in danger, when despite its state of crisis the French cinema is one of the last to survive, it appears to us necessary to redefine the idea of a French film with the intention to promote films expressed in French.]

However, such developments did not pass without controversy and counterargument. Louis Malle asserted that, although his new film *Damage* had used English, it remained French. He threatened that if the exclusion of such 'French films in English' continued then he would no longer enter any works in the César competition. Claude Berri supported Malle's position. He justified his using English in *L'Amant* (1992, Jean-Jacques Annaud), which he had produced, by explaining that commercial reasons were the motive behind the decision. He protested that the choice of English did not mean that French directors and French films lost their soul or their essential French and European identity.[45]

Finally, speeches and intellectual polemics have sometimes shifted from the language of war to genuine if minor diplomatic incidents. In the run-up to GATT, reform tensions escalated dramatically when, in 1989, Mayor of Paris Jacques Chirac threatened to expel U.S. film crews working in his city. He explained that this was in retaliation for the U.S. embassy's refusal to give visas to French technicians waiting to join director Élie Chouraqui to work in Chicago on the film *Miss Missouri*. Jack Lang added to the controversy by officially declaring that if the visas were not granted within twenty-four hours the French would be forced to take further measures.[46] Years earlier there were tensions too when Claude Chabrol's political thriller *Nada* (1974) included scenes in which a fictional U.S. ambassador to Paris visits a brothel, shortly before he is kidnapped by a leftist terrorist group. The film's release was delayed because the Quai d'Orsay (the foreign office) requested it not be shown to the public before being fully approved by Maurice Druon. They did not want it to offend the U.S.A., described by them at that time as a 'grande nation amie'.[47]

In the tense year of 1968, it was the French who were concerned by the filming of a U.S.-produced spy film in their country. Often overlooked because Hitchcock was so admired in France, Minister of Culture André Malraux temporarily forbade him from location shooting for espionage thriller *Topaz* because it was felt that it was too negative towards Gaullist policy. Donald Spoto outlines the crisis that followed:

A hasty meeting was arranged with the American Ambassador in Paris, Sargent Shriver, who was somewhat puzzled to find himself in the role of movie agent. Was this a matter for the embassy? He wanted to know. It was indeed, Coleman [Assistant Producer] insisted, since the French government had raised it to that level by complaining that Universal and Alfred Hitchcock were producing an anti-French film. ... The possibility of

*international intrigue had moved from the story to real life just long enough
to cause him [Hitchcock] anxiety.*[48]

In conclusion, the selected anti-American film events illustrate how relatively frequently France spiralled into imagining its cinema to be under threat. One can say that this encounter with America has been experienced negatively and that the metaphors of invasion and resistance regularly feature. These are, I suggest, important less for what they reveal of people's genuine attitudes towards the U.S.A. and more as an assertion of a continued image of France as the independent, feisty resister. The above pages have, however, also highlighted two important caveats to this generalization. (1) There were usually tensions and contradictions in the protests and there were refined positions on the left and right. Here one should follow Ralph Sarkonak who so helpfully underlines in a special issue of *Yale French Studies* dedicated to 'France/U.S.A.: The Culture Wars' that the Franco-American dialogue is not only about the international exchange but also about internal politics and two localized culture wars.[49] Certainly, in Cold War France such matters were a chance for the left to demonstrate its patriotism and to indulge in populism. It was also a space where left and right could compete with each other, egging each other on to new rhetorical heights. This was certainly the case in the GATT disputes, since Mitterrand was a socialist president working with a conservative Prime Minister (Balladur) and Minister of Culture (Toubon). As discussed in my earlier reading of the reception of *Un homme et une femme*, detailed content of films did not always matter because reviewing and politico-intellectual response was part of a wider framed discussion.

(2) It is a genuinely difficult judgement to identify where enthusiasm for independent cinema ends and where the more xenophobic discourse about fear of Hollywood begins. In periods of direct economic debate on trade, these lines are sometimes deeply blurred. A case-by-case analysis is the key to differentiate between a passionately cinephile 'making of' work, like Assouline's book about *Germinal*, and a more reactionary intervention, such as Blain's polemic against Hollywood in *Le Monde* (1981). It is also worth pointing out here that the general public have often read French protectionism as a positive force for all of European cinema, and that to some extent the French approach developed towards Hollywood has been taken in some countries as something of a universal model to defend against so-called cultural imperialism. Such

matters go beyond the terms of reference of this book. What one can add here is that in these larger, international discussions, the localized French nationalism is itself quite often very simplistically, romantically read, neglecting the intense Parisian press and film scene that has over the years offered up offensive xenophobia under the banner of protecting freedom from Hollywood.

Metaphors of Metaphors: Implications and Codifications Onscreen

In the public debates against Hollywood very little detail is ever given about the enemy. Hollywood is menacing, anonymous and powerful. Extremists sometimes used the slang term 'ricains' to put down the U.S.A., but otherwise it is noticeable that the rhetoric lacked any real detail. Nevertheless, three individuals were regularly targeted. James F. Byrnes (of Blum–Byrnes notoriety) is repeatedly attacked and French critics note how he was employed in the U.S. film industry shortly after his diplomatic career ended. It is implied that this was his reward for trying to 'kill French cinema'. Second, MPAA chief Jack Valenti is similarly characterized as a scheming and hostile player during the GATT disputes, as well as before. Finally, it was two films from Steven Spielberg (*Raiders of the Lost Ark* [1981]; *Jurassic Park*) that were premiered at Deauville when the major controversies of the 1980s and 1990s flared up. Already, before Deauville 1981, some on the left had criticized his work and taken him as a negative example of low-quality but highly commercial U.S. filmmaking. For instance, when his *Jaws* was released, the critic at the socialist-leaning newspaper *Libération* underlined that it was only pretending to be critical of American corruption and that Peter Benchley (author of the novel from which the film is adapted) was linked to the CIA.[50] When Spielberg attempted serious works, these too were harshly treated in France. Generally speaking, *Schindler's List* (1993) was roundly viewed as too melodramatic a vision of history to be appropriate for the subject it was treating. However, this was a view that many intellectuals in the U.S.A. shared with their French counterparts and which was widely circulated in cultural magazines such as *The Village Voice*.[51]

If the film events are high on passion and rather low on detail, there is an even greater fogginess about anti-Americanism in cinema itself. What is suggested in the next pages is that films themselves were far more ambiguous and heavily coded political communication than the polemics and controversies discussed above. Certainly, filmmakers did evoke and loosely mirror some of the crises described above; however, this was through muted inference and reference. Where one might have expected series of quite explicit fictions made against Hollywood, such direct attacks were seemingly non-existent. In their place were metaphorical critiques, plays on the bolder 'U.S. invasion metaphor/French resistance' theme so prominent in public debates (circa Blum–Byrnes and recurrent).

As David Bellos and others have highlighted in their work, when the anti-Blum–Byrnes campaigns were at their height, famously, Jacques Tati's cinema played with the anxiety of Americanization.[52] His first major work, *Jour de fête* (1949) is the most explicitly ideologically coloured of his career and is replete with amusing anti-American imagery and plot. A postman in a rural village (Tati) observes in an imported U.S. film clip how the American mail service has modernized and improved their delivery system. Taking the U.S. film images as a literal truth, the French postman attempts to import the new American lessons to his round. The result is a series of accidents and disasters that make fun of the Frenchman who thought he could adapt U.S. practices to the Hexagon. Tati's political subtext is that if France copies the American way of life then only horrible failure will result. The director's thesis is that the mixing of American ideas with French society is a recipe for disaster.

The same coded message runs through several of Tati's subsequent works. In *Mon oncle* (1958), for instance, Tati juxtaposes an idealized depiction of small-town France with the horrors of the modern Americanized suburbs. Here he imagines the consequences of Americanization: odd modernist architecture, people in a hurry without time to talk, and so on. Unsurprisingly, the communist critic Georges Sadoul adored it, telling readers of his column in *Les Lettres françaises* that the film was made for them, the ordinary people of France.[53] In his next film, *Playtime* (1967), Tati mocks the standardization of international tourism. Therein he imagines a world where every service is so similar and therefore bland that there is almost no national-cultural identity left to enjoy. In a moment of pure pathos the Eiffel tower is glimpsed, but only as a reflection in the shiny windows of a hotel. The director's vision of a Parisian suburb that looks like any other modern city functions to criticize mass culture, and the film works well as an appeal for a return to a world where national differences exist.

Tati's France is a nation living in fear of cultural mixing, modernity and change inspired by U.S. practices. As has been said before, it chimes quite directly with the Blum–Byrnes era rhetoric against cultural standardization but cleverly avoids any political heavy-handedness. His cinema is important because it provided images that simply hinted at the fantasy idea of the American invasion, which never actually occurred but was standard in writings and newspaper opinion pieces of the Blum–Byrnes period. His exaggerated presentations of modern urban life showed audiences what the future negative modernity could be like and not what it was like. These were comedies but they were science-fiction parables too. The almost surrealist subtext to many of the films enhanced this aspect, as did the famous use of silent comedy. *En passant* one can note that in Hollywood Chaplin had made similar fun with modernity in his *Modern Times* (1936) and that this was surely an influence on Tati.

Other less famous comedy directors employed narratives that had similarities with the Tatean political imagination. For instance, *La Grande lessive* (Mocky, 1968) explains the frustrations of a hardworking schoolteacher who is tired of his pupils watching too much television. To counteract these pitiful educational circumstances, he begins a campaign to destroy the medium by breaking television aerials and transmitters across Paris. He and a band of other traditionalists take on the television authority, which is modelled on a U.S. corporation. In brief, the film narrates a French counterattack after the successful invasion of the television. One can recall too *Les Gaspards* (Tchernia, 1974), which describes how a group of Parisians who are hostile to contemporary urbanization of their community take action into their own hands by kidnapping international tourists and holding them to ransom. This was all familiar territory for co-scriptwriter, René Goscinny, the author of the *Asterix* comics. After all, in the comics he had imagined the besieged Gauls fighting off the stupid but hegemonic Romans. However, here too we should recall Klein's *Mister Freedom*, which is discussed in the opening pages of this book. In light of the films discussed here, one realizes how clever that work really is. In its over-the-top aesthetics, it at once provides the perfect fantasy of an American invasion (*Mister Freedom* is here to save France) and at the same time because of this exaggeration it is also a brilliant satire on the comedy tradition discussed above.

To digress a little here, Jean Renoir's *Le Déjeuner sur l'herbe* (1959) merits renewed viewing because it works in similar ways to the above films but its target is the nascent European Union and not the U.S.A. Shot on location in the hills above Nice, at the Renoir family home, the story mocks a European scientific commission and the Germans who work for it. The film is the only known example I have found of a postwar comedy where a modernist invasion is not attributed to the U.S.A. but rather to a European neighbour. It is also distinctive in its simplicity and the relative openness of the hostility towards the German characters.

Through the 1950s and 1960s, other genres repeated a vague impression that U.S. power was eradicating sovereignty. Clouzot's noir spy thriller *Les Espions* (1957) is a very different film from Tati's work, but it is another fascinating retelling of a coded U.S.-invasion political myth. In *Les Espions*, Clouzot narrates the story of a young French doctor, Dr Malic (Gérard Sety), who runs a private mental asylum. Facing hard times and therefore needing monies to maintain this establishment, he is bribed by an American intelligence agent to use the facility to house an important secret guest. Detailed scenes from the film underline its implicit political message. For example, American agent Colonel Howard warns the doctor that his life is at risk by accepting the arrangement. Innocently, Dr Malic asserts that nothing untoward will happen to him because, 'we are in France and not Chicago'. Ominously Howard replies that this may be so but that there are ruthless people from Chicago, Madrid and Moscow at work in France and that no one can stop them. The political integrity of France is insecure and even though Dr Malic is on home soil, his government has no power to protect him.

Les Espions includes another important theme that chimes with some of the tone of anti-Americanism in protests, policy and the press: the nation's control and protection of technology. As the narrative develops through a series of twists and turns, the audience discovers that Dr Malic must try to help a European scientist, Professor Hugo Vogel. Vogel is a great man whom both of the superpowers (the U.S.A. and the U.S.S.R.) wish to capture and control to exploit his knowledge for military purposes. There are echoes here of anxieties that were rife inside the film industry. Since the 1920s, cineastes perceived technical development as part of an international competition for success and they commonly believed that Hollywood had been empowered by the invention of sound. In 1946 Pagnol wrote that U.S. colour film would destroy French cinema unless the industry mastered the new technology. Writing in private in his notebooks, he jotted a series of quite wacky military-technological interpretations of recent history. For him the final part of the Second World War was shaped by a race for German colour-film technology and the U.S.A. and the U.S.S.R. invaded Germany in 1944/1945 with a top priority of capturing the Agfacolor studios in Wolfen.[54]

New Wave cinema is not usually associated with anti-Americanism; quite the contrary. Nevertheless, some of the corpus did have a quite complex ideological colouring. Re-viewing *À bout de souffle*, it is plausible to interpret it as a very subtle, cut-up reworking of the standard American invasion mythology voiced more clearly in intellectual and political debates. Paris is still Paris but dotted about the city are the invader's bastions, a U.S. travel agency, ugly modern architecture (explicitly highlighted) and the offices of the *International Herald Tribune*. Eisenhower is in town and uniformed American soldiers are walking on the streets. Frenchman Michel (Belmondo) is in awe of American culture, cars, clothes, gangster films and his girlfriend, Patricia (Seberg). Moreover, Godard suggests that this fascination with America is his downfall, after all pretty Patricia reports him to the police. A death that is foretold by the visiting intellectual Parvulesco (played by Melville) who when asked about the difference between American and French women, remarked: 'There's no comparison between French and American women. The American woman dominates man. The French woman doesn't … yet'. The famous jump-cut editing makes the narrative a loose and highly ambiguous affair but the anti-American subtext is surely identifiable when one begins to explore the film for the theme. Besides underlining the American military-political-economic presence in Paris, Godard implies that Patricia doesn't give much of a damn about her Frenchman. To repeat his love is rewarded with a phone call to the police. Dying, Michel moans 'c'est dégueulasse' ['it's disgusting'] and the treacherous American girlfriend is informed he has called her 'dégueulasse' ['you're disgusting']. She states 'What is dégueulasse?' This could be taken as sorrowful guilt, sudden existential confusion. Or, alternatively, it underlines Patricia's complete superficiality and willingness to instantly forget all that has occurred, in the cliché, to go on to another 'frontier', to betray another Frenchman. It also highlights her linguistic incompetence, as Michel has used the term already in her company, but she was not listening.

Godard's presentation of the film on its release lends this interpretation some credibility. Speaking to Yvonne Baby, he commented: 'On this theme of Truffaut I told the story of an American girl and a Frenchman. Things couldn't go well between them because he thinks about death all the time, while she never gives it a thought'.[55] *À bout de souffle*'s hidden politics are not so far removed from those that shape Tati's or Clouzot's earlier films. This is not the only way to watch *À bout de souffle*, to be sure; the work is open to many forms of analyses, including Godard's fascination with American modernity which is also there.[56] What I simply want to draw attention to is that maybe on a very crude level one can map together traces of Blum–Byrnes rhetoric in this significant and brilliant work.

Plainly the New Wave was a highly sophisticated and complex aesthetic and historical moment that is about many different things: changing generations, liberalization, decolonization, youth, modernity and style. A part of this richness is some ambivalence towards the U.S.A.; fascination and contempt need not be contradictory emotions. Part of the brilliance of Godard is to weave such complexity into a single groundbreaking film that cannot be pinned down to a single simplistic meaning.

Tracking through films made in the modern period (1945–1995), one can suggest that selected examples of portrayals of American men do focus on the military (as in *Les Espions*) or ruthless big business. Jean-Luc Godard's imagined Hollywood film producer Prokosch (Jack Palance) is the definitive example of the latter type: a monster worthy of brave resistance if ever there was one. Throughout *Le Mépris*, the American mocks fine art, teases European director Fritz Lang and humiliates French scriptwriter Paul (Michel Piccoli). He asserts his loathing of culture and freely quotes Goebbels, thus blurring the lines between Hollywood and the Third Reich. He is proudly monolingual, barking out orders in English to all the French speakers who work for him (Palance provided a wonderful performance of arch villainy). An element of the narrative of *Le Mépris* is again about the invasive, negative presence of U.S. power in France and Europe. Let us recall, it is partly implied that because French scriptwriter Paul panders to Prokosch, he loses the respect of his girlfriend Camille (Bardot). His feeble resistance to Hollywood is further punished when she gravitates towards Prokosch. And Godard shows that, unlike the ponderous Frenchman Paul, Prokosch is pleased to just take her for himself. Perhaps I am reading too much into all this but my central point is that the filmic treatment is more ambiguous and sophisticated than the protests and campaigns analysed earlier in this chapter.

It is less widely acknowledged that Truffaut poked fun at corporate America. Ten years before Jack Lang's boycott of the Deauville film festival, he made *Domicile conjugal*, a work replete with edgy comment on U.S. business culture. Memorably, the director's alter ego Antoine Doinel (Jean-Pierre Léaud) is employed by an American corporation to radio-control absurd model electronic boats around its ridiculous mock-up of a modern port. It is a stupid job that is utterly pointless. Moreover, Doinel is only employed by the company because the Americans hire people who they think are anticommunist, preferably with links to fascism. In an extremely funny scene Truffaut portrays the U.S. company director believing he is recruiting a good anticommunist. In a nod to Tati's set designs for *Mon oncle* and *Playtime*, and Godard's *Alphaville* (1965), the architecture of the American corporate headquarters is ugly modernism, the military compound look, a Pentagon by the Seine if you like. In case audiences didn't fully recognize the homage to the great director-comedian, Tati appears in a two-minute cameo for Truffaut, passing Antoine Doinel on the Denfert-Rochereau metro platform.

American women are not negatively portrayed in quite the same way as men. When they feature they are treated as exotic and erotic love interests for Frenchmen to seduce or enjoy looking at (the experience for the male audience). Jean Seberg set the tone in *À bout de souffle* although, as noted, her treachery lends the role a potentially nationalistic as well as sexist element. Sadoul's review captures the ambiguity rather well: 'it was certainly quite an achievement to transform Jean Seberg, a cold fish in *Bonjour tristesse*, into a brightly coloured, scintillating and lissom trout wriggling in a stream. However attractive she may be her character turns out ... to be a perfect "bitch"'.[57] Jane Fonda followed in her footsteps, as did Candice Bergen, each starring in major works from Godard and Lelouch respectively. In short, the U.S. women are represented as trophies for Frenchmen to pursue, sometimes with fatal consequences and sometimes not. Generally speaking, though, these portrayals of American women contrast rather favourably with the depictions of English women. Following her contribution to *The Night Porter* (Cavanni, 1974), for a while Charlotte Rampling was repeatedly cast as a pervert living in Paris. Jacques Deray's *On ne meurt que deux fois* (1985) remains the classic example. Therein Rampling plays temptress to a police officer (Serrault) while indulging in incest with her brother. However, one should acknowledge that this film is based on the grimy crime novel, *He Died with His Eyes Open*, written by British author Derek Raymond.

The films that placed French characters in America inverted parts of the narrative pattern of U.S. invasion by highlighting how displaced the citizens of

France are when they visit the United States. The famous example is *Le Gendarme à New York* (Girault, 1965), wherein amusing *flic* (Louis de Funès) is sent to New York to solve a mystery. When the cops are in New York they assert their Frenchness by eating well and, like Jacques Tati before them, failing to understand modern technology. This is all very funny; however, the premise remains that France and America are distinctive and that the two cultures cannot mix.[58] Works of more serious cinema were also vectors for similar impressions of the U.S.A. Thus, Jacques Deray shot *Un homme est mort* (1972) on location in California. It is a brilliant if bleak gangster film that reveals Los Angeles's criminal underbelly. Herein the French assassin (Trintignant) dies in the city, slumped at the wheel of his Cadillac: a bleak if poetic ending to a fast-paced film that casts a critical eye over the contemporary American city.[59] In a different genre, Alain Resnais included images of North American city slums in his philosophically inflected melodrama, *Mon oncle d'Amérique* (1978). The thesis of his film is that humans function like animals and that they are aggressive or self-harming when they are provoked. As this argument is fully elaborated in the final minutes of the film, via a voiceover from Resnais, one is shown the mean streets of urban decay. The allusive message seems to possibly be that France will soon face this miserable future, because it is also experiencing a comparable modern social development.

Conclusion

Anti-Americanism expressed in public debates around cinema issues (mainly around economics and trade) was a powerful conduit for nationalist ideology, ruling out mixing of cultures and, for our concerns just as importantly, imagining France as independent, pure and resistant to a domineering cousin. The metaphor of invasion and response was set up during the Blum–Byrnes dispute and has recurred on several significant occasions. However, I believe that the above attitudes were far more common in general political, economic and intellectual debates than in any individual works of cinema. There are examples of some mocking images of American business people, corporate life, the military, but these matters are framed through genres such as comedy, spy and science fiction that lend an absurdity to the political undergirding. This implicit critique of American culture was demonstrated through set design and images of modernist architecture and art, rather than more explicit narrative emphasis. These are therefore themselves metaphors of the invasion metaphor, what in semiotics one might call at the very least a third-order form of communication, after primary and secondary meaning is established. Here *Le Mépris* does draw one's attention because Prokosch (Palance) does so directly resemble the feared invader of Blum–Byrnes lore.

Why would such a divergence between offscreen rhetoric and onscreen material occur? Commercially there was no market for self-serving propaganda, and American films were very popular. Directors, cameramen and others were admirers of impressive American examples of their chosen art, including *Gone with the Wind*, Hitchcock and Raoul Walsh, to name a selection featured herein. And what is important is that this admiration of professional talent was very usually maintained, even when criticizing Hollywood. Similarly, it is noticeable that the most vehement anti-Americans in film events were not often the filmworkers (directors or actors or technician), but politicians, intellectuals, academics and journalists. One might speculate to suggest that their hostility was sharper because they felt no direct affiliation or common bond with fellow film people. They were also never likely to seek employment in the U.S.A.

To repeat a conclusion already drawn in the previous chapter, the film event discussion on the imagined U.S. menace was not necessarily about the reality of content of a film or an economic policy. Rather, it was also about publicly demonstrating a symbolic position for other political groups to understand and then respond to. In other words, we are in a world of layers and shadow games where language and imagery connote subtle stances around left–right politics, rather than to be always taken at immediate face value as being explicitly about cinema.

Notes

1. For the January 1948 rally see G. Leclerc, 1948, 'Tous unis, nous sauverons le Cinéma Français', *L'Humanité*, 4/5 January, 1; 'Pour sauver le cinéma Français', 1948, *Le Monde*, 6 January, 1; 'Tous ceux qui font le cinéma français s'unissent pour le défendre', 1947, *L'Écran français*, 20 December, 131; F. Timmory, 1948, 'Le problème du cinéma français est désormais du domaine public', *L'Écran français*, 13 January, 2–3; H. Magnan, 1947, 'L'Agonie du cinéma français', *Le Monde*, 14

November, 3; P. Ory, 1992, 'Mister Blum goes to Hollywood', in M. Boujut and J. Chancel (eds), *Europe-Hollywood et retour*, Paris: Autrement, 100–111.

2. F. Timmory, 1947, 'Quand vedettes et techniciens s'en vont de salle en salle', *L'Écran français* 143, 23 March, 1.

3. P. d'Hugues, 1999, *L'Envahisseur américain: Hollywood contre Billancourt*, Geneva: Favre, 61.

4. Renoir, *Letters*, 181.

5. See 'Le 14 Juillet a réuni les vedettes et leur public', 1948, *L'Écran français* 166, 20 July, 7.

6. See R. Vautier, 1998, *Caméra citoyenne: mémoires*, Paris: Apogée, 19–23. Concerns about the Americanization of film were voiced as early as 1945, before the accords were ever settled; see for example, 'Défense du cinéma français', 1945, *L'Écran français*, 2, July 11, 2.

7. M. Thorez, 1963, *Oeuvres*, Paris: Éd. Sociales; G. Soria, 1948. *La France deviendra-t-elle une colonie Américaine?*, Paris: Éd.du Pavillion.

8. G. Sadoul, 1938, *Ce que lisent vos enfants*, Paris: Bureau d'éditions.

9. V. Kravchenko, 1948, *J'ai choisi la liberté!*, Paris: Self. For anti-Kravchenko material in the film press, see Barrot, *L'Écran français*, 257–59.

10. E. Gilson, 1948, 'La poutre et la paille', *Le Monde*, 6 January, 1; 'Le comité de défense met les choses aux points', 1948, *L'Écran français* 143, 3 March, 2.

11. Vincendeau, *Jean-Pierre Melville*, 84.

12. P. Laroche, 1946, 'Pour un mort anonyme', *L'Écran français* 51, 19 June, 6; M. Pagnol. 1946, 'Lettre ouverte de Marcel Pagnol', *France Soir*, 29 June.

13. 'Il n'est pas possible d'imaginer que des acteurs français acceptant de rendre "français" un tel film', 1952, *L'Écran français*, 30 January, 6.

14. See BFI Press Pack File: *The Desert Fox*. Clippings there indicate protests around Europe, as well as in South Africa. This coverage is mainly offered in the leftist press, *Daily Worker* and *Tribune*.

15. L. Daquin, 1952, 'Lettre ouverte à un technicien', *L'Écran français*, 23 January.

16. See 'Les policiers qui torturent, les bourreaux qui exécutent se placent eux aussi sur le plan professionel', 1952, *L'Écran français*, 5 March, 10.

17. H. Decae, 1952, 'Je n'entends assumer que la qualité technique des prises de vues', *L'Écran français*, 5 March, 10.

18. See Sadoul, *French Film*, 110–13; J. Davidson, 1954, *Correspondant à Washington, 1945–53*, Paris: Seuil; J-P. Rioux, 1987, *The Fourth Republic, 1944–58*, Cambridge: CUP, 40; for a revision of the standard mythology see J. Portes, 1986, 'A l'origine de la légende noir des accords Blum-Byrnes', *Revue d'histoire moderne et contemporaine* 33, 314–29.

19. See 'Manifeste contre l'invasion des ondes et pour la diversification des échanges audiouvisuel', 1985, *Le Monde*, 24 January. See also 'La Chanson francophone menacée', 1985, *Le Monde*, 26 January.

20. Cited in D. Looseley, 1995, *The Politics of Fun*, Oxford: Berg, 77; See also, 'Un entretien avec M. Jack Lang', 1981, *Le Monde*, 5 September; J. Siclier, 1981, 'Deauville au soleil', *Le Monde*, 8 September; Cld, 1981, 'Les voyages de M. Jack Lang', *Le Monde*, 11 September.
21. Lang remembers selectively. In his 2009, *Demain comme hier*, Paris: Fayard, 144, he recalls visiting a number of French heritage-cum-folkloric sites during the weekend of the Deauville festival but overlooks his reported trip to Rome to watch Gance. For further contemporary accounts see G. Dumur, 1981, 'Eviva Buonaparte!', *Le Nouvel Observateur*, 14 September.
22. See V. Luksic, 1981, 'Première réunion à Rome de la Fédération européenne des réalisateurs', *Le Monde*, 8 May.
23. A. de Baecque and S. Toubiana, *Truffaut*, 728–29.
24. See R. Dumas, 2007, *Affaires étrangères: 1981–1988*, Paris: Fayard.
25. L. Martin, 2008, *Jack Lang: une vie entre culture et politique*, Paris: Complexe, 242–44; A-D. Bouzet, 1992, 'Mexico et après...', in M. Boujut and J. Chancel (eds), *Europe-Hollywood*, 183–84.
26. See 'Cinéma Français et Cinéma Américain', 1981, *Le Monde*, 29 October.
27. See J. Thibau, 1979, *La France colonisée*, Paris: Flammarion; H. Gobard, 1976, *L'Aliénation linguistique*, Paris: Flammarion; and H. Gobard, 1979, *La Guerre culturelle*, Paris: Copernic.
28. See P. de Saint Robert, 1981, 'Cosmopolitisme ou francophobie?', *Le Monde*, 24 April; where de Saint Robert attacks Scarpetta for his 1981, *Éloge du cosmopolitisme*, Paris: Grasset.
29. G. Blain, 1981, 'Le poison américain', *Le Monde*, 19 September.
30. See M. Marmin, 1970, *Raoul Walsh*, Paris: Seghers, 1.
31. See A. Rollat, 1981, 'Le GRECE prêche la 'guerre culturelle' contre les civilisations 'américano-occidentale', *Le Monde*, 20 May.
32. A. Halimi, 1985, *Touche pas à l'Amérique*, Paris: Plon; J-P. Manchette, 1997, *Les Yeux de la momie: chroniques de cinéma*, Paris: Virages, 471–73.
33. R. Kuisel, 2012, *The French Way*, London: Princeton University Press, 50–54.
34. Toubon cited in 'La guéguerre des étoiles', 1993, *Le Nouvel observateur*, 23 September.
35. See M. Guilloux, 1993, 'Le cinéma a ses prédateurs', *L'Humanité*, 19 October. See also P.P., 1993, 'Dinomania: comment l'invasion a été programmé', *L'Événement du jeudi*, 26 August; G. Lefort and O. Seguret, 1993, 'Écran total pour Jurassic Park', *Libération*, 20 October.
36. Cited in J-P. Jeancolas, 1998, 'From the Blum–Byrnes Agreement to the GATT Affair', in G. Nowell-Smith and S. Ricci (eds), *Hollywood and Europe*, London: BFI, 59.
37. E. Balladur, 2009, *Le Pouvoir ne se partage pas*, Paris: Fayard, 134.
38. D. Toscan du Plantier, 1995. *L'Émotion culturelle*, Paris: Flammarion, 110.

39. Kedward, *La Vie*, 578; Drazin, *French Cinema*, 370–76; A. Murray, 2003, 'Film as National Icon: Claude Berri's *Germinal*', *The French Review* CXXVI/5, 906–15.

40. L. Pauwels, 1993, 'L'Assommoir', *Le Figaro*, 16 October; A.D.G., 2008, *Papiers gommés*, Paris: Le Dilettante, 56, originally published in *Le Libre journal de la France courtoise*, 7 October 1993.

41. T. Jousse, 1993, 'Vices publics et vertus privées', *Cahiers du cinéma* 472, 4–5.

42. P. Assouline, 1993, *Germinal: l'aventure d'un film*, Paris: Fayard.

43. du Plantier, *L'Émotion*, 73.

44. 'CESARS 93: LA POLEMIQUE', 1993, *Le Technicien du film et de la video*, 421, 4.

45. 'CESARS 93', 4.

46. M-C.A., 1989, 'Miss Missouri: incident diplomatique entre la France et les U.S.A', *Le Film français* 2261, 1 September, 1, 37.

47. C. Chabrol, 1974, 'Ce qui m'intéresse, c'est l'imbécilité', *Cinématographe* 6, February/March, 4.

48. D. Spoto, 1984, *The Dark Side of Genius: The Life of Alfred Hitchcock*, New York: Plexus, 532.

49. R. Sarkonak, 2001, 'Just How Wide is the Atlantic Anyway?', *Yale French Studies*, 100, 5.

50. See P. Gavi, 1976, '"Jaws", le requin qui menace l'Amérique', *Libération*, 2 February.

51. 'Myth, Movie, and Memory', 1994, *The Village Voice*, 29 March, 24–31.

52. See D. Bellos, 1999, 'Tati and America: *Jour de fête* and the Blum–Byrnes Agreement of 1946', *French Cultural Studies* X/29, 145–59; Ross, *Fast Cars, Clean Bodies*, 42–43, 171–74.

53. G. Sadoul, 1979, *Chroniques du cinéma français*, Paris: Union Générale d'Éditions, 162.

54. M. Pagnol, 2008, *Carnets de cinéma*, Paris: Privé, 143.

55. Godard with Yvonne Baby in *Le Monde* (18 March 1960), cited in D. Andrew, 1987, *Breathless: Jean-Luc Godard, director*, New Brunswick: Rutgers University Press, 165.

56. For an excellent reading that is informed by philosophy and historical context see D. Morrey, 2005, *Jean-Luc Godard*, Manchester: Manchester University Press, 8–15. A further discussion of 'America' and genre film influence on French cinema, including Godard, is provided by G. Vincendeau, 1992, 'France 1945–1965 and Hollywood: the *policier* as International Text', *Screen* 33.1, 50–80.

57. G. Sadoul, 2009, 'Les Quais des brumes 1960', in P. Graham and G. Vincendeau (eds), *The French New Wave: Critical Landmarks*, London: BFI, 235.

58. G. Vincendeau, 2000, *Stars and Stardom in French Cinema*, London: Continuum, 151.

59. See also Drazin, *French Cinema*, 353–54.

CHAPTER FIVE

The Maintenance of Neocolonial Attitudes

In the highly regarded art film *Caché* (Haneke, 2005), a middle-class Parisian family is thrown into turmoil as scenes from their past filter back into their memory, prompted by being seemingly stalked by an Algerian immigrant. As any sense of security painfully unravels, images from a deeply repressed historical episode flash before the principal character's mind. Blocked out from his recollection are the days of his youth when his family took brief custody of an Algerian child who was orphaned after his parents mysteriously disappeared, probably murdered by the police in the violent roundups that infamously took place in Paris in October 1961. This is not the time or place to add to an ongoing and intellectually rich debate on this much-analysed work. What follows, however, is a subtle rethinking and revision of Haneke's aesthetic emphasis on concealment, repression and displacement as being the appropriate modes to think about filmic representation of empire and decolonization. In this chapter it is argued that a more nuanced picture than that emerges, which suggests that the cinema did not simply hide colonial and postcolonial history from all view. The first part below discusses how from the 1960s to at least the 1980s popular genre films and more serious melodramas perpetuated patriotic and defensive colonialist myths and stereotypes. Ex-colonial territories did not therefore disappear from cinema screens altogether but rather were frozen in tropes more reminiscent of the realm of earlier colonial cinema and pulp fiction. The second part of this chapter reconstructs how the right wing reacted to Pontecorvo's *La Bataille d'Alger* and how, there, one discovers an extensive, systematic and very public campaign of hostility. This right-wing repression of the film was not an internalized psychological defence mechanism. On the contrary, it was an open and public display of political commitment and defiance.

Saturday Night at the Movies: Implicit Myths of National Superiority

Neocolonial adventure cinema that implied a national ethnic superiority over non-white, non-Christian 'outsiders' continued for several decades after decolonization, probably only falling out of fashion towards the end of the 1980s. Just sampling the titles from some of these films offers a good indication of their more general tone. For instance, there was an early Yves Montand film *Les Héros sont fatigués* (Ciampi, 1955) that was filmed in Parisian studios and the Camargue but which is set in Liberia. *Congo vivo* (1962), *Safari diamants* (1966), *Soleil noir* (1966) and *Les Aventuriers* (1967) are similarly evocative of the types of work that were being made. Some of these were of little note, minor B-movies, while others pulled in significant audiences. Piecing together the repetitious narrative patterns from this broad corpus, one can discern two common conventions. First, this kind of cinema continued to describe action and adventure in exotic locations, unnamed tropical sites or more barren desertscapes. No matter which landscape was onscreen, and for whatever reason (criminal, economic, espionage), French men found romance, action and adventure around the world. Second, some action thrillers adopted a quite different geographical approach: these works were set primarily in France but featured characters who for brief passages of the work were sent to Africa, but then most of the action followed them back home to the Hexagon. This variant did not require extended location shooting, even in the Camargue, but it did include significant colonialist reference points or backstories.

Henri Verneuil's *Cent mille dollars au soleil* (1964) is exemplary of the first type of work, the 'action in the sun' films. Set in Morocco, Rocco (Jean-Paul Belmondo), Plouc (Lino Ventura) and their friends drive truck convoys for *Transports Transsaharien*. They work hard and play hard but, because Rocco has fallen in love, he is willing to break with his male companions to steal a vehicle with a cargo worth one hundred thousand dollars. When this work was premiered at Cannes (1964), its director Henri Verneuil described it as being an authentically French interpretation of the western.[1] The use of the barren, often beautifully photographed, Moroccan landscapes is reminiscent of this genre. So too is the macho banter between the truck drivers, and Jean-Paul Belmondo wears something akin to a cowboy hat and through much of the action he smokes a cheroot. Be that as it may, Verneuil's work implied that North Africa remained a playground for fun-loving young Frenchmen. Rocco and Plouc race their powerful modern trucks through the countryside and towns of southern Morocco as if they own the country. They assert themselves over the local people, showing no concern for the Moroccans. The picture treats the Moroccans as an anonymous mass of no individual worth who are used as props, adding to the exotic scenery that includes imagery of stereotypical minarets and mountains.

The depiction of drivers racing modern trucks through Africa also directly recalled the famous colonial documentary film, *La Croisière noire* (1926, Léon Poirier). This described how the Citroën car company mounted an automobile expedition across Central Africa, passing through exotic landscapes and filming the Africans for added interest. Citroën made several of these colonial car rallies and they had even attempted to set up automobile tourist routes linking French Algeria to French West Africa.[2] Similarly, Verneuil's work continued Henri-Georges Clouzot's 1953 truck-driving adventure *Le Salaire de la peur*. It was probably the success of that film that made the subgenre of truck movies in the tropics popular in the early 1950s and 1960s. For instance, Jean Gabin played a tough-man driver alongside Jeanne Moreau in Gilles Grangier's *Gas-Oil* (1955). And following *Cent mille dollars*, truckers had further mileage to run (excuse the pun) when in 1967 the Belgian B-Movie director Wily Rozier extended the tradition with *Les Têtes brûlées* (1967).

The 1981 hit film *Le Professionnel* (directed by Georges Lautner and scripted by Michel Audiard) is illustrative of how colonialist and xenophobic themes recur in thrillers that are set mainly in France. This work has an especially thin plot line: French secret services hire Beaumont (Belmondo) to assassinate an African politician. Throughout the film neocolonial prejudices are offered implicitly and presented as normal attitudes for everyone to enjoy. In very brief snippets the film shows that Africa is essentially corrupt, chaotic and therefore an inferior place. The depiction of the black African diplomats who are visiting Paris is especially reactionary: they are characterized as being vain and obsessed with their own importance and they speak in an odd dialect that is supposed to be amusing but is only demeaning. As Yannick Dehée underlines in his impressive study *Mythologies politiques du cinéma français*, there is also an explicit crude racism in the work. For example, when Beaumont kills one African he mutters, 'Tu vois, malin comme un singe' ['You see, cunning like a monkey']. When he throws a policeman onto a group of Arab characters, who are eating together, he quips: 'Et un couscous poulet!' ['Couscous with a cop'].[3] In 1981 this material did receive some critical responses in newspapers such as *Libération*, but the film was nonetheless a huge commercial success, for a time being the highest-earning picture of the decade (5.2 million tickets sold).[4] For what it is worth, and putting the explicit violence of the film to one side for a moment, in many respects *Le Professionnel* closely resembles the Tintin comic books and especially one of their live-action filmic adaptations, *Tintin et les Oranges Bleues* (Condroyer, 1964). Therein, Tintin and his faithful companion Snowy the dog gleefully thwart a menacing and corrupt Middle Eastern conspirator. To paraphrase, set in Valencia, Spain, Tintin confronts the evil machinations of Emir Sadek el Benzine that threaten not only the peace of Franco's happy land but also all of Western Europe. As in the original comic strips, Tintin is the white francophone hero defending the West from a pernicious outsider. As such he is the boyish younger brother to the role in cinema that was often attributed to Jean-Paul Belmondo.[5]

In the later period there were half-hearted attempts to update these kinds of film. The Alain Delon vehicle, *Parole de flic* (Pinheiro, 1985) merits discussion because superficially it appears to be an antiracist film, explicitly different from *Le Professionnel* and the like. Delon plays tough cop Daniel Pratt who is embroiled in another tale of corruption and vengeance. Living in retirement in West Africa, Pratt is informed that his daughter, who is studying in Lyons, has been murdered by a group of extreme right-wing vigilantes. As cop-thriller connoisseurs will have already recognized, it is very close to being a French remake of Clint Eastwood's second Dirty Harry picture, *Magnum Force* (1973). Sadly, despite its best efforts to take the genre in a new direction, the Delon film rehearses numerous paternalistic clichés. For example, Pratt is a friend to all the Africans and he is consistently pictured teaching their children through playing games with them. He smiles benignly at groups of black women and they beam back at him. In addition, he is depicted as being the dominant male in Africa and in Lyons. For example, in the first shots of the film he proves his physical superiority by winning a wrestling match with an African, and with traditional colonial power relations thus established he sets off to Lyons to tame the fascists.

The recurrent subtext of these works is that French male authority is maintained and that Africans (Arabic or black) are the inferior party. The French male is constructed as the force of power, excitement and visual entertainment while the foreigners are the brunt of jokes or enemies to be eliminated. The films continued the old tradition of colonial filmmaking by offering action and adventure that implied a French national supremacy over non-Europeans. Certainly absolutely no significance is placed on non-French culture, values or history. The world is still made for action men (usually Belmondo, sometimes Delon, often also Ventura) to roust about in. Nonwhites are almost always corrupt politicians, thuggish brutes or eroticized pin-up girls. In Africa and Indochina the sky is either blue (or sodden with tropical rain) and the desert or the beaches golden. As we know, representation of landscape is an ideological matter and in these films the setting seems to intimate that everything would still be paradise if it were not for the troublesome locals and one or two corrupt politicians back in Paris. Importantly too, no mention is ever really made of how Empire has ended in military humiliation, complicity in torture and tragic deaths of civilians, among other aspects. The films offer only a symbolic gloss on this history, with their fantasy images compensating for the reality. As might be expected from the above, not a single work features a heroic non-white character. Whereas films in the U.S.A. such as *In the Heat of the Night* (1968), *Shaft* (1971) and *Beverly Hills Cop* (1984) introduced black action heroes (not without their own stereotypes of course), in the same period in France no directly equivalent works were ever made.

The point of the genre was to be suspenseful or fun, not critical or in any way historically accurate, let alone discursive. This was the mode through which the OAS terror campaign in favour of Empire and against decolonization was famously represented on the big screen in the Anglo-French co-production *Day of the Jackal*, in France titled just *Chacal* (Zinnemann, 1973). This was the first major work devoted entirely to the subject of the OAS and mainly it neglects to provide a contextual commentary on the wars of decolonization. Emphasis is placed instead on the game of chess between French policeman (Michael Lonsdale) and English assassin working for the OAS (James Fox). The critics in Paris quite admired the movie and enjoyed its suspense-filled two hours, although they often noted that Frederick Forsyth's original novel was far superior to the film. Consistently they praised the contribution of the two homegrown stars, Lonsdale and, in the role of a sexy aristocrat, Delphine Seyrig (a casting that was not very original following her role in *L'Année dernière à Marienbad* [1961]) and the same critics mocked the British acting talent on show. Similarly, during the location shooting the French film community were upset at how much access the state had given Zinnemann to film on Parisian streets. It was claimed that as a foreigner he was receiving privileged treatment, including special rights to use live footage of 14 July parades.[6] These were the safe patriotic angles taken by journalists to represent *Chacal* to the public in the early 1970s. In short, little in the press or on the screen provided any details about the politics of decolonization.

Besides the action film genre, through the 1970s, some upmarket melodramas also added to the mythology of national racist domination over non-white non-Europeans. The well-known but ambiguous example here is Francis Girod's *L'État sauvage* (1978). It is illustrative of how even quite serious works that were seemingly made to demonstrate a sophisticated approach to representing the non-French world were marked with colonialist prejudices. For, on the one hand, its makers were adamant that their depiction of romance (featuring a historical first, a mixed-heritage sex scene), politics and intrigue in a postcolonial African state was a liberal work, while, on the other hand, the content and general reception of the film evidences that this was largely an unsuccessful ambition.

At a premiere of the film held in Nantes, Girod explained what he had wanted to contribute with *L'État sauvage*. He elaborated: 'J'ai voulu faire un film populaire pour sensibiliser un maximum de gens aux problèmes que pose le racisme.... J'ai justement voulu rappeler deux choses qui sont pour moi essentielles: la nécessité d'être tolérant et de refuser la caricature'[7] ['I wanted to make a popular film to heighten public awareness of the problems created by racism ... I just wanted to recall two things that for me are essential: the importance of tolerance and to reject caricatures']. Speaking to *France Soir,* actor and producer Michel Piccoli confirmed that the film was a condemnation of the racists, any white or black people who had prejudices against sexual relationships between people from different cultures, one of the main themes of the film.[8] Nonetheless, the francophone-African press was highly critical of *L'État sauvage.* In *Demain L'Afrique,* Mourad Bourboune offered a witty and sarcastic review. Here he suggested that with the invention of international tourism the average French man or woman who had experienced an 'exotic' holiday would enjoy the clichés in the film. They would love the scenery that was shown and would not be bothered that the work had been shot in French Guiana, South America, and not in Africa at all.[9] Same N'Gosso at *Afrique-Asie* was disheartened by the dangerous paternalism of the work. He wrote that he was disgusted by the way in which Girod had imagined African politics. Focusing on a scene that depicts a black African government cabinet meeting descending into a farcical exchange of insults, he asked, 'N'est-ce pas là un beau tableau symbolique de l'Afrique tam-tamesque de papa et des nostalgiques du bon vieux temps' ['Is not that scene a pretty symbolic picture of how Daddy imagined tom-tom beating Africa and for those nostalgic for the good old days?'].[10]

Furthermore, the black actors' group, 'Pour les comédiens noirs travaillent en France', directed by Robert Liensol, called on all black actors from Africa and the West Indies to protest together against the racist caricatures found in Girod and Piccoli's film. Their statement highlights that the pernicious aspect of the work was that it had claimed to be antiracist, only with the intention to freely trade in hateful fantasies.[11] Evidence from a provocative media stunt mounted by *L'Express* magazine adds to this picture of the work's failed good intentions. Thus, journalist Michel Delain and the novelist and scriptwriter for the film, Georges Conchon, were flown to Senegal to interview President Léopold Sédar Senghor to find out his response. In the company of the President and Senegalese Prime Minister Abdou Diouf, they watched it at a private screening. As the final reels of the work were spooling through the projector the President intimated that it was appropriate to applaud. However, this was only a diplomatic nicety and when the President further elaborated his judgement was critical. Senghor underlined to his Parisian guests that the image of Africa presented in the film had nothing to do with his country. For example, he highlighted that the scene in the film that showed an African governmental meeting was entirely different from his experience of leadership. He continued that when in 1962 and 1967 there had been some instability in his country, it had not been at all violent. Senghor communicated politely but firmly to his guests that Senegal was not a 'savage state' like the one portrayed in the film. He concluded: 'Mais soyez certains qu'au Sénégal on dira que pareille situation est dépassée pour nous. Nous verrons *L'État sauvage* comme un documentaire sur d'autres pays ... ailleurs' ['But be certain that in Senegal one can say that for us a comparable situation is out of date. We watch *L'État sauvage* as a documentary about other countries ... elsewhere'].[12]

Despite its liberal intentions, *L'État sauvage* does perpetuate significant colonialist attitudes and myths and it is little wonder that it sparked critical press reception. In her discussion of the film, Dina Sherzer suggests that it is replete with stereotypes of race and sexuality. She explains, 'This particularly violent film, which victimizes both the white and black women, repeats the familiar Africanist topoi about black men's sexuality, white women's hysteria in Africa, the accessibility of black girls, and the right of white men to do as they please with black girls'.[13] The film's concluding visualization of the aggressive mobs that attack the two main protagonists is important, too, for reasserting another longstanding colonial and nationalistic stereotype. It is a repetition of the trope that positions Africa as irrational and therefore inferior, and awaiting Western control through supposedly rational assertions of order. The depiction of the African political elite in the film adds to the same notion that the postcolonial state is an anarchic place. Girod and his scriptwriter Conchon did not invent this wider political discourse: it was a common prejudice dating from at least the late nineteenth century, and which had gained new currency during decolonization, not only in France. For example, when in 1959 the Congo gained independence from Belgium, a standard European-metropolitan interpretation was that those Congolese who were fighting for independence were disorderly children; their very revolutionary actions confirmed that they would be incapable of future self-control and self-governance. It is a political myth that implies self-governance is impossible outside of Western Europe and that therefore forms of paternalistic control were legitimate in the past and even that new interventions are always possible in the present.[14]

One should add here that the history/heritage films set in the Imperial past contribute to this same mythology. Probably the first nostalgic and glamorous colonial heritage film in the French language was the Swiss director Daniel Schmid's *Hécate* (1982). It is a lush and romantic melodrama about a French officer falling madly in love while he is posted on a mission to Morocco. Adapted from a novel by the extreme right-wing writer and diplomat Paul Morand, it mixes intrigue, drama and eroticism. It and some of the more famous heritage works of the 1990s imply that the diplomatic and military elite of colonial French rulers, the rich, sophisticated and stylish, did provide some legitimate order and control. The political relationship between a representation such as that provided in *L'État sauvage* and a heritage film such as *Hécate* is therefore dialogic: in the former the cinema shows how chaotic independent states in modern Africa seem to be after decolonization, while in the latter heritage film the historical conditions of Empire are reduced to romantic tales and intrigue among the elite, who are taken as still good enough to rule. In other words, there is some synchronicity between the formats' treatments of past and present. Equally, they share a rejection of exploring how Western policies and actions limited the conduct of democratic politics and economics in the non-European world.

Coincidentally, just one year before the release of *L'État sauvage*, Minister of Foreign Affairs Louis de Guiringaud anticipated its supremacist subtext when he remarked that Africa was the only place in the world where five hundred French soldiers could change the course of history.[15] Indeed, the cinema commemorated one of the more significant of these armed interventions in *La Légion saute sur Kolwezi* (Coutard, 1980). It reconstructs how the Foreign Legion rescued European workers in Kolwezi, Zaire, from an attack mounted by rebels based in Angola (May 1978). In the film, when the Legion lands and a group of black and white prisoners are liberated, they break out into a rendition of the 'Marseillaise'. The film's director Raoul Coutard had hoped to film in Africa but no state was willing to participate so he shot on location in Guiana instead.[16] The work is a straightforward blending together of existing neocolonial approaches, being a mixture of the action-film celebration of French machismo and the assertion that independent African states are anarchic and need re-controlling. *En passant* (and maybe this should be just a footnote), on some albeit rare occasions film people and intellectuals were themselves embroiled in modern African politics. Thus, in 1972 the actor Maurice Ronet and writer Dominique de Roux travelled to Mozambique to make a documentary on the war there. Photographs suggest that they looked the part, Ronet wearing sunglasses and a white foulard and de Roux thinking himself the new Hemingway. Afterwards de Roux fantasized in print that the maintenance of the Portuguese empire would be beneficial for the world.[17]

Finally, let us draw attention to Bertrand Tavernier's *Coup de torchon* (1981), which is of special note here because it can be interpreted as one convincingly original anticolonial treatment. It is important because it so thoroughly deconstructs the neocolonial attitude that the Westerners are sane and the local population is savage, discussed above. Set in the 1930s, and adapted from a novel by Jim Thompson that was originally set in the Deep South, U.S.A., it portrays life in the 1930s in a rough, dusty colonial outpost.[18] The principal protagonists are crude, ugly unfortunate people and here Noiret gives one of his finest ever performances as a world-weary police officer. Throughout this unusual film, Tavernier destroys any glamorization for a golden age of Empire and the idea that it is the Africans who are uncivilized. Cleverly he highlights that the white colonialists are the ones who are slowly going insane. The idea that Africans are the irrational community, so central to *L'État sauvage*, among others, is thereby powerfully inverted in this impressive film. In my opinion, to this day, Tavernier's film is one of the most radical treatments of colonialism ever to be shown in cinemas. It is a work that certainly stands the test of time far better than any others discussed in this section of the book. Moreover, besides its political radicalism it works as a visceral piece of cinema that achieves more impact than several other comparable adaptations from Jim Thompson's oeuvre, including the recent *The Killer Inside Me* (Curran, 2010).

In summary, the cinema provided a variety of filmic works that continued to depict French characters in colonial and postcolonial settings. The discussion offered above provides a sidelight on Haneke's approach in *Caché* in three significant ways. (1) Decolonization was denied mainly through the perpetuation of colonial-era storytelling in the action movies. This did not mean that former colonial spaces simply disappeared from cinema screens but that they were for an extended period frozen in old-fashioned clichés, which many audiences continued to flock to until at least the mid to late 1980s. Such narratives were not found in only colonial-era cinema, being also common in pulp fiction such as the OSS117 and 'SAS' paperbacks, as well as of course in comics such as Tintin.[19] And one might add very quickly here that readers should not think that I believe that French cinema was alone in mining this popular culture – English-language films include *The Wild Geese* (1978), *The Dogs of War* (1980) and so on. (2) Films with greater ambition and indeed antiracist intentions provided images of postcolonialism, but they were also marked with discourses of xenophobic nationalism, especially around themes that juxtaposed ideas of order (equated with France) and chaos (usually standing for the newly independent African states). (3) Perhaps most different from the implications found in a film like *Caché*, where an emphasis on French guilt and repression is uppermost, some of these neocolonial works of cinema were themselves openly contested by, among others, black actors' organizations, politically committed journalists, African leaders who were embroiled in Parisian press stunts, and in a limited number of works of non-nationalistic cinema, notably *Coup de torchon*.

Censorship, Shunning and the Recovery of National Honour: *La Bataille d'Alger*, 1966–1981

Nothing fully prepared French audiences for the Italian–Algerian co-production *La Bataille d'Alger* (henceforth *La Bataille*). Directed by the Italian Gillo Pontecorvo and produced by Yacef Saadi, *La Bataille* is a neorealist depiction of the Algerian independence movement's fight against French troops for Algiers (1956–1957). Actor and producer Saadi was a key figure in these historic events and the film is a loose adaptation of his memoirs, *Souvenirs de la Bataille d'Alger*.[20] Pontecorvo considered it a manifesto for national independence movements around the world. He explained:

> In times like these when so many countries are still grappling with the problems of the struggle for independence and freedom we thought it both stimulating and important to focus not only on the techniques of urban guerrilla warfare and partisan war but also on how, with the right timing, a people or an ethnic group need simply set its mind on independence in order to begin an irreversible process which will eventually achieve that goal despite momentary defeats and setbacks.[21]

Scenes from the film do elicit sympathy for the Algerians and antipathy for the French. This is, however, relatively carefully established and it is not uncommon for the work to be read as being politically neutral. I disagree there and to discuss this issue a little further let us consider one or two scenes here, if only briefly. Typically, in one section of the film Pontecorvo shows the Algerian community working together to clear rubble after the French have bombed a building. Ennio Morricone's rousing soundtrack heightens the drama as the men and women work together to rescue their comrades. Pontecorvo's camera sweeps down from above and then on over the people to pan out across the city to a view of the harbour and the sea. Through this type of material the viewer is aligned in sympathy with the suffering of the Algerians. In effect, one is invited to be a part of their community at war. Next, Pontecorvo focuses his camera on a mutilated child who is carried out from the rubble. A close-up on the child's face allows one to witness his agony. In this sequence there is little doubt as to who the (noble) victims are and who the (evil) oppressors are. Contrast these images with the director's handling of French victims of the Front de Libération Nationale's (FLN's) violence that features in another section of the work. These deaths are portrayed as matter-of-fact assassinations, unstylized by the camera, cold and neutral pictures. No specific images of French children suffering are included in the work, even though of course they were severely injured in some of the FLN terror actions that are openly shown in the work, notably the Milk Bar Café bombing in Algiers in 1956. For example, in the scene where Pontecorvo depicts an FLN bombing of a racecourse, he presents the French and Europeans' fears and frustrations and then quickly re-depicts them as the aggressor by illustrating how quickly and unfairly they turn in anger against an innocent Algerian boy. The published script locates this sequence at a football ground but the director moved it to a racetrack. Subsequently, he explained that he believed 'it would have been like planting a bomb among the common people by having it at the soccer stadium'.[22]

Moreover, Pontecorvo and Saadi's film shows and denounces the French military's methods of warfare, including the use of torture. The depiction is philosophically important for it highlights that the French, enlightened power is quite capable of deploying methods dating from the medieval period to defend its status. This depiction of torture revises the idea that France is a benign and civilizing nation. Here, colonialism is associated with the violent use of force and not the rational organization of society (a great counterpoint to the tropes discussed earlier in this chapter in the context of *L'État sauvage*).

Reception of Pontecorvo's film in France was deeply negative and it is important to detail this long and often violent example of another kind of film event, quite different in its brutality from those discussed in previous chapters. French nationalists found the film impossible, ugly and unfair. For nearly twenty years different groups mounted public and extremely violent campaigns against the picture. This was not a repression that was in any way comparable to the tormented dilemmas of the characters in Haneke's *Caché*. On the contrary, organized protest groups were mobilized in the street, cinemas bombed and other comparable works also attacked. As we will read in the next pages, it is the case too that some brave voices spoke out in favour of the film, notably through the early 1970s when it had passed the state censorship process but when many of its screenings, especially in Paris, were stopped by mob rule.

The long and protracted hostility towards *La Bataille* began at the Venice Film Festival of 1966. Officially representing France, there was Robert Bresson's *Au hasard Balthazar*, and also in the competition, in the British delegation's participation, there was Truffaut's *Fahrenheit 451*. Bresson and Truffaut were both internationally recognized artists working at the height of their careers and there were good grounds to believe one of them would win the Lion d'Or. However, *La Bataille* was also entered in the competition and as the festival progressed the French found this offensive. Reporting from Venice, Henry Chapier warned readers of *Combat* that they should expect the worst from the

Italian–Algerian film.[23] Yvonne Baby of *Le Monde* reported that *La Bataille* appeared to be a neutral depiction of history but it was nothing of the sort. Baby underlined that Pontecorvo's work invited sympathy for the Algerian independence movement.[24] Next, the official French delegation to Venice boycotted the film when the head of delegation Philippe Erlanger refused to attend its screening.[25] When rumours circulated among the international delegations that *La Bataille* was likely to win the coveted Lion d'Or, the French were further perturbed. The prospect of sharing a film festival soirée with a former enemy who had committed indiscriminate assassinations of French citizens, and who was now displaying these acts in an internationally recognized film, was too much to contemplate. Thus, the delegation officially left Venice before *La Bataille*'s victory was confirmed.[26]

The patriotic pressman Henry Chapier revealed to his readers back in Paris that he knew that the prize jury had been divided over crowning *La Bataille* over Bresson's *Au hasard Balthazar*. He reported that when the prize was announced many in the room had declared their disquiet with shouts of 'salauds' ('bastards'). Chapier wrote that he considered this appropriate behaviour, adding to boot that the jury had acted in complete ignorance. It was clear for him that Bresson's film was the superior work in the competition that year.[27] Moreover, Chapier believed that *La Bataille* had won the competition because of the role of the social democratic mafia. He claimed the entire festival had been staged to celebrate Pontecorvo's film and that the chair of the jury, Luigi Chiarini, was employed to fix the result. Chapier concluded that a dishonest chauvinism always held sway in Venice.[28] Out of interest, Patrick Gibbs of the London *Daily Telegraph* shared some of Chapier's dismay. He explained: 'The French attitude, therefore, is understandable, especially in view of the insidious way this picture is presented … working a confidence trick on the audience'.[29] (Finally on Venice 1966, let us also note here that some time later, for charitable purposes, Pontecorvo auctioned his Lion d'Or trophy. A little bizarrely it was a young Steven Spielberg who bought it and then returned it to him at the Venice Festival in 1993.)

The controversy of the Venice Film Festival (1966) was quickly debated in the Assemblée Nationale (French national parliament) where the right-wing politician Pierre Pasquini brought the subject of the film and the festival prize forward for discussion. He requested that the Gaullist government defend the national interest by stopping the film. He added that the Minister of Culture,

Malraux, should also cease French participation in future Venice Film Festivals. Pasquini contended that the Italians would do better to explore historical subjects from their own past (by implication Mussolini and fascism) rather than treating wars of which they had no knowledge.[30] The government agreed to prohibit the film from display in France. Days after the parliamentary debate a quasi-diplomatic incident occurred when Saadi attempted to visit Paris to discuss making a possible adaptation of Albert Camus's *L'Étranger*. Reuters reported that when Saadi had landed at Orly he was refused entry into the country and was turned away for fear that his presence would incite disturbances.[31]

In 1970, France recognized Algeria as a sovereign nation-state and lifted its censorship of *La Bataille*. On the eve of the film's release in Paris, a military veterans' group opposed its screening. The Union Nationale des Combattants d'Afrique du Nord announced their disappointment that the film was being permitted display. They requested that all veterans, including those of the resistance movement (1940–1945), campaign against it. They explained that the film was an insult to France and likely to provoke public disorder. A second organization, the Association des Combattants de l'Union Française, declared that anyone who watched *La Bataille* was an anti-national subversive. A *pieds-noirs* organization interpreted the film as an insult to their history. Speaking on their behalf, Marc Lauriol highlighted that it hampered reconciliation between 'rapatriés' and the metropolitan French.[32] Prominent spokespeople from the former *Algérie Française* movement intervened as well. For example, General Jacques Massu labelled Pontecorvo's film a false representation of history. He emphasized that it wrongly implied that the FLN had won the battle of Algiers. In addition, Massu believed that Saadi's role in the war was most brutal. He recalled that Saadi had employed young women to place bombs in cafés and bars to kill Europeans. Massu was aggrieved by the negative depiction of the French army: his men were never duped by pretty girls working for the FLN, as is suggested in the film.[33]

The Parisian premiere of the now four-year-old film was stopped because of anonymous threats to destroy cinemas. According to the contemporary press, the first French screening occurred in the small provincial town of Coutainville, Normandy, on 20 August 1970. Daniel Jouland, director of the Drakkar cinema, programmed it for a series of midnight screenings for holidaymakers. He scheduled it alongside the pro-American Vietnam War film, *The Green Berets* (John Wayne, 1968), thereby balancing a leftist film with a rightist one.[34] A review of contemporary press coverage reveals that royalist youth groups (Restauration Nationale) and others mounted violent demonstrations wherever the film was being programmed, all around the country in fact. For example, in Lons-le-Saunier, an extreme right-wing group daubed graffiti on the Regent film house and the owner of the cinema, César Carboni, was warned that if he continued to programme Pontecorvo's film then smoke bombs would be released in his auditorium. Carboni did not withdraw the work and a group of trade union and secular organizations called on the citizens of Lons to watch the film together to demonstrate their disgust with the fascists. Nevertheless, Carboni's cinema was attacked: vandals rendered his screen unusable. Bravely, Carboni's colleagues at the neighbouring picture house, Le Palace, put on *La Bataille* there instead.[35] In Laval, it seems that extreme right-wing students from Paris and Nantes shouted throughout a screening and then threw ink bombs at the screen.[36] In Orléans, at the Rio house, the screen was vandalized as well, here more viciously, with acid being used to destroy it. The most violent incident, however, was in Saint-Etienne at the 'Le Méliès' cinema on the rue Gambetta in the centre of the city. There the cinema owner protected his house from destruction by discovering an explosive device before its detonation.[37]

At the same time, the official television channel censored the broadcast of clips from *La Bataille*. The television show Panorama, directed by Olivier Todd, dedicated an episode to *La Bataille* and had recorded a debate between Yacef Saadi and the French military veteran Colonel Trinquier.[38] Hours before the programme was scheduled for broadcast, the director of Conseil d'Administration of the ORTF, Monsieur Desgraupes, refused permission for extracts from *La Bataille* to be included. Subsequently, he explained that the office of Jacques Chaban-Delmas (the serving Prime Minister) had 'asked the Government Agency to ban the entire segment ... and the ORTF council had shown its independence by airing the debate portion of it'.[39] In an honest and brave decision that showed great integrity, Todd resigned in protest at being censored.

Generally speaking, the nationalist protesters achieved a significant victory in limiting the screening of Pontecorvo's film in France. Cinemas did not screen *La Bataille* without facing overwhelming intimidation. It was not presented in Paris for some time, only returning to the capital in October 1971. Then it was programmed at the Studio Saint Séverin, the art house in the Latin Quarter that had also offered a home to Marcel Ophul's exposé on wartime collaboration, *Le Chagrin et la pitié* (1971). This belated run was conducted without any advance publicity: one can conclude that it was a quasi-clandestine release. In addition, the cinema considered it necessary to use volunteers to protect its premises from attack and to ensure security for its audiences. When its own amateur security force was not on duty and only the police force were providing protection, an attack did occur.[40]

The historian Benjamin Stora describes French neocolonialists as 'les hommes du Sud', after the U.S. Deep South racists. He suggests that these groups were united by their mutual hostility towards the independence of Algeria, opposition towards African immigration into France and the presence of Muslims in Western Europe. To paraphrase further, he argues that they believed that colonial rule had been a great national achievement and that the loss of Empire had endangered metropolitan France because losing control in North Africa made the country more vulnerable to invasion from the southern shore of the Mediterranean.[41] Stora highlights also that de Gaulle shared some of their attitudes. For example, Alain Peyrefitte's memoirs of his conversations with the President emphasize how de Gaulle held anti-Islamic views – he feared that Arab migrants would, through greater sexual reproduction, outnumber the French. In the 1970s, it was this broad 'Southernist'-revisionist coalition of right-wing nationalists that defeated *La Bataille*. Gaullists, royalists, neofascists all wanted to believe that the Algerian war had been fought honourably, even if they also disagreed on much else about it and indeed hated each other. They did not want to allow an enemy depiction of a French defeat to be shown. Nor did they wish to see what brutal tactics the French army had used in the 1950s and early 1960s. For them, stopping *La Bataille* was a struggle to protect an image of national military honour. Meanwhile repressing it also maintained the fantasy that colonialism had been a *mission civilisatrice*. In fact, the hatred continued for years and in 1981 a new terror attack hit a cinema in the Latin Quarter that was screening Pontecorvo's film.[42] In 1993 unidentified reactionary assassins of a veteran *pieds-noirs* leader, Jacques Roseau, declared that, among his other misdemeanours, Roseau had shared a platform with Yacef Saadi.[43]

Let me strongly underline, and explain further, that many professionals from the film industry were shocked by the reception meted out against *La Bataille* and did attempt to protect screenings of the work in 1970. Notably, veterans of the May 1968 États Généraux du Cinéma published a petition calling for its full release. A Comité de Défense du Cinéma supported the film and several prominent filmmakers defended it, signatories of this petition including film journals *Positif* and *Jeune Cinema*, as well as Jean-Luc Godard, Louis Malle, Jean Buñuel and Marie-France Pisier. Their petition said that the state was complicit in reactionary terrorism because it had provided insufficient security for a safe dissemination of the work. They contrasted this casual approach to protecting *La Bataille* with the way in which official security was provided to defend John Wayne's *The Green Berets* from leftist agitation that had disliked that film's depiction of the Vietnam War. In summary, they called the government's position 'fascisation' ('turning fascist') and, invoking a slogan from the streets of May 1968, they appealed for everyone to recognize that, 'Vous êtes tous concernés' ['You are all involved!']⁴⁴

Petitions, the bravery of the individual cinema owners and their families who fought to keep *La Bataille* available for audiences to watch, and the bold actions of a figure like Olivier Todd prepared the way for new films that critiqued imperialism and military conduct during the war in Algeria. In May 1972, the Cannes Film Festival's 'semaine de la critique' welcomed the first significant French film to condemn the Algerian war, *Avoir vingt ans dans les Aurès*. Directed by Vautier, who in 1963 had assisted in the production of *La Bataille* itself, it depicts the chaotic and brutal experience of a group of Breton soldiers fighting in the deserts of Algeria. At the beginning of the work, Vautier highlights that each scene is based on a minimum of five eyewitness statements from men who had fought in the war. The scenes that feature are harrowing and include a soldier raping a Muslim woman, the French use of torture and images of extremely violent desert combat. Vautier's work was rewarded at Cannes 1972 with the Prix de la Critique Internationale.⁴⁵ Months after this success, in January 1973, Vautier continued his campaigning by going on hunger strike to pressurize for release of the banned radical documentary *Octobre à Paris* (Panijel, 1963), which is about how police brutality dealt with Algerians in the capital in 1961.⁴⁶ Vautier's hunger strike lasted thirty-one days, gaining public support from Claude Sautet, Robert Enrico and Alain Resnais.⁴⁷ It was a successful intervention with Panijel's film consequently obtaining its first official visa for display a decade or so after its completion. However, it achieved only a limited distribution and it was not widely available for viewing until its release on DVD in 2012.

In the early 1970s, brand new works with themes relating to the Algerian war, immigration or violence were still being censored by the Gaullist state, despite the complaints from Vautier and others. For example, in 1977 the short film by Frank Cassenti, *L'Agression*, was prohibited from cinemas. Officially, it was forbidden because of its perceived violent content. However, the film association SRF identified that it was being suppressed because it offered too disturbing a picture of modern society. The SRF wrote to trade magazine *Le Film français* to complain and they wondered if the Giscard presidency was trying to stop people from watching films in which France looked an ugly place. In addition, the SRF bemoaned the fact that a Kafkaesque situation was developing since officially there was no longer censorship yet the state was still stopping releases such as Cassenti's film.[48]

In 1977, a film adaptation of Henri Alleg's political tract against torture, *La Question* (Laurent Heynemann, produced with assistance from Tavernier), was released. It was widely supported by the press as a major work of cinema.[49] The nationalist neocolonialists reacted strongly against it and scenes reminiscent of the aggression mounted against *La Bataille* were repeated. For instance, Minister of Culture Michel d'Ornano forbade it from viewing by under-eighteens.[50] This was an odd and no doubt politically motivated decision because it was nowhere near as violent as Don Siegel's *Dirty Harry* (1971), which had recently been restricted to adults on these same grounds. Less subtly, fascistic terrorists sent death threats to the director of Gaumont so as to intimidate him from releasing the work, and after just two days of general release the company withdrew it from its cinemas. Street protests against the film that few people would ever be able to see also occurred, some becoming quite aggressive and akin to the treatment of *La Bataille*. In Paris bomb scares closed cinemas down and in Montpellier the extreme right-wing Front National (FN) demonstrated outside a cinema that had scheduled showings.[51] There, a brave local newspaper editor condemned the violence and encouraged readers to support the film. In the same article it was also noted that the attacks on *La Question* had followed anti-Semitic and anticommunist intimidation of staff from the University of Montpellier, as well as vandalism against bookshops in the town. The journalist called on people to watch *La Question* so as to defend their freedoms. In contrast to this antifascist movement in Montpellier, in Marseilles the reservist Association des Sous-officiers de Réserve de Marseille circulated the following statement against *La Question*:

Est-il nécessaire de rappeler qu'à travers l'Armée de la Nation, c'est la France, notre Patrie, qui est également attaquée, ce sont ceux qui ont versé leur sang pour notre liberté qui sont bafoués. Nous dénonçons ici, cette action antifrançaise permanente, alors que dans d'autres pays … la Patrie et l'Armée sont respectées et ont rang de valeur morale intangible … Le peu de succès de ce film, pour ne pas dire son échec, ne fait aucun doute et laisse espérer le retour d'une saine conscience de tous envers l'Armée de la Nation garante de l'indépendance de la Liberté et de l'Honneur.[52]

[Is it necessary to recall that through the national army, it is France, our country, that is also attacked, that it is those who have shed their blood for our liberty who are being scorned. Here we denounce this permanently anti-French action, while in other countries … the nation and the army are respected and have an intangible moral rank. … The limited success of this film, if not to say its failure, leaves no doubt, and lets one hope for, a return to a clean conscience towards the national army, protectors of our liberty and our honour.]

Similarly, in Strasbourg thirty veterans, sporting military berets and medals, made a disturbance in a cinema foyer, where they pasted their tracts over the posters for *La Question*.[53] Down in the industrial heartland of Saint-Etienne the protest was less sophisticated when two hand grenades were thrown into the foyer of the Alhambra-Gaumont.[54]

In the cinema itself in the 1970s and early 1980s there were of course the genre films discussed at the beginning of this chapter. However, as has been underlined, these were studiously careful not to make direct political statements. Their mode of political mythmaking was around recycling many existing colonialist stereotypes while foregrounding action, adventure or romance. It is worth reflecting then on whether the protests against *La Bataille* and *La Question* ever received an onscreen equivalent – a work that chimed with the thinking behind the protests? As Bénédicte Chéron writes in her recent work, one director did become increasingly associated with a filmmaking that provided a defensive and sometimes patriotic imaginary centred on the wars of decolonization: the writer and director, Pierre Schoendoerffer.[55]

In a series of successful films, Schoendoerffer asserted pride in French military conduct during the wars in Indochina and Algeria. To that extent the subjects and treatments in his major works did directly counter the narrative balance of *La Bataille* and *La Question*. Notably, in 1982 the former military cameraman completed *L'Honneur d'un capitaine*. Scripted by Schoendoerffer himself, the film begins with images of a television documentary dedicated to the history of the Algerian campaign. The talking heads on the couch turn their attention to the role played by a fictional military figure, Captain Marcel Caron (Jacques Perrin). This discussion becomes heated when a historian, a thinly disguised version of Pierre Vidal-Naquet, asserts that Caron is guilty of having committed torture. Through the rest of the film Schoendoerffer narrates the struggles of Captain Caron's widow (Nicole Garcia) to sue for defamation against the historian who has caused offence. Slowly but surely the audience is treated to a courtroom battle for the historical truth. On the one side, there is the story of the honourable widow and her barrister who aim to establish Caron's innocence. On the other side, there is the historian and his legal team, who are depicted as being determined to taint a man who, through Schoendoerffer's vision, the audience is encouraged to believe only wished to serve his country. Thus, Schoendoerffer employs flashbacks to events during the Algerian war to depict the Captain's activities there. The viewers learn that Caron is a former resistance fighter and also a veteran of the Indochina campaign. His service in Algeria is presented as successful, albeit tragic. The film concludes with victory for those who have defended his reputation. In this fashion Schoendoerffer implies that military honour was not tarnished in the battlefields of Algeria. The left intelligentsia's interpretation of the war is presented as a deception that has unfairly blemished the nation. For Schoendoerffer, the French troops, symbolized by Caron, were fighting a hard campaign but were acting in good faith. Similarly, the implication is that individual soldiers were not responsible for being placed in intolerable situations of mortal danger where normal morality could not function. For him it was the politicians at home who had guided the military campaign that created these circumstances, not the soldiers or the army. Caron's widow and friends, veterans of the war, are presented as bringing truth against the lies that have besmirched the individual's and the nation's records.

Schoendoerffer is no simple propagandist and this work leaves room for a little ambiguity. The material marshalled to establish the historical record for the defamation trial implies that the war was a miserable business in which some wrongs were committed on all sides. Nonetheless, Caron's reputation is proven sufficiently clean for his widow to win her case.

In public interviews and statements Schoendoerffer has explained that the army was nervous about his film and hence did not let him use their equipment. This statement plays on the idea that he was breaking taboos and that his film was revealing a politically sensitive truth. However, the comment is somewhat misleading. State television channel TF1 produced *L'Honneur d'un capitaine* and the conservative press heaped praise upon it, and so it was not far outside the mainstream. *Le Figaro* critic Claude Baignères described it as 'un plaidoyer superbe' [a superb speech for the defence] and argued that Schoendoerffer had contributed a balanced and objective film.[56] *Figaro magazine* commissioned Académie Française member Michel Droit to write on it. He thanked Schoendoerffer for his film and explained how he was one of the few people to address the subject with dignity and insight. Arguably the conservative press's support for the film was to be expected. Journalists at *Le Figaro*, *Combat* and *Carrefour* had been relatively sympathetic to Algérie française and the OAS during the war.[57]

In contrast, intellectuals from the left-of-centre of the political spectrum highlighted the reactionary nature of Schoendoerffer's work. Henri Alleg was interviewed in *L'Humanité* where he argued that the film was a complete misreading of history. He underlined that Schoendoerffer had completely overlooked the huge numbers of Algerians who had died at the hands of the French military, up to one million. In addition, he suggested that the *L'Honneur d'un capitaine* repeated numerous stereotypes about the conflict, all of which were erroneous, albeit commonly disseminated in writings by veterans like General Massu.[58]

Let us next recall that Schoendoerffer's first treatment of decolonization was *La 317ᵉ Section* (1964), a more personal film, inspired by his own experiences of service in the military in the war in Indochina. It too stars the actor Jacques Perrin, cast this time as a young officer leading a small troop of men in Indochina in 1954. As in *L'Honneur d'un capitaine*, the central theme of the work is the assertion that, although the experience of war was hard and often ugly, the nation's soldiers were essentially good men who had served admirably. They had fought for what they had believed in and despite defeat they had added to the annals of national military glory. Whereas the later film offers a retrospective, meta-historical discussion on the Algerian war through the structure of the trial, here the audience is plunged directly into the valleys and forests of Indochina. The underlying message is that the national army had done wonders under difficult circumstances and that good men had suffered greatly and been sacrificed for scant reward. The idea of retention of military and national honour in circumstances of humiliation and defeat was again the theme for *Le Crabe tambour* (Schoendoerffer, 1977). This film focuses on the memories of three naval officers and their attitudes to politics and the recent past. Sitting together on a naval vessel patrolling the mid Atlantic, en route to the French territory of Miquelon, they remember a comrade, Willsdorff. He is a mythical character who is the epitome of French masculine courage and honour. However, he has suffered at the hands of state politics because he had supported the OAS rather than remaining loyal to the official military during the Algerian war. The sailors who remember him idealize him as a great warrior, a national hero, who has been lost because of decolonization.

The main fictional protagonists from *Le Crabe tambour* have sometimes been described as being based on two historical protagonists from the navy: Jean-Marie Guillaume, who had supported the OAS, and Admiral Querville, who had followed his chain of command to remain loyal to de Gaulle.[59] The theme of a comrade supporting the illegal OAS is also one close enough to Schoendoerffer's own milieu to merit comment. In 1956 he worked with fellow military filmmaker Jacques Dupont, and the cameraman Raoul Coutard, Joseph Kessel and the producer Georges de Beauregard, on the docudrama about tribal culture in Afghanistan, *La Passe du diable* (1956). Several years later Jacques Dupont was suspected of supporting OAS terrorism, for which he was tried in September 1961.[60] Schoendoerffer's producer, as well as the figure behind the making of several famous works associated with the New Wave, Georges de Beauregard, had helped in vain to hide Dupont from the police. It also seems likely that Dupont's daughter was a member of the same far-right-wing terrorist organization.[61]

Schoendoerffer's works provided a sense of honour for the military and its supporters, even while acknowledging defeat and the divisions that emerged as a consequence of OAS terrorism. His works were not always critically well received, *L'Honneur d'un capitaine* especially sparked hostility from the left. Nonetheless, it is worth recalling that in the same year that *La Question* was forced off cinema schedules, it was his *Le Crabe tambour* that was feted at the César awards ceremony, receiving six nominations and being singled out for praise by organizer Georges Cravenne.[62]

Conclusion

In our period, and as might be expected, cinema did offer a patriotic response to the loss of Empire. By showing French action heroes, often portrayed by Jean-Paul Belmondo, fighting Africans or chasing around in trucks or other vehicles, they kept alive the idea that the nation and its men were superior to those who lived on the other side of the Mediterranean. This kind of genre cinema was a fantasy consolation for the end of imperial grandeur. In addition, the longstanding myth that Africa was a childlike, crazy, inferior society was maintained through the 1970s and early 1980s. This was an important narrative or myth because it further legitimated notions of superiority.

The genre works discussed in the first part of this chapter do not present theoretical claims to French-white superiority. In that sense they are not examples of race theory, but that is not the purpose of this kind of entertainment cinema. What they do is to repeatedly tell narratives in which white French male film stars defeat non-Europeans, played by unknown actors who in some cases never even have a voice in the film, let alone a nuanced characterization. The mythmaking function of the 1950s to 1980s action movies is to imagine an idea of a good, traditional and white France, combating non-white foreigners. Today, this material is ripe for satire and this process has begun with the clever comedy pastiches OSS117 *Caire nid d'espions* (2006) and OSS117 *Rio ne répond plus* (2009). These are amusing films that hit the mark, but they are also sometimes too close to repeating neocolonial racism for my own comfort.

A discourse of reluctance to witness the history of decolonization is further evidenced in cinema that directly referenced the Algerian war. To repeat, in some quarters images of French suffering and defeat were hated material to be simply and literally destroyed. As I have narrated, there were significant episodes of public disorder when *La Bataille* came to French screens in the 1970s. Nonetheless, some directors stand out for their challenge against the state censorship and lack of policing and the nationalist far-right intimidation. Vautier's commitment to showing and discussing historical footage about the Algerian war went as far as the act of hunger strike. Until 2012, Vautier's *Avoir vingt ans dans les Aurès* was unavailable for wide public distribution. Apparently, for some time its rights were not owned by the director and, for whatever reasons (political or commercial), it did not receive a release on DVD. Bertrand Tavernier's work is also a fascinating example of a counter-discourse to neocolonialism, and provided another critical acknowledgement of the meaning of Empire and decolonization. He co-produced *La Question* and, to repeat, *Le Coup de torchon* is a work that profoundly unsettles most, if not all, neocolonial attitudes. Though not discussed at length here because of my focus on the period 1945–1985, it was of course also Tavernier who made the most sensitive and intelligent documentary work *La Guerre sans nom* (1992). That is a film which can be seen as the culmination of his intelligent and open-minded approach to addressing the painful and genuinely complex historical experiences of Empire and decolonization, themes that he acknowledges always attracted him from the time when he had sought out samizdat screenings of the banned *Octobre à Paris* and early works from Vautier and Paul Carpita.[63]

Conceits and language from psychoanalysis provide fascinating and poetic modes through which to engage with France's difficult and continued journey from Empire towards multiculturalism. Little wonder then that Haneke's *Caché* was so powerful and thought-provoking a film. This chapter has expanded on the issues raised in that work by suggesting that experience in this area was subtler than might be imagined. Films perpetuated myths dating from colonial days of the 1880s to the 1930s but they were also sometimes contested (as noted in the paragraph above). It is also important to acknowledge that stopping films such as *La Bataille* and others was not a clandestine or covert mode of repression, nor was it psychoanalytically complex. Instead, this repression was public, political and a process that combined state censorship with street-level violence.

In conclusion, I would like to think that readers find that the material offered in this chapter has in some small part enriched and deepened our continued understanding of the 'film event'. In these pages we have charted Parisian and regional experiences of cinema owners in the face of intimidation and noted the political subvariations and the power of reactionary protest groups. Again the role of film festivals is underlined, with Venice 1966 being a significant moment in the history of the reception of *La Bataille*. It has also been possible to further internationalize the concept of the film event by showing how a film such as *L'État sauvage* prompted ambitious Parisian journalists to fly to Senegal to watch that film in the company of President Senghor. As it happened, when they had made their rather crazy journey they did not find a significant story to report on and instead only a very diplomatic response to the work. In hindsight it was a remarkably silly stunt that showed little if any sensitivity towards postcolonialism. Yet it seems to me a pertinent and suitable episode on which to conclude this chapter. After all, one could suggest that the journalists had travelled in an old fashioned spirit of adventure but all they had really discovered, if they chose to look, was the hollowness of their own metropolitan mindset.

Notes

1. Verneuil quoted in R. Quinson, 1963, 'Henri Verneuil tourne "Cent mille dollars au soleil"', *Combat*, 17 September.
2. A. Murray, 2000, 'Le Tourisme Citroën au Sahara (1924–1925)', *Vingtième siècle* 68, 95–107.
3. Dehée, *Mythologies politiques*, 554.
4. C-M. Bosséno and Y. Dehée, 2004, *Dictionnaire du Cinéma populaire français*, Paris: Nouveau Monde, 641.
5. For further on colonial ideology of Tintin, and comics more generally, see M.Mckinney, 2011, *The Colonial Heritage of French Comics*, Liverpool: Liverpool University Press.
6. R. Dunkley, 1994, 'On Location', *The Sunday Telegraph*, 25 September, 21; R. Chazal, 1973,'Chacal', *France Soir*, 24 September; 'Chacal', 1973, *L'Express*, 16 September; G. Charensol, 1973, 'Chacal', *Nouvelles littéraires*, 24 September.
7. Cited in '"L'état sauvage": haro sur le racisme', 1978, *Presse Océan*, 28 April.
8. Cited in 'Les quatre hommes de "L'État sauvage"', 1978, *France Soir*, 16 April.
9. M. Bourboune, 1978, 'Requiem pour un business', *Demain l'Afrique*, 9 May, 50–52.
10. S. N'Gosso, 1978, 'L'État sauvage: un paternalisme dangereux', *Afrique Asie* no. 12, June.
11. 'Raciste', 1978, *Rouge*, 10/11, June.
12. See 'Senghor: La France sera peut être plus choquée que nous', 1978, *L'Express*, 2 May, 129.
13. D. Sherzer, 1996. 'Race Matters and Matters of Race', in Sherzer (ed.), *Cinema, Colonialism, Postcolonialism*, Austin: University of Texas, 241. No acknowledgement is made of the antiracist intentions behind the work.
14. For further on this aspect see also B.B. Diop, O. Tobner and F-X. Verschave, 2005, *Négrophobie*, Paris: Les Arènes; K.C. Dunn, 2003, *Imagining the Congo: The International Relations of Identity*, New York: Palgrave.
15. Cited in A. Bourgi, 2011, 'Insupportable néocolonialisme français', *Le Monde*, 16 April, 18.
16. See M. Perez, 1980, 'La Légion saute sur Kolwezi', *Le Matin*, 10 January; J. Pouget, 1980, 'La Légion', *Le Figaro*, 9 January; J. de Baroncelli, 1980, 'La Legion saute sur

Kolwezi', *Le Monde*, 16 January. Certainly there were criticisms too. Leftist critic Vincent Kermel called on all anti-Imperialists to protest. See his 1980, 'Cinéma et impérialisme', *Rouge*, 11 January.

17. See D. de Roux, 1973, *Ne traversez pas le Zambèze*, Paris: L'Age d'Homme; see also J-Luc. Barré, 2005, *Dominique de Roux: Le provocateur, 1935–1977*, Paris: Fayard, 464–72.

18. J. Thompson, 1964, *Pop 1280*, Greenwich: Gold Medal.

19. See for example J. Bruce, 1961 *OSS117 au Liban*, Paris: Presses de la Cité; Josette Bruce,1966 *Congo à gogo,* Paris: Presses de la Cité. Alternatively 'SAS' titles include work such as, De Villiers, 1967, *SAS aux Caraïbes*, Paris: Presses de la Cité; and, 1973, *Mourir pour Zanzibar*, Paris: Presses de la Cité.

20. Y. Saadi, 1962, *Souvenirs de la Bataille d'Alger*, Paris: Julliard.

21. Pontecorvo in P. Solinas, 1973, *Gillo Pontecorvo's The Battle of Algiers*, New York: Scribner, 165.

22. Pontecorvo in Solinas, *Battle of Algiers,* 183.

23. H. Chapier, 1966, '"La Bataille d'Alger" de Pontecorvo', *Combat*, 2 September.

24. Y. Baby, 1966, 'Vulgarisation historique avec "La Bataille d'Alger"', *Le Monde*, 2 September.

25. Baby, 'Vulgarisation'.

26. S. Passeur, 1966, 'Malaise à Venise', *Aurore*, September. One understands that *Aurore* tended to be read by *pieds noirs*. Also for the record, it is suggested by a historian of CIA influence on cultural politics that French delegation leader Erlanger, is not simply a cultural diplomat and historian. In her work Stoner Saunders describes him as a French liaison officer to the CIA. See Stoner Saunders, *Who Paid the Piper?*, 270.

27. H. Chapier, 1966, 'Un verdict de 'salauds' à Venise', *Combat*, 12 September. Chapier's 'bastards', the jury, were: Giorgio Bassani, Lindsay Anderson, Lubos Bartosek, Michel Butor, Lewis Jacobs, Lev Kouleshov and Joris Yvens. See also D. Robinson. 1966. 'Prizes at the Venice Film Festival', *Financial Times*, 12 September.

28. In 1964, Chiarini had rejected the American *Lilith* from the competition. The U.S.A. boycotted Venice that year.

29. P. Gibbs, 1966, 'Row over award of anti-French film', *The Daily Telegraph*. No date on original microfiche.

30. 'Pierre Pasquini (député UNR) demande l'interdiction du film "La Bataille d'Alger"', 1966, *L'Humanité*, 23 September.

31. See 'Film producer from Algiers barred', 1966, *The Times*, 23 September; 'French Eject Yacef Saadi Whose "Battle of Algeria" Topped Venice', 1966, *Variety*, 28 September.

32. 'Rapatriés: L'A.N.F.A.N.O.M.A. proteste contre la sortie du film "La Bataille d'Alger"', 1970, *Le Figaro*, 3 June; 'La sortie à Paris du film "La bataille d'Alger" retardée', 1970, *France Soir*, 4 June; F. Maurin, 1970, 'Laissera-t-on l'O.A.S. dicter sa

loi?"', 1970, *L'Humanité*, 4 June; M. Lauriol, 1970, 'Le communiqué de la délégation nationale sur "La Bataille d'Alger"', *L'Aurore*, 5 June.

33. J. Massu, 1971, *La Vraie bataille d'Alger*, Paris: Plon, 191; countered in J. Roy, 1972, *J'Accuse le Général Massu*, Paris: Seuil.

34. 'Première projection publique de "La Bataille d'Alger"', 1970, *Le Monde*, 20 August.

35. Quite erroneously historian Langlois reports, 'The film was also shown without incident and for several days in a cinema in Lons-Le Saunier', see his 2002, 'La bataille d'Alger', *CinéAction* 103, 88. Contemporary accounts include, 'Le film "la Bataille d'Alger" est retiré de l'affiche à la suite de manifestations hostiles', 1970, *Le Monde*, 8 September; '"La Bataille d'Alger" à Lons-le-Saunier: nouveaux incidents', 1970, *Le Monde*, 10 September.

36. 'Incidents à Laval au cours de la projection de "la bataille d'Alger"', 1970, *La Croix*, 22 September.

37. 'Plastic contre "La Bataille d'Alger"', 1970, *L'Aurore*, 22 September.

38. Clips from this programme are available to view on youtube: see www.youtube. com/watch?v=mckpbjQH4HQ extract titled 'Débat Colonel Trinquier et Yacef Saadi 1970 (last consulted October 2012).

39. See 'M. Olivier Todd déclare ne plus pouvoir assumer la responsibilité de "Panorma"', 1970, *Le Monde*, 14 June; Garreau, *Archives secrètes*, 241.

40. Vautier, *Caméra*, 200.

41. See B. Stora, 1999, *Le Transfert d'une mémoire. De l'Algérie française au racisme anti-arabe*, Paris: La Découverte.

42. 'Deux personnes ont été blessés lors d'une attaque contre le cinéma Saint-Séverin', 1981, *Le Monde*, 14 January.

43. Stora, *Le Transfert*, 64–65

44. See 'Pourquoi vous n'avez pas vu *La Bataille d'Alger*', 1970, *Positif*, 119, 73.

45. Vautier, *Caméra*, 233–34.

46. Bickerton, *Cahiers du cinéma*, 34–5; Vautier, *Caméra*, 101

47. See Garreau, *Archives secrètes*, 248; Vautier, *Caméra*, 5–7.

48. 'Opinion de la SRF', 1974, *Le Film français*, 15 February, 8. See also '"L'agression" censurée', 1974, *Le Film français*, 15 February, 1, 7; 'Éditorial', 1974. *Cinématographe* 7, 1.

49. J. de Baroncelli, 1977, 'Résistance d'un intellectuel', *Le Monde*, 5 May; J.F. Vilar, 1977, 'Torture: les témoignages de la douleur', *Libération*, 2 May; K. Kaupp and H. Alleg, 1977, 'Henri Alleg', *L'Express*, 25 April; A. Cervoni, 1977, 'L'expéreince d'Alger', *France nouvelle*, 11 July; R. Chazal, 1977, 'La Question', *France Soir*, 5 May.

50. 'La Question: toujours la censure', 1977, *Le Matin de Paris*, 30 April.

51. See M. Douin, 1998, *Dictionnaire de la Censure au Cinéma*, Paris: PUF, 363; 'A propos de la projection du film La Question', 1977, *Midi libre*, 11 June.

52. 'Double protestation contre la projection du film, "la Question"', 1977, *La Marseillaise*, 13 June.

53. 'On vous dit tout, on vous cache rien', 1977, *Rouge*, 30 June; 'Strasbourg: manifestation contre la projection du film *La Question*', 1977, *Le Quotidien de Paris*, 30 June.

54. See 'Revue de presse 1977', 2001, *L'Avant-Scène cinéma* 506, 133. For reaction in Bordeaux, see 'Au Marivaux, "*La Question*" n'a pu être projetée', 1977, *Sud Ouest*, 18 June.

55. B. Chéron, 2012, *Pierre Schoendoerffer: un cinéma entre fiction et histoire*, Paris: CNRS.

56. C. Baignières, 1982, 'Un plaidoyer superbe', *Le Figaro*, 2 October.

57. A-M. Duranton-Crabol, 1995, *Le Temps de l'OAS*, Brussels: Complexe, 106–8.

58. 'Le témoignage d'Henri Alleg', 1982, *L'Humanité*, 1 October.

59. R. Kauffer, 2002, *OAS. Histoire d'une guerre franco-française*, Paris: Seuil,185–86.

60. M. Cottaz, 1962, *Les Procès du putsch d'Alger*, Rennes: NEL, 224–25.

61. C. de Beauregard, 1991, *Georges de Beauregard: Premier sourire de Belmondo...dernier de Bardot*, Nimes: Lacour, 103.

62. G. Cravenne, 1978, 'Positivement vôtre', *Le Film français*, 1709, 1.

63. B. Tavernier, 2011, *Le cinéma dans le sang*, Paris: Écriture, 66–67.

CHAPTER SIX

The Persistence of Anti-Semitism

The chapter begins with a detailed consideration of a major film event: the six month period when in 1989 the veteran director Claude Autant-Lara was elected to the European Parliament as a representative of the far-right-wing Front National and, secondly, it then discusses the longer and more covert twists and turns of anti-Semitic nationalism as expressed in postwar cinema debates and selected individual films from 1945 to 1989. Autant-Lara's public anti-Semitic rhetoric was all the more scandalous and inflammatory because for much of the postwar period, with the exception of Michel Audiard, no major figure from cinema had so openly expressed this form of racist hatred. In other words, the scandal Autant-Lara engineered in 1989 gained attention precisely because superficially it looked unusual. However, writing the longer history of prejudice suggests such a judgement needs qualification. Examples of limited and coded nationalist anti-Semitism do predate the Autant-Lara scandal. While nothing quite so shocking occurred in earlier postwar decades, forms of anti-Semitic xenophobia are present.

The Claude Autant-Lara Affair (1989)

On the veteran director Claude Autant-Lara's election to the Académie des Beaux-Arts (19 April 1989), he reported to journalists that the officials of the academy had ordered him to drop twenty-two pages from his speech to them because it was too controversial. Subsequently, a small publishing house provided the full text, now titled *Le Bateau coule*. It is composed of a series of criticisms of Hollywood and it also includes quasi-coded quasi-explicit anti-Semitic statements. In this publication Autant-Lara argued that there was a mysterious world conspiracy behind capitalism, but he did not name the conspirators. Readers with an anti-Semitic mindset would have been quick to identify the conspiracy to which he was referring, that is a Jewish world-power group. Indeed Autant-Lara implicitly encouraged this interpretation. In addition, he praised Louis-Ferdinand Céline, author of notorious anti-Semitic polemics in the 1930s. Apparently, in his opinion, he was the last great writer to have published in France. Furthermore Autant-Lara mocked other groups, including sufferers of AIDS. He joked that the modern art of Picasso was a greater poison for humankind than the virus.[1] Such remarks were not uncommon in some quarters. As the historical record from the 1980s indicates, it is the case that his bitter word games were similar to common banter among extreme right wingers. For example, also in 1989, Jean-Marie Le Pen warned his supporters that France was suffering from 'sida mental'.[2]

It was the publication of *Le Bateau coule* that announced a long summer of anti-Semitic polemic from Autant-Lara, which culminated in speeches and statements on his election to serve the FN at the European Parliament and then his subsequent resignation from that post. Matters unfurled in a series of stages and are best reconstructed chronologically. Thus, by autumn 1989, Autant-Lara, representing Le Pen, gained sufficient votes to serve as an MEP. As the eldest elected member of the European Parliament, by convention, Autant-Lara was entitled to make an inaugural address to open the new parliamentary session. Original video footage of the whole occasion can be rewatched and analysed. Reviewing the 'live' DVD of his address made available to me thanks to the EP library (London), one sees the elderly, pompous, Autant-Lara reading out his speech in a tranquil voice, making new insults against his imagined Jewish conspirators. The MEPs watch on astounded at what they are witnessing. The director is utterly unconcerned by their protests and continues to make his speech. His thesis there is far more explicit than earlier in the year, and as laid down in *Le Bateau coule*. It is direct and offensive: that the French and all of the Europeans must shield themselves from American influence and that the real danger for Europe is American culture and not Soviet military power. Reflecting on being in Strasbourg, he invited young French to put down their bottles of Coca-Cola and to savour a good local wine, a Traminer or a Riquewihr. He added next the implication that U.S. cultural influence and 'Jewishness' were one and the same. In an almost throwaway but certainly a calculated remark (he reads from a script), he claims that all he wants is that, 'Shylock's teeth to be filed down a bit'.[3]

Anyone who may have missed the snippet of brutal anti-Semitism in Strasbourg had it re-mediated via the FN's own extensive press coverage of their politician. For example, Gabriel Domenach explained in the party's weekly newspaper, *National Hebdo*, that the reason why the filmmaker was so unique and precious was that he was not only criticizing America but that he was also identifying the enemy as being capitalist-Jewish America.[4]

Shortly after Autant-Lara's speech, Henri Elkaim of the mainstream news magazine *Globe* interviewed him about it. Editor-in-chief at *Globe*, Georges-Marc Benamou, looking back, explained that his publication had wanted to investigate the elderly FN supporter who had given the anti-Jewish speech in Strasbourg. It was this material that Benamou published as selected extracts, directly from the taped telephone interview. Benamou added that Autant-Lara had been making similar remarks for years and that they needed to be stopped, which would only occur if they were aired. In the interview Autant-Lara raged against prominent French Jews, far more horribly than on the two previous occasions. He explained that he had joined the FN because they were the only party working for France. He believed the left was currently dominated by 'la juiverie cinématographique internationale, par le cosmopolitanisme et par l'internationalisme' ['international Jewish cinema groups, by cosmopolitanism and internationalism']. Next, when asked what he thought of the cinema of Claude Berri, who recently had completed *Jean de Florette* (1986) and *Manon des sources* (1986), he stated that his cinema lacked 'francité'. Thus, Autant-Lara implied that Berri, a French citizen of Jewish religious and cultural background, was incapable of capturing Frenchness in his adaptation of Pagnol's novels. Similarly offensive commentary followed when Autant-Lara discussed the politician Simone Veil. Autant-Lara explained (and Benamou published) that he disliked her because she was part of an ethnic group that was domineering. When Elkaim responded to that remark by asking if Autant-Lara felt that Veil exploited her status as a Holocaust survivor he replied: 'Oh elle joue de la mandoline avec ça. Mais elle en est revenue, hein? Elle se porte bien ... Bon, alors quand on me parle de génocide, je dis: en tout cas, ils ont raté la mère Veil!' ['Oh she plays the violin with that. But she came back, eh? She is in good health ... Good, when people talk to me about genocide, I say, in any case they missed mother Veil']. Earlier in the interview Autant-Lara had declared his sympathy for historical revisionism, the euphemism for Holocaust denial.[5]

When *Globe* published these remarks Autant-Lara was disowned by the Académie des Beaux-Arts. Subsequently, he resigned from the European Parliament, explaining that this had always been his intention (the FN politician Jean-Claude Martinez took his seat). Autant-Lara added that he had not been informed that his conversation with Elkaim was for publication. He complained that he had been set up and that he was the victim of a media entrapment. Thus in the same summer of the bicentenary of the French revolution (see chapter 2), Autant-Lara employed every opportunity to combine anti-Semitism with populist anti-Americanism. The filmmaker's point was to bluntly exclude prominent French Jews from the national community. For Autant-Lara the true France was being undermined by conspiracy. His tone and psychology are classic racist nationalism, akin to the anti-Dreyfusards of 1898. Throughout the various scandals and interventions the discursive strategy was that Autant-Lara portrayed himself as an honest man who was being unfairly treated for expressing patriotism. Extreme right-wing intellectuals repeated and developed his rhetoric and disseminated it to their readerships. For example, the new-right, intellectual magazine, *Éléments*, dedicated the cover and much of its winter 1989 issue to defending him. The film critic, and one of the leading thinkers in this small group, Michel Marmin, explained that the elderly director had been tricked and discredited because he was telling the truth about 'cosmopolitan' Hollywood. In the same publication, historian Jean-Claude Valla argued that *Globe* had acted irresponsibly in obtaining Autant-Lara's comments. He bemoaned the fact so many politicians were lining up to attack Autant-Lara without appreciating the nefarious manner in which the interview was conducted. The veteran director had made one mistake and that was to attack Simone Veil. Valla branded her the 'Miraculée d'Auschwitz' ['Miraculous Survivor of Auschwitz'] and stated that it was a pity that the political class were so distracted by the Autant-Lara scandal. For him other controversies were more important, notably, that the Holocaust denier Robert Faurisson had been violently assaulted in Vichy. From Valla's perspective Autant-Lara and Robert Faurisson were victims meriting support.[6]

The FN's own weekly newspaper *National Hebdo* ran stories that explained how the left-wing journalists from *Globe* had entrapped a harmless film director. Roland Gaucher highlighted the inglorious spectacle of leftist politicians rushing to condemn an eighty-eight year old. He suggested that *Globe* journalists had already been trying to set up other members of the FN by not being explicit about which publication they represented. Gaucher acknowledged that Autant-Lara was mistaken to accept a telephone interview. There was also a half apology to Simone Veil: 'à 17 ans, elle a été expidiée à Auschwitz, lieu qui était plus proche de l'enfer que d'un palace cinq étoiles. Quiconque a vécu cela, s'il a eu la chance de s'en tirer, en restera marqué à vie'

['At seventeen she was sent to Auschwitz, a place that was closer to hell than a five-star hotel. Anyone who lived through that, if they had the chance to get out, stay marked for life'].[7] In his regular column in the same newspaper, François Brigneau argued that Autant-Lara was being subjected to a witch-hunt and that in essence his remarks about Veil were correct.[8] Officially the FN noted that Autant-Lara was not an official party member and hence no formal declarations about him were necessary.[9]

I bring this raft of FN material to attention here for two reasons. First, it shows how the initial scandal facilitated much more publicity and how a variety of further offensive and xenophobic material was peddled on the back of Autant-Lara's own intervention. Second, as in recent years the FN has attempted to modernize and appear a more mainstream party of the right, it is a historian's task to explain their prior antics for readers to understand their world in 1989. It is also significant and important to note more generally that Autant-Lara's intervention echoed Le Pen's own wider strategy to gain media attention in this period. Throughout the 1980s, Le Pen used offensive public statements to generate press coverage. When the centre-right and centre-left press protested against him, he retaliated by claiming he was being persecuted. One can plausibly suggest then that Autant-Lara's actions were *lepeniste* in their form as well as their content. His handling of his period of high media attention repeated almost precisely the techniques used by the party leader on previous occasions. Each used xenophobic and racist expression to gain public attention, then, as the mainstream rightly denounced them, asserted how badly they were being treated. The 'Autant-Lara affair' was a film event that was carefully engineered, and not a spontaneous reaction.

Next, it is important to further discuss Autant-Lara's own background and the deeper historical backdrop to his anti-Semitic commentary on cinema. This is helpful for several reasons that are equally pertinent to this chapter as a whole. (1) The polemics of 1989 restaged prejudices that were first popularized in the 1930s and 1940s, precisely when Autant-Lara entered his profession. It is sometimes assumed that Autant-Lara was a befuddled pensioner manipulated by the FN to make that speech in Strasbourg. To see matters more clearly it is therefore essential to underline that Autant-Lara had lived and worked with other cineastes in the 1930s who held views close to those he expressed in the late 1980s. (2) The relatively brief historical digression to the interwar and Vichy periods (1918–1944) is also important for context on the second part of this chapter. Some sense of how common anti-Semitic views were among the film community in the 1930s and 1940s allows a better appreciation of its recodifications in the postwar period.

In the 1930s, Autant-Lara's first mentor Marcel L'Herbier had held similar opinions to those advocated in Strasbourg decades later. L'Herbier, founder of IDHEC, the national film school, openly believed that French cinema in the interwar period had confronted an excessive and overwhelming invasion of foreign migrants who were fleeing from persecution in Nazi Germany. Reflecting on the interwar years in his memoirs (published in 1979) he identified the 'invasion from the East' of migrant workers as having been quite as disheartening as competition from Hollywood. According to him, some immigrant artists had been competent but many had come to France solely for profit. L'Herbier considered them incapable of addressing French themes and values and put forth that the scripts that these 'Russians' were bringing to France were inappropriate.[10] L'Herbier believed that in the 1930s the cinema had faced a terrible threat, being dispossessed of 'SON cinématographe'. Looking back he explained too that he had believed that France was being colonized, with the French makers of film being expelled from their own homeland by the refugees from Germany.[11]

Colin Crisp notes in *The Classic French Cinema, 1930–1960* that L'Herbier's prejudice is remarkably similar to the views expressed by other writers who were publishing under the Nazi occupation and the Vichy regime.[12] One can add here that in the 1930s and 1980s respectively, L'Herbier and Autant-Lara denied Jewish filmmakers the ability to make works of art for France. Their vision of the Jewish community was as an alien grouping hostile to cinema and nation. Neither director was very clear as to what values were purely French but they knew, instinctively, that an artist or producer from Central Europe, of Jewish faith or cultural tradition, or in their implied discourse, race, was unable to express them.

In 1989 in his public statements it is intriguing that Autant-Lara overlooked the words of his former colleague, L'Herbier, preferring instead to cite the novelist Céline as his inspiration. Céline was a more famous cultural figure than the cineaste and maybe this was why he was added to the rhetoric. In fact, we can add here for historical clarity that in the 1930s Céline had made much the same arguments as L'Herbier. In *Bagatelles pour une massacre* (1937, reprinted under Vichy 1943), he espoused polemical opinions that associated Jewish power with the winning of control of filmmaking from nations. Céline rants that, 'Le Juif est à 'l'origine de tout le cinéma … il est au milieu dans les salles 'circuits', dans les rédactions … les critiques … il est au bout … à la caisse … Il est partout'. ['The Jew is the origin of all cinema … he is in the milieu in the cinema circuits, in editing … the critics … in the end … at the till … he is everywhere'].[13] His thesis is that the Jews use cinema to make the Aryans lose all their traditions, to destroy their religions and their history and to replace that with a preference for everything Jewish.[14] The argument is the blunt core of Autant-Lara's own views: the cinema is a means of Jewish power and it is used to undermine French and European culture. Céline expels the French Jewish community from his vision of the national community. They are stigmatized as conspirators. In the same pamphlet he attacked Renoir's *La Grande illusion* (1937), which provided too positive an image of a French Jew for his taste. Thus, Céline describes Renoir's character Rosenthal (Marcel Dalio) as a terrible landmark, the beginning of a Jewish control of images of themselves in French cinema.[15]

By the mid 1930s it was relatively commonplace to assert that Jewish groups were damaging the cinema. In May 1934 the film trade union was campaigning against 'foreigners.' In 1935 when the Gaumont production company collapsed through bankruptcy, journalists from across the press held Bernand Natan, a French Jew, responsible.[16] Before the Natan affair, novelist Paul Morand used the cultural form of the novel in his *France la doulce* to decry how non-French immigrants were exploiting the cinema to the detriment of the domestic industry. *France la doulce* is a bitter satire on German and East European Jews in the French film business. In its preface, Morand claimed he had written it to defend national cinema from foreign interference.[17] Infamously, in the final lines of the novel, which was published in 1934, the happy immigrant filmworker concludes that unlike Nazi Germany, France is 'God's own concentration camp'. As a matter of fact, Paul Morand, whose novels inspired several film adaptations in the 1970s, and who was close friend to scriptwriter Pascal Jardin, seems never to have changed or updated his views about people he considered different to him and his notion of French society. Thus, at the present time, his postwar correspondence with scriptwriter, editor and novelist Roger Nimier is unpublished because of their offensive anti-Semitic banter.[18] Nimier was himself an important right-wing novelist of the 1950s whose works set out to shock (another right-wing anarchist like those noted in chapter 2 herein). As readers will recall, besides editing fiction at Gallimard he wrote the script for Louis Malle's *Ascenseur pour l'échafaud* and had some of his own fiction adapted to cinema by Jean Valère.

Renoir's reputation has been glossed over, few critics or scholars noting his anti-Jewish thinking as regards the management of cinema in France even though he was also a victim of Céline's wrath. Thus, in 1940 he attacked the Jewish influence in cinema along similar lines to in Morand's earlier novel. When the Vichy regime was established, he visited the new seat of government and was interviewed in the newspaper *La Semaine à Vichy* (21 September 1940). There he complained about producers having been 'en majorité étrangers et israëlites'. He remarked in the press that it was for the best that they were being removed by the new state. Later that same autumn, Renoir had attempted to create his own studio at Valbonne, near Cannes. Vanessa Schwartz summarizes the premise of the project very clearly and well, 'Basically with the corrupt Jews gone, people like Renoir would revitalize the French film industry'.[19] Matters were no doubt complicated. The defeat of 1940 was a terrible shock and in reality Renoir was in Vichy sounding out what future role he might play. He was also there enquiring for a visa to travel to work in the U.S.A., something encouraged by his partner Dido Freire. His letter of 14 August 1940 to Vichy's new director of radio and cinema is probably the most telling document of all, however. There he plays to the anti-Semitic gallery ('The riff-raff known to you continue to cause trouble. And I still don't foresee a way of getting rid of them'), raises the possibility of staying in France to 'be involved in the rebirth of our national cinema', and also sounds out the minister as to his views on his possible departure for Hollywood.[20] It seems Renoir was hedging his bets, testing how the new state might view his departure to the neutral U.S.A. while also seeing if there was work to be had in Europe, where it was assumed that war would end shortly with an Axis victory.

In cinemas Marcel Pagnol's comedy *Le Schpountz* was the significant work to address comparable issues and, given how unusual Autant-Lara's words sound in 1989, it is helpful for further historical context to return again to the 1930s. For *Le Schpountz*, Pagnol cast the comedian Fernandel in the role of rustic youth Irénée. He is the central character of the film, a dreamy youth who has fantasies of becoming a film star (he is *Le Schpountz* of the title). When a film crew visits his village and they play a trick on him, he readily believes that he has gained an opportunity for fame and fortune. Next, Irénée leaves for

Paris thinking a prominent film producer, Meyerboom, wants to make him a star. Following a number of misadventures, romantic twists and turns, Irénée is a hit. In one of the final scenes from the film, Irénée, encouraged by his girlfriend, strikes a hard bargain with Meyerboom. Pagnol's portrayal of the producer Meyerboom (Léon Bélières) is plainly an anti-Semitic treatment. Moreover, Pagnol was perturbed himself to discover that some reviewers considered his work anti-Semitic.[21] In response he reedited the film, cutting out some of the scenes described above. Extreme right-wing film critic François Vinneuil (also known as Lucien Rebatet) expressed his disappointment at this reworking. For Vinneuil the subject of the Jewish film producer needed airing and Pagnol was wrong to tone down his work. In fact, Pagnol maintained all the fundamental stereotypes in the revised work, including the character of Meyerboom. For example, in a scene from the edited film a French film technician asks who the director is for the epic they are working on. Another replies: 'Bogidar Glazounow. C'est un Allemand ou un Turc ... Enfin il a pris un nom russe, et il parle avec un accent italien; ça lui a permis de devenir un grand metteur en scène français' ['Bogidar Glazounow. He is German or a Turk ... Finally he took a Russian name, and he speaks with an Italian accent, that's what let him become a great French director'].[22] Many other slyly ethnocentric passages mock Meyerboom, even in the supposedly new version.

For comprehensiveness and a duty to the victims of racism let us note briefly that the anti-Jewish film material from the 1930s was also a prelude to the actions of the Vichy regime (1940–1944). Weeks after Philippe Pétain's takeover, the new state promulgated the *Statut des juifs* (3 October 1940) imprisoning all non-citizen Jews in France, and established a *numerus clausus* for French citizens of Jewish faith employed in administration and the arts, including cinema. Vichy Minister Paul Baudoin explained to the American press association, whose own country was not at war at the time, that, 'we have decided to limit the action of a spiritual community that, whatever its qualities, has always remained outside the French intellectual community'.[23] Shortly afterwards, the Institut d'Études des Questions Juives, mounted exhibitions and made cinema that targeted Jews as being members of an enemy religion, an anti-French culture and race.[24] Actor Dalio's image was ripped from the context of his appearances in Renoir's films and used as an anti-Semitic poster. Nazi anti-Semitic cinema was distributed and dubbed into French. On the radio, the film actor Robert Le Vigan featured in popular anti-British and anti-

Jewish comedy shows *Rythme du Temps*, wherein he played the part of Baron Rothschild. In the field of film criticism works were circulated that advanced anti-Jewish arguments. The Occupation era reedition of Maurice Bardèche and Robert Brasillach's *Histoire du cinéma* attacked Jewish filmmakers and praised Nazi filmmaking.[25] In 1941, Vinneuil (also known as Rebatet) published the book *Les Tribus du cinéma et du théâtre* where he highlighted how Jews had invaded cinema and theatre. In that quite lengthy work Rebatet accused the Jewish film producers of depravity: they had used their wealth to buy the prettiest girls in Paris, a moral fear he shared with Céline. *Arrondissement* by *arrondissement*, he listed individual Parisian cinema owners by name, calling for them to be removed from business.[26] This very public list circulated in April 1941, just under a year before French police rounded up Jewish people for deportation and death at the hands of Nazi executioners.

Autant-Lara's comments against Jewish influence in 1989 repeated the interwar debates on film and the language behind the Vichy era policy. The influence of L'Herbier, Céline's pamphlets, Paul Morand's fiction and Pagnol's filmmaking is evident in the backdrop to Autant-Lara's incitement to hatred. These figures established a paradigmatic model, which was reworked in new language in 1989, that evoked the idea that 'Eastern' Jewish foreigners were exploiting the national cinema and that the French were losing control of the power to make their own films. The anti-Semites of the 1930s and the 1980s implied that foreign and Jewish involvement in French cinema was illegitimate. The political fantasy was that Jews were exploitative and lacked indigenous values. The same political myth took for granted that 'true French' film was an art form that aimed for high cultural value and not for exclusively commercial success. Outsiders, either Jewish migrants from Central and Eastern Europe, or from North America, were labelled a threat to that imagined approach. Not that one should mistake 1989 for 1939; plainly substantial differences between the content of arguments from the periods can be identified. Autant-Lara weaved together anti-Semitism with anti-Hollywoodism. Wrapping anti-Semitism into populist anti-Americanism made it sound more palatable for a late 1980s public. In the 1930s this had not been necessary, or even always the case. Pagnol did work those two themes together in *Le Schpountz*, whereas Morand and L'Herbier had stigmatized Eastern European Jewish migrants quite specifically as the single enemy. They did not bother to adopt anti-Americanism to support their anti-Semitism.

Anti-Semitism after 1945

After the Liberation no new works of the equivalent of *Le Schpountz* were produced. A concern to avoid raising explicit issues associated with Jewishness and Germany developed in relation to mainstream cinema. Notably, when Renoir's *La Grande illusion* was rereleased in August 1946 the work was no longer seen as a classic of internationalism and pacifism, but rather as a threatening precedent for pro-Germany Vichyite collaboration, suffused with latent anti-Semitism. In 1945, the French censors considered the film from the 1930s about First World War French prisoners of war in Germany as inappropriate for audiences that might include survivors of Second World War death camps.[27] Rerelease was delayed. When it was eventually brought out cuts were made to improve the representation of French Jewish prisoner of war, Rosenthal (Dalio). Prefects were given the right to ban it from their regions if they considered it too disturbing.[28] In fact, it became a popular hit, Renoir's theme of working-class heroism matching popular communist rhetoric of the period. It was also something of a classic for the 1950s and 1960s with its celebration of Franco–German harmony corresponding neatly to the new and genuine postwar rapprochement, as well as wider European integration – an internationalist aspect that was further advanced by the fact that the scriptwriter was the francophone Belgian, Charles Spaak.

As is well known, Marcel Carné's *Les Enfants du paradis* was the triumph of the Liberation, proof that France remained a significant force in the realm of cinema. In its initial casting, the anti-Semitic actor and radio broadcaster Robert Le Vigan played the malicious character Jéricho. However, as fortunes of war shifted Le Vigan fled from France to Southern Germany, joining other collaborators in Sigmaringen, including Céline. After losing Le Vigan, Carné preserved the character of Jéricho – the villain of the piece was needed for the plot – and offered the role to Pierre Renoir, older brother of Jean. This was a less provocative casting than the initial plan; without Le Vigan the depiction was less charged with references to anti-Semitism (besides playing Rothschild on Vichy radio 'comedies', Le Vigan was also famous for portraying the highly 'Aryan' Jesus Christ in Duvivier's *Golgatha* [1935]). However, the anti-Semitic subtext from the Vichy era version did not disappear altogether with the change of actors. Biographer and Carné specialist Edward Baron Turk underlines:

> [I]n Les Enfants du paradis *the bend of his body, the croak of his voice, and the configuration of his facial hair make Renoir's portrayal of the film's only true villain conform all too uncomfortably to distorted images of Jews propagated in notorious German films such as Fritz Hippler's,* Der Ewige Jude *and Veit Harlan's* Jud Süss.[29]

Because it was a melodramatic epic, set in the early nineteenth century, this imagery was not treated with concern in the way that *La Grande illusion* had been in the months and days after the Liberation. The idea that theatrical villainy could be linked to non-Gallic body features, stereotypes from the long anti-Semitic tradition, did not perturb anyone in 1945. On the contrary, as readers will know, the film was much loved and has been considered a treasure of the nation's cinema ever since. Audiences in 1945 were certainly unperturbed: seemingly they were so used to negative images of Jewishness that they did not see the stigmatizing stereotype in front of them, or they did not mind it. Of course comparable works with similar stereotypes were made in Britain, notably David Lean's *Oliver Twist* (1948). France, Britain, Western Europe, did not stop using softened anti-Semitic clichés after the Holocaust. Implicit racist caricatures from the literary and visual cannons remained broadly acceptable at least in the 1940s and 1950s. Only in the late 1970s and early 1980s did this kind of anti-Semitism start to be questioned, and then not in all quarters. For example, in 2005 Patrick Brion continues to gloss over the subject when offering another standard celebration of Carné's famous film. According to his *Cinéma français 1895–2005*, published in association with the French foreign office, *Les Enfants du paradis* is simply a much-loved classic. Therein context and political content are replaced with regarding film as a national heritage site, a position also discussed in chapter 1's treatment of the 1995 Centenary of Cinema commemorations.[30]

Julien Duvivier's adaptation of Georges Simenon's *Les Fiançailles de M. Hire* (film 1946; source novel 1933) is in many regards exemplary of the ambivalence of the immediate postwar years. Shot as *Panique* (1946), it recounts the story of Hire, an ordinary working-class man living in the suburbs of Paris. He is framed for a murder that he has not committed. It is implied that Hire is French Jewish, and the film illustrates how the community quickly suspects him of murder. In the horrific final scene they turn against him and an unruly crowd attack him. The film is a critique of mob rule, by implication a statement against prejudice. However, Duvivier also laces the work with anti-Jewish stereotypes that go unquestioned. Hire is associated with esoteric and occult activity, a reference that hints at the anti-Jewish slander of ritual child murder. He is pictured as being physically unattractive. Duvivier's new work therefore continues his interwar cinema, which had depicted Jewishness through popular clichés, for example, *Le Golem* (1935). It would also stand good comparison with Karen Adler's meticulous discussion of the ambiguities of Clouzot's film *Manon* (1949) and the public responses that film stimulated through its representations of Jewishness, Zionism and Israel.[31]

Offscreen, the critic Vinneuil (Rebatet) stood trial for collaboration. Colleagues from the film industry supported him despite the fact that he had published denunciation of Jewish film owners during the occupation, some of whom were almost certainly killed in the Holocaust. For example, the scriptwriter to *La Grande illusion*, Charles Spaak, attended the trial and testified for him on 22 November 1946. He noted that anti-Semitism had been 'notre honte à tous' ['our collective shame'], not only Rebatet's, and one does not disagree completely with that historical assessment.[32] Letters from René Clair, Jacques Becker, Jean Grémillon, Claude Autant-Lara and Louis Daquin were submitted in favour of the critic, pleading for his life to be spared. Novelist and scriptwriter Marcel Aymé attended all of the proceedings. Rebatet was imprisoned and later he continued his career as a writer and critic, using a variety of pseudonyms. In 1953, the right-wing literary periodical *La Parisienne* offered him the opportunity to reflect on his career and imprisonment. He recalled that while he served his prison sentence his wife had kept him informed about new films.[33] He concludes by praising Clouzot's *La Salaire de la peur* (1953). As many contemporary readers would have surely appreciated, Clouzot had himself been blacklisted by the resistance at the end of the war for his work with Nazi production house Continental and for his negative depiction of France in *Le Corbeau* (1943). Selecting him to review first was not an innocent coincidence. Probably, it can be taken as a statement of defiant loyalty to his past politics. It did not signify any new self-critical development in light of his trial and imprisonment. It was a way of saying that others with dubious war records were also now well regarded and working again.

It seems to me that the late 1940s show confused attitudes that blurred together residual anti-Semitic prejudice with some self-censorship and a vague awareness that what had occurred was barbaric, but not really about

France or French life per se. Nonetheless, it is also important to add that this period also saw development of coded and left-leaning anti-Semitic discourses around the subject of the film industry. Thus, during the Blum–Byrnes dispute (1946 to 1948, see also chapter 4), the film community's anti-Americanism blurred into forms of new anti-Semitism. At the first meetings of cineastes opposed to the accords (1946), the sharpest criticisms were reserved exclusively for Jewish politician Léon Blum. Repeatedly, the film protesters and the communist press asserted that it was Blum who had betrayed the nation by agreeing to the trade deal in Washington.[34] Communist daily L'Humanité focused on Blum's role in supposedly destroying the domestic cinema. For example, in L'Humanité, 8 January 1948, Guy Leclerc alleged that Blum had sold off France's second most important national industry – cinema – to the Americans.[35] A day later, emblazoned on the front page of the same newspaper, André Marty accused Blum of a new, different treason. He highlighted that Blum was siding with Gaullism and fascism by arguing for a normalization of Franco-Spanish relations. The same writer accused Blum's socialist party of being the 'Americans in France' and the representatives of the Rothschild's bank.[36] Thus, the communists tarnished Blum's reputation as a patriot by questioning his loyalty to the people and by inferring complicity with international banking. Clearly, these are anti-Semitic propensities. Pierre Hervé developed this argument further; he accused Blum of being a 'treacherous serpent' whose politics favoured Wall Street over national economic recovery.[37]

The communist attacks continued through into 1948 and included not only written argumentation but also satirical caricatures. These intimated that Blum was working for foreign interests and was not 'truly French'. The cartoonist 'Donga' provided a particularly cruel piece for L'Humanité (15 January 1948). There Donga depicts Blum and his group listening to the national anthem 'Allons enfants de la patrie', with text beneath that asserted that none of these pro-Americans understood the song. The message was explicit: Blum and his colleagues were unable to be French. Donga caricatured the socialists with grotesque features, large pointed noses and sporting strange spectacles that concealed their eyes. It is a visual imagery that draws on anti-Semitic racial stereotyping from an earlier period of illustration and newspaper cartooning.[38]

When filmmakers, including Autant-Lara, and the PCF attacked Blum they repeated abuse that was originally made by the extreme right-wing Vichy regime. Throughout the 1930s Blum had suffered greatly at the hands of anti-

Semites and under Vichy he was made to stand trial for betraying France, before the Nazis deported him to Buchenwald.[39] Moreover, the frequency and ferocity of the attacks on Blum circa 1946 to 1948 were so great that it was all too easy to believe that Blum was solely responsible for the hated postwar trade and film quota deal. In fact he was acting as a delegate on behalf of President Félix Gouin, accompanied on his mission to the U.S.A. by Jean Monnet, whose economic recovery plan for France was the essential element of the diplomatic mission. Furthermore, Blum never literally signed the annex of the Franco–American agreement covering the cinema. To be precise it was Henri Bonnet (the French Ambassador to the U.S.A.) and the Deputy Secretary of State William Clayton who had concluded the agreement. The PCF even conveniently forgot that they were full members of the coalition government in 1946 when the accords were negotiated. The historian Georgette Elgey highlights that in 1946 the PCF had claimed to be influential in achieving a positive agreement for France in Washington![40]

Some film journalism in specialist periodicals for fans and critics added to the climate of suspicion that implied that U.S.-Hollywood-Blum and 'the Jews' working in Hollywood were the number one threat to France. For instance, L'Écran français blurred its increasingly negative Cold War reporting on Hollywood with the accusation that the home of filmmaking in the U.S.A. was also a site of a Jewish cabal. In 1947 it published translated extracts from Budd Schulberg's novel What Makes Sammy Run? Schulberg had set this fictional work in Hollywood and in it he charted the rise of a ruthlessly ambitious New York Jew, Sammy Glick. The French journalist Jean Vidal presented the novel to his readers as a quasi-factual insight into the dubious world of American cinema. According to Vidal, Schulberg's novel was a realistic insider's account of Hollywood life. It illustrated the true face of Hollywood, its monstrous artificiality. It was presented as being an edifying read for French film enthusiasts wanting to understand its setting. [41] Claude Roy, also writing for L'Écran français, shared this reading of the novel and repeated it in his column.[42] Thereby a complex work of fiction was represented as a quasi-factual insight into the alleged seamy side of Hollywood. That this was a highly ambiguous novel, which can be read on several different levels, is overlooked. Readers of L'Écran français were encouraged to simply believe that Hollywood was run and controlled by scheming people like Sammy Glick.[43] Indeed, others in the industry seemed to believe that Hollywood was intimately connected to New

York finance. When Jean Renoir wrote to Saint-Exupéry about a possible U.S. adaptation of his *Terre des hommes* (1939), he expressed suspicion that decisions on production did not come out of California at all. Instead, Renoir remarked in correspondence dated 26 May 1941 that:

> [L]es entreprises un peu exceptionnelles dans l'Industrie Cinématographique, se décident non pas à Hollywood, mais à New York. Je n'ai aucune preuve pour soutenir cette théorie, mais j'ai la sensation que, ici, c'est l'Usine, avec ouvriers, les ingénieurs, et des grands Directeurs; bref, les exécutants. Mais les financiers, ceux qui alimentent la machine et en tirent des bénéfices, sont à New York.[44]

> [The ventures that are a little exceptional in the cinema industry are not decided in Hollywood but in New York. I have no proof to support this theory but I have the feeling that here is the Factory, with its workers, its engineers and the great Directors, the makers. But the financiers who feed the machine and take the profits are in New York.]

Extreme anti-Jewish prejudice was never as explicitly made public as it had been previously in the interwar period. Anti-Blum–Byrnes campaigners mixed anticapitalism with anti-Americanism and this is the ideological space where their anti-Semitism was demonstrable. The communist journalists identified themselves with the resistance and antifascism, yet in their anti-Americanism and anticapitalism they implied that it was Jewish politicians or business groups who were menacing France. Winock summarizes helpfully, 'Without doubt the most receptive to anti-Semitism were among the PCF's electorate where there was acceptance of the old nineteenth-century equation: Jews equal capitalism'.[45]

Filmmakers who engaged in radical political protest through the 1960s and early 1970s deployed historical analogies that trivialized or diminished the Holocaust. Trite comparisons between U.S. intervention in Vietnam and Nazi genocide were regularly voiced, including in the filmmaking community. The reactions of the PCF and a group of filmmakers to John Wayne's take on the Vietnam War, *The Green Berets*, is exemplary. In *L'Humanité*, Madeleine Riffaud argued that the same financial sources that had paid for napalm bombing in Vietnam were behind Wayne's film. She described the Green Beret regiment as the 'Gestapo de l'impérialisme', and stated that the film was a work of propaganda to make Goebbels proud.[46] Cineastes agreed and reused the historical analogy. Robert Enrico, Louis Malle, Pierre Kast and Doniol-Valcrose petitioned for censorship of the picture. They invited cinema managers not to become complicit in what they called the 'génocide américain au Vietnam'.[47] Such was the language of the times and Godard did more than most to make this kind of rhetoric fashionable. In his commissioned film for the PLO, *Ici et ailleurs* (1976), he helped establish the propaganda claim that Israel's defence and foreign policies were equivalent to Nazism.[48] For what it is worth, Godard has continued this rhetoric into the 2000s. In autumn 2009 his inflammatory remarks about Israel and the history of the Holocaust reached the French press. Alain Fleischer's *Courts-circuits* revealed a new angle on his attitude. According to Fleischer, Godard had suggested to him that Palestinian suicide bombers attacking Israel were comparable to the Jewish 'sheep' who had let themselves be exterminated in the gas chambers to bring about Israel, '[S]e sacrifiant ainsi pour parvenir à faire exister l'État d'Israël' ['Sacrificing themselves this way to bring into being the state of Israel'].[49] Let us also recall that years earlier Truffaut had taxed Godard for his anti-Semitism. In his polemical letter to Godard of May 1973, Truffaut accused him of describing film producer Braunberger as a 'filthy Jew'.[50] This insult related to a dispute that had taken place between Godard and the producer, and that Braunberger had complained about to Truffaut.

Besides the more public radical-left discourses, right-wing extremists interested in cinema returned after 1945. For much of the postwar period, the film historian Maurice Bardèche edited a marginal fascistic periodical, *Défense de l'Occident*, and was instrumental in developing Holocaust denial thinking. *Défense de l'Occident* was not a film-related publication, being dedicated to promoting extreme right-wing ideology rather than culture. Nonetheless, from time to time, Bardèche included film criticism. Short articles by Michel Mourlet, critic from *Cahiers du cinéma* and *Présence du cinéma*, featured in the periodical in 1962. Other items about the cinema were also occasionally published. In 1959 an anonymous contributor warned that Jewish pressure groups were ruling over all independent thinking in Europe. The writer explained that these groups had unfairly stopped the former Nazi filmmaker Schaffer from making a scientific documentary film about wildlife in the Congo, which had been commissioned by the Belgian royal family. According to the anonymous author the 'Jews' were also creating unjustified hostility against Veit Harlan (veteran Nazi filmmaker). His postwar work was being censored as well. The same anonymous author concluded that it was a curious psychological instability that made Jews wish to stop directors working again. He threatened that their actions would only promote renewed antipathy towards their community. The article was however a fringe piece situated on the political margins.[51]

Much more significantly, Bardèche and Brasillach's *Histoire du cinéma* was reedited and newly published in 1948. This edition continued to express anti-Semitism and was unedited. For example, it retains the authors' attack on Marcel Carné, describing his work as 'trop longuement associé à une esthétique judaïsante' ['too long associated with a Jewish aesthetic'].[52] Subsequent paperback editions revised this section completely. In the 1964 reprint for the mass-market 'Poche' printing, the former judgement on Carné's work is modified to read: 'trop longuement associé à une esthétique contestable' ['too long associated with a questionable aesthetic'].[53] People with far greater influence on the arts than Bardèche were also attempting to bring Nazi filmmakers back to public attention: it is a matter of record that Jean Cocteau entered into correspondence with Leni Riefenstahl and he actively campaigned for her to be given the right to show *Tiefland* at the 1954 Cannes film festival. His efforts failed.[54]

To review, the immediate postwar anti-Semitism is significant because of its different mode to from before the Liberation. The Morand-Pagnol-Céline vision of the 1930s and early 1940s was in retreat. In the final analysis, Bardèche cut a lonesome and eccentric figure, despite his connections to one or two *Cahiers du cinéma* people. Political and cultural power had switched from the right to the left wing. It was on the left that vicious antipathy towards Blum revived old prejudices. It is also the case that by the late 1960s trivializations of the Holocaust were relatively common in polemics that used historical analogies. This material evidences a complete lack awareness of what this history meant to survivors.

A decade before Claude Autant-Lara was elected a Member of the European Parliament, popular director Michel Audiard made a series of racist and anti-Semitic attacks that were relatively similar to what followed in 1989. Speaking on France-Inter radio, he suggested that he liked 'nègres' because unlike 'juifs' they were more easily identifiable to him.[55] Writing in his published essay *Vive la France* (1973) he quipped that the only reason anyone ever had for joining the resistance during the occupation was because they were trying to escape being hunted down by the Nazis.[56] The film of the same title that Audiard directed in 1973 was a further reactionary attack, especially against de Gaulle. Philippe d'Hugues notes that at the time critics accused him of Poujadism, but that the film was more right wing than that.[57] One of his next films included further snippets of crude anti-Semitic content. *L'Entourloupe* (1975, directed by Pirès, who went on to make *Taxi* [1998], the script is from Audiard) contained brief material of this same type. There the main character, a medical-dictionary salesman, bandies racist language, muttering anti-Semitic defamations to one of his team.

Readers should understand that Audiard wrote for high-circulation newspapers *L'Aurore* and *Le Matin* and he used this opportunity to again denigrate the Jewish community. In his column for *Le Matin* of 6 August 1980 he composed a series of cynical remarks about Nazism and the Holocaust. Here, he discussed a recent television documentary on the subject of Nazi doctor Mengele. To paraphrase, he had found it informative: Mengele was an excellent doctor and a philosopher who had opened the door to progress. People like Audiard, who were stupid and ugly, could not oppose Mengele's wish to make people more intelligent and pretty. Audiard added that what was ugly in the documentary was the ungrateful deportee who the doctor had saved.[58]

Some of the above remarks did provoke criticism, and increasingly Audiard was identified as being too old-fashioned. Such criticisms must be balanced by the fact that months after the *Le Matin* article Audiard was hard at work with director Georges Lautner on the script to *Le Professionnel* (see chapter 5). Between 1980 and his death in 1983, Audiard collaborated with Yves Boisset, Claude Miller, Jacques Deray and Henri Verneuil. Likewise, in 1982, he was feted at the César awards ceremony for his script on Miller's film *Garde à vue*. In the year of the Centenary of Cinema, 1995, Audiard was also commemorated as part of the great family of cinema. That same year the trade journal *Le Film français* advertised the collected writings of the director, *Audiard par Audiard*, on its front cover. For Audiard, expressing reactionary polemics were all one and a part of a successful and prolific career.[59]

Further context assists this discussion. Notably, Audiard imagined and described himself as a follower and popularizer of Louis-Ferdinand Céline. His crude anti-Semitic humour and love of Parisian slang marked him out for this role. This was a literary-political passion Audiard shared with many others working in cinema. Jean Gabin learned pages of Céline's writings by heart and with Audiard and another friend, Gilles Grangier, they would test each other's knowledge of the writer's work. Jean-Paul Belmondo was another admirer of the author of *Voyage au bout de la nuit* and Audiard considered casting him in an aborted adaptation.[60] Childish and sometimes cruel joking about the Nazi period was a part of this subculture. When Jean Gabin asked his friend André Pousse if he was 'still a fan of Hitler', Pousse enjoyed replying that he continued to appreciate his authoritative leadership style. Audiard and René Fallet enjoyed similar 'witty' repartee together. Playing with Proust's question, 'Quelle est votre occupation favorite?', the standard reply was 'L'occupation allemande'.[61] In Audiard's circle, crude racist humour was treated as normal and acceptable. Scriptwriter and novelist Pascal Jardin remarked of Gabin, 'I know Gabin the misanthrope, the pessimist, the misogynist, who regards two-thirds of humanity as swine and the other third as fools, who thinks that Europe is done for and that the "yellow men" are going to checkmate us, who considers nearly all women to be butches, bitches and witches'.[62] The wider subculture of reactionary high jinks is further discussed by outsider to that world Simone Signoret in her memoirs, *Nostalgia Isn't What it Used to Be*. Signoret's comments on the director Clouzot, and the life off-set during the filming of *Le Salaire de la peur* add more evidence to the above picture. Thus, Signoret recalls that most evenings after dinner there would be a fun mock fight about cinema and history with cheap plates brought from Prisunic so they could be smashed up in exaggerated anger. Signoret writes:

> I often quarrelled with Clouzot but that was part of the fun. He got a kick out of it. If perchance, I wasn't aggressive fast enough, he would provoke me. It generally started with 'Poor Brasillach ... so sensitive, so delicate'. So sensitive and so delicate that he wrote for Je suis partout. That would make the evening.[63]

Anti-Semitism, racism, they rely on the continuity of precisely these supposedly less harmful and 'funny' perspectives. Such *petit-Celinien* humour asserts clear in- and out- group dynamics for the national community. On the one hand, there were the artists who find themselves witty and humorous people who are able to laugh at anything, including genocide. On the other hand, there is the rhetorical creation of the out-group being generated, they are the people who do not laugh or who are the focus of the so-called joke. Trivialization is a powerful political device because it turns negative attention towards the group being mocked (the victims of Nazism, the Jewish community) and distracts from the shameful role played by the national group (Vichy France) with whom the joker is identifying. Audiard took this private subculture and put it into his films and scripts. He thrived on looking radical by challenging good taste.

Michel Audiard is an especially significant case when considering this aspect because he had also been active under the Nazi occupation, writing fascist leaning and anti-Semitic journalism for the collaborationist newspaper *L'Appel.* Yet such details were never discussed in any detail in Audiard's lifetime.[64] His blustering and offensive mode of operations distracted attention from any focused and serious historical research because no one would suspect anyone with direct roots in the politics of the Vichy period to be so audaciously offensive. Audiard was just too successful a player in the industry to have youthful indiscretions raised against him while he was alive. Certainly, his record sheds new light on his son's film, a work beyond the immediate remit of this book, *Un héros très discret* (1996). That work is about the fabrication of history, a young man inventing a record in the resistance. It is usually discussed as a film about collective memory but must have also been a son's reflection on a complicated family history as well.[65]

Art cinema in the 1970s was marked by a different kind of anti-Semitism to Audiard's form of badinage. Here, when high-profile directors addressed the meaning of Vichy France, fascism and the Holocaust, they sometimes slipped into making anti-Semitic stereotypes or paid too favourable attention to fascism. Louis Malle's *Lacombe Lucien* is the classic example of the tendency. Let me explain why. In that work Malle's primary intention was to show audiences painful truths about their national history and to undermine the notion of certainty in historical understanding per se. All other matters were secondary to him. Because of this, his work missed out on making any kind of nuanced interpretation of the Jewish protagonists. Malle's primary male Jewish character in *Lacombe Lucien* is represented as a rich tailor who can pay bribes to protect himself and his family from deportation. His daughter, France (Aurore Clément), is quickly willing to sleep with collaborator Lucien (Pierre Blaise). Malle's work was sloppy in its use of these clichés, and focused too intensely on the subject of fascism to address French Jewish experience in any concerned or intelligent mode. It is only the brilliant cinematography and fine performances from the actors that make an otherwise grotesque narrative function for its purposes.

Insensitivity to the Jewish historical experience was relatively commonplace in some quarters of art filmmaking in the 1970s. The film community's reactions to Rainer W. Fassbinder and Daniel Schmid's *L'Ombre des anges* (1976) are a further noteworthy example. Based on a script by Fassbinder, Schmid's film describes a series of encounters between a German prostitute and a central protagonist who is named as 'Le juif riche'. This protagonist is portrayed as a powerful and exploitative businessman who is running an unnamed German city. He uses the prostitute and ultimately he murders her, attributing his violent act to another man. Repeatedly, other characters in the film describe him as the 'juif riche' or 'le chef', and on occasions they make sexually explicit jokes against him. In one scene a former Nazi – the father of the prostitute – regrets that he had not gassed the rich Jew during the Holocaust.

Fassbinder and Schmid assert that they were exploring the complex themes of power and Germany's Holocaust guilt. It is not a realist work and is self-evidently Brechtian in its aim to unsettle audiences.[66] The French film community hailed the significance of *L'Ombre des anges*. In addition, they defended it from criticisms made by many other commentators who felt it was significantly wide of the mark. Even though the work was banned in West Germany, the Cannes Film Festival organizer, Maurice Bessy, accepted it to represent Switzerland in the 1976 competition. The festival organizers were unwilling to listen to complaints from the Israeli delegation. Spokesperson Zohar Bar-Am declared that his country was deeply offended by Schmid's film and that it should not be screened. The managing clique at Cannes ignored these protests and the Israeli group quit Cannes in protest.[67] When *L'Ombre des anges* went on general release in Paris most of the film community defended it from criticism. On the 21 February 1977, producer Bojilow issued a press statement in the newspaper *Libération* in which he and a group of sixty intellectuals and filmmakers proclaimed that the work was not anti-Semitic and that its censorship was unacceptable. The signatories of the petition include Gérard Blain, Gérard Depardieu, Sami Frey, Peter Handke, Clara Malraux, Vincent Malle, Eric Rohmer, Gilles Deleuze and Frédéric Mitterrand.[68] In addition, Gilles Deleuze wrote in *Le Monde* to promote Schmid's work. Using the deliberately provocative title 'Le juif riche', he claimed that the film merited being excused a little bit of anti-Semitism because it was so beautiful.[69] In Paris there was something of an unseemly rush to celebrate Schmid's work. For example, the much-respected film critic at *France Soir*, Robert Chazal, argued that it was absurd to view the film as being anti-Semitic and that it worked best for those audiences interested in the artistic development of its director. Articles in film magazines *Positif* and *Cahiers du cinéma* were similarly supportive.[70]

The film did offend the French Jewish community who requested that it not be shown in their country because of its anti-Semitic content. Legal representatives for LICA (Ligue International Contre le Racisme et l'Anti-Sémitisme), Henri Hajdenberg, Philippe Ryfman and Serge Klarsfeld, wrote to the film's producer and director to explain how the work was offensive for Jewish and non-Jewish audiences. Jean-Pierre Bloch, the president of LICA, writing in *Le Monde*, explained that *L'Ombre des anges* combined so many hateful discourses that it was intolerable. He underlined that throughout the film the highly offensive and clichéd terminology 'rich Jew' was repeated. He noted that Fassbinder and Schmid had deployed the traditional stereotype of the successful, ruthless, Jewish capitalist. For Bloch these images were unacceptable in a film that was set in West Germany, the Nazis' homeland, the place where the Holocaust had been ordered. Double standards were at work in Paris too. The same cineastes that were calling for freedom of expression in favour of *L'Ombre des anges* had done nothing to defend a documentary film about Vichy France, *Chantons sous l'occupation* (Halimi, 1976), when it was forced off the screen because of threats from extreme right-wing student groups. Nor had they reacted when anti-Zionist protesters had stopped the action film *Raid on Entebbe* (1977).[71] Nonetheless, Claude Lanzmann gained a right to reply to Gilles Deleuze's essay and his views were disseminated in *Le Monde*. Lanzmann reiterated how the film was offensive and misguided. He argued that the philosopher Deleuze was wrong to defend it.[72]

In hindsight, the cineastes displayed a lack of understanding of the French Jewish community's experience and memories of the 1930s and 1940s. It is striking that the film community refused any dialogue with the French Jewish community about Fassbinder. No public statement from the defenders of Schmid and Fassbinder acknowledged the hurt that the content of the work caused, even unintentionally. On the contrary, the film was championed and any criticism of it was repelled as unwarranted. Why so? The intellectuals and artists speaking up for the film prioritized their own interpretation of the work as superior to that of the spokespeople for the French Jewish community. They elevated their ability to read the film as a work of art as preferable to the French Jewish citizens' viewpoint that it was a hurtful recycling of anti-Semitic insults. The intellectuals, actors and directors failed to consider how a Jewish survivor of Nazi or Vichy persecution would interpret Schmid's work. Furthermore, the film continued to be admired and defended long after the controversy abated. For example, Jean Tulard writes in his widely read dictionary of filmmakers aimed at students and general readers, 'There was a really unfair trial of Schmid on grounds of anti-Semitism in his adaptation of Fassbinder's play'. Tulard, who is also an eminent historian of the Napoleonic era, offers more of the same in his entry on Claude Autant-Lara where he also expresses sympathy for the director. He reviews the scandal from 1989 most oddly, or at least that is what it seems to me: 'Des propos imprudents lui [Autant-Lara] ont valu des attaques non moins excessives qui ont précipité sa retraite' ['Imprudent remarks from him (Autant-Lara) cost no less excessive attacks which precipitated his retirement'].[73]

Conclusion

Before reviewing the discussion above it seems important and sensible to add some meta-commentary on the material included and left out in the above pages. Because I have wanted to detail and analyse evidence pertaining to issues of anti-Semitism, I have not included any extended discussion of Holocaust cinema in France, including the two major documentaries, Resnais's *Nuit et brouillard* and Lanzmann's *Shoah* as well as works on which I have written before and much admire, such as Malle's *Au revoir les enfants*. I was reluctant to discuss those films in this context because I do not believe anti-Semitism as a discourse is the same subject as Holocaust film, although of course negative reception of such a film could evidence the former. When researching precisely that question at BIFI Paris, the film-review files relating to *Shoah* reveal no evidence whatsoever of neofascist violence being launched against the work. On the contrary, the film was identified as a landmark work and received support from the state, including from President Mitterrand who wanted to campaign for Lanzmann to receive a Nobel Prize. Four further remarks seem helpful for readers, especially university students wanting to work with this book in their courses and maybe in more wide-ranging study of postwar France and the cinema than I approach herein. (1) Obviously, not all French cinema was anti-Semitic (coded or uncoded) and indeed in the above pages I have been making quite a different argument about how the ideology of nationalist anti-Semitism retreated to a more rearguard or coded discourse after 1945, with notable exceptions. (2) Postwar France was a site for some of the best examples of Holocaust documentary work. Political and intellectual elites have supported these works and they are a regular feature in the antiracist campaigns of the late 1980s and 1990s. For example, Resnais's work was rebroadcast on National Television as educational response to neo-Nazi outrages such as the vandalism of French-Jewish graves in Carpentras (1990). The three films noted above also point to new directions in French cinema more evident in the 2000s than maybe for the period which I am discussing. Thus, in only the past few years two major and powerful works have addressed the Vichy Police roundup in Paris, the Rafle de Vel d'Hiv (16 and 17 July 1942). (3) That Resnais and Lanzmann achieved their works is all the more significant because they were being made in parallel to the dispositions and discourses analysed in this chapter. (4) To repeat, this book focuses on a selection of sites of nationalism and these are distinctive and different from sites of resistance to that disposition. This work has highlighted only briefly sites of dissonance and discussed them so as to acknowledge that perspective and often its role in film events (for example, in the last chapter the black actors' campaign against *L'État sauvage* or Tavernier's *Coup de torchon*, are good examples). My analysis stands or falls on its ability to deconstruct and reveal the sites of nationalism, political myths and film events, not in the analysis of different counter-ideologies, which merit detailed study in their own right.

To return to the subject one has written on, it is worth underlining here that anti-Semitism was an open and important part of cinema-related debates, circa 1930 to 1944. Regularly, writers, critics and cineastes asserted that the national cinema was threatened when too many Jewish filmmakers found work in the pictures. Pagnol's advice in *Le Schpountz* that the French were better off looking after themselves rather than allowing producers such as 'Meyerboom' too much power was one common attitude. The idea of an excessive Jewish employment in film and other arts directly informed Vichy policy. In the 1980s the extreme right wing repeated these ideas. Autant-Lara's speeches and interviews represent a historical residue of opinions that were once popular. Such attitudes faded after 1945 but were not entirely removed from society or cinema. Anti-Americanism in the days of the Blum–Byrnes accords filtered latently anti-Semitic prejudices back into press circulation. Then, leftist anti-Semites reimagined Jewish power reasserting control over filmmaking and economy. By the 1970s, reactionary Michel Audiard insisted on keeping 1930s attitudes alive. Few in the film industry were concerned when offensive rhetoric was hurled. This was true whether its origin was either populist (Audiard) or avant-garde (Fassbinder and Schmid).

Louis-Ferdinand Céline's influence on cineastes is worth underlining further here, as it does appear as a common factor in the mythic discourses and film events discussed in this chapter. Autant-Lara cited him as the last great national writer; Audiard imagined he would be able to film his novels and to continue his tradition. Famous film artists supported Céline in the postwar years, including Arletty, Gabin, Belmondo and others. In the 1950s, Gallimard editor and novelist Roger Nimier suggested that Louis Malle would be an appropriate director of a film adaptation of *Voyage au bout de la nuit*.[74] Autant-Lara was mooted as being another possibility to direct a work of this kind. Truffaut's correspondence from 1964 also notes that he too was once asked to film the novel.[75] No film was ever made; however, Godard's *Pierrot le fou* is in part a mash-up of Céline's vision. Godard had also hoped to cast Céline in *À bout de souffle*. He had wanted the author to play the role of the celebrity writer being interviewed at Orly airport by Patricia (Seberg). Céline declined the offer and Godard persuaded Jean-Pierre Melville to take the part instead.[76] Céline counted among his inner circle important figures from the cinema. Notably, he was close to the actor Robert Le Vigan, and includes depictions and commentaries on him in his *D'un château l'autre* (1957). They had fled France together in 1944 and had briefly stayed in Germany awaiting the conclusion of the war. When living in exile in Argentina, Le Vigan made recordings of readings from Céline's texts for commercial sale. Le Vigan was an anti-Semite and a crude racist, especially fearing Chinese power. He won a minor cult following inside the postwar film industry. Publications evidence that Maurice Ronet and Arletty, among others, attended the Mass held to commemorate his life.[77] We can add that Arletty described Céline as being like a brother to her. She had enjoyed the war in the company of a German lover, attending a reception at the German embassy in 1941 in the company of Göring. At her trial for collaboration she explained, 'In my bed there are no uniforms', and 'My heart is French but my ass is international'.[78] For what it is worth, some years later, Hollywood cast her as a French resistance fighter in *The Longest Day* (1962).

In the 1930s, Céline was one among many writers and artists who expressed anti-Semitism through discussion of cinema. Then, for the film community, Paul Morand and Marcel Pagnol were quite as influential as he was. Céline's influence was therefore far greater on the postwar generation that followed, who used his literary credentials to legitimate the continuation of right-wing anarchism and anti-Semitism in the 1970s and 1980s. The prominence that Céline's writing had gained by the end of the twentieth century, the literary value placed by critics on *Voyage au bout de la nuit*, made referencing him far more useful and populist an intertextual gesture than any fidelity to Morand, Rebatet or Pagnol.[79] It is also worth underlining that Céline's status as the 'star' anti-Semite focused historians attention away from the ambivalence of work made by the national treasures Carné and Renoir.

Did the anti-Semitic rhetoric ever develop into populist violence, akin to the extreme right-wing attacks on *La Bataille d'Alger*? There were some comparable extreme film events, though no single work attracted the violence that was directed against Pontecorvo's work. In 1976, presentation of the documentary on wartime collaboration among the artistic community in Paris, *Chantons sous l'occupation* (Halimi) was disrupted. On its release, a smoke bomb was thrown into the Capri cinema on the Champs-Elysées. Distribution agents Parafrance withdrew it from all seven other Parisian cinemas where it was scheduled. No group, extreme left or extreme right, claimed responsibility.[80] A group calling itself 'Le Collectif d'Offensive Communiste' sabotaged showings of the action movie about Israeli special services, *Victoire à Entebbe* (1977).[81] This took place at the Paramount-Montparnasse where a witness added that the youths distributed leaflets explaining their complaints. It denounced the film for being a stupid glorification of Israel and accused the French state of complicity with it because of arming Phalangist Lebanon and for arresting Palestine Liberation Organization (PLO) leader Abou Daoud. In 1994 the extreme right-wing student group Groupe Union Défense (GUD) threw smoke bombs into two cinemas showing Lanzmann's documentary about the Israeli army, *Tsahal*.[82] The anti-Semitic violence mounted against film theatres was therefore sporadic and far smaller in scale than the treatment towards critical cinema relating to the Algerian war. However, leftists as well as right-wing groups conducted these raids on the cinemas. One can underline that this left–right ideological confluence did not occur in the terrorism mounted against *La Bataille d'Alger* or for that matter in the attacks on *The Last Temptation of Christ*, which will be analysed in the next chapter.

Notes

1. C. Autant-Lara, 1989, *Le Bateau coule*, Paris: Liberté, 44–5, 97.
2. See O. Biffaud, 1989, 'Selon M.Le Pen la société française est atteinte du "sida mental"', *Le Monde*, 3 October, 12.
3. Full film record of the episode is available from the European Parliament Library, London, U.K. For a written transcript see *Official Journal of the European Communities: Debates of the European Parliament*, no. 2–379, 1989–1990 Session, 'Report of Proceedings from 25 to 28 July 1989'.
4. G. Domenach, 1989, 'Celui par qui le scandale arrive', *National Hebdo* no. 263, 3 August, 24.
5. For the interview see 'Claude Autant-Lara: encore plus loin que Le Pen', 1989, *Globe*, 40, 37. See also L. Joffrin, 1996, 'La tache brune', *Nouvel Observateur*, 14 September, 34–35; H.G. Simmons, 1996, *The French National Front*, Oxford: Westview Press, 126–27.
6. See M. Marmin, 1989, 'Autant-Lara: L'enjeu d'une affaire', *Éléments*, 67 (Winter), 5–8; J-C. Valla, 1989, 'Le faux interview d'Autant-Lara', *Éléments*, 67 (Winter), 9–10. For the Faurisson affair see 'L'agression contre M. Robert Faurisson revendiquée par "les fils de la mémoire juive"', 1989, *Le Monde*, 19 September, 14; L. Greilsamer, 1989, 'L'obstine négateur du génocide', *Le Monde*, 19 September, 14.
7. See R. Gaucher, 1989. 'Autant-Lara et les globuleux', *National Hebdo*, 14 September, 2.
8. See F. Brigneau, 1989, 'Le Journal d'un homme libre', *National Hebdo*, 21 September, 4–5; Brigneau, 1989, 'Autant-Lara et Cie', *National Hebdo*, 21 September, 23.
9. See 'Autant-Lara, suite', 1989, *National Hebdo*, 4 October, 23.
10. M. L'Herbier, 1979, *La tête qui tourne*, Paris: Pierre Belfond, 204; see also C. Crisp,1993, *The Classic French Cinema, 1930–1960*, Bloomington: Indiana University Press, 170. See also S. Lindeperg, *Les Écrans de l'ombre*, 288–89, where the influence of the First World War on Autant-Lara's politics is underlined.
11. L'Herbier, *La tête*, 244–45.
12. Crisp, *French Cinema*, 170.
13. L-F. Céline, 1943, *Bagatelles pour un massacre*, Paris: Denoël, 58.
14. Céline, *Bagatelles*, 160.

15. Céline, *Bagatelles*, 269. See also A.Y. Kaplan, 1987, *Relevé des sources et citations dans 'Bagatelles pour un massacre'*, Tusson: Lérot, 193–94.

16. See J. Ulff-Moller, 2001, *Hollywood's Film Wars with France: Film Trade Diplomacy and the Emergence of the French Film Quota Policy*, Rochester: Rochester University Press, 118–99.

17. P. Morand, 1934, *France la doulce*, Paris: Gallimard, 11.

18. See P. Assouline, 'Faut-il publier toutes les lettres de Paul Morand', *Le Monde. fr*.; see http://passouline.blog.lemonde.fr/2010/07/06/faut-il-publier-toutes-les-lettres-de-paul-morand (last accessed October 2013).

19. For Renoir's article in *La Semaine à Vichy*, see M. Cointet, 1993, *Vichy Capitale, 1940-1944*, Paris: Perrin; 134; Schwartz, *It's So French!*, 69, 216–17.

20. Renoir, *Letters*, 75, Letter to Director of Radio and Cinema, 14 August 1940.

21. M. Pagnol, 1970, 'Le Schpountz', *L'Avant Scène du Cinéma*, July/September, 51.

22. See C. Beylie, 1986, *Marcel Pagnol ou le cinéma en liberté*, Paris: Atlas, 93.

23. Cited in M. Marrus and R. Paxton, 1981, *Vichy France and the Jews*, New York: Basic Books, 20.

24. See Hayward, *French National Cinema*, 197.

25. M. Bardèche and R. Brasillach, 1942, *Histoire du cinéma*, Paris: Denoël, 350–52, 355–61.

26. L. Rebatet, 1941, *Les Tribus du cinéma et du théâtre*, Paris: NEF, 58–60.

27. M. O'Shaughnessy, 2009, *La Grande illusion*, London: IB Tauris, 102.

28. See Ferro, *Cinéma et histoire*, 187–98; J. Jackson, 2009, *La Grande illusion*, Basingstoke: BFI, 95–99. See also the extensive discussion in Lindeperg, *Les Écrans de l'ombre*, 209–20.

29. E.B. Turk, 1992, *Child of Paradise: Marcel Carné and the Golden Age of French Cinema*, Cambridge: Harvard UP, 266.

30. P. Brion, 2005, *Cinéma français, 1895-2005*, Paris: ADPF, 37–38.

31. See S.P. Sibelman, 2000, 'Jewish Myths and Stereotypes in the Cinema of Julien Duvivier', in E. Ezra and S. Harris (eds), *France in Focus: Film and National Identity*, Oxford: Berg, 79–95; F. Wild, 1996, 'L'Histoire ressucitée: Jewishness and Scapegoating in Julien Duvivier's *Panique*' in S. Ungar and T. Conley (eds), *Identity Papers: Contested Nationhood in Twentieth Century France*, Minneapolis: University of Minnesota Press, 178–92. See also Adler, 'Nation and Alienation', 326–53

32. Cited in R. Belot, 1994, *Lucien Rebatet: un itinéraire fasciste*, Paris: Seuil.

33. F. Vinneuil, 1953, 'Le cinéma retrouvé', *La Parisienne* (June), 845–53.

34. See M. Dreyfus, 2009, *L'antisémitisme à gauche*, Paris: La Découverte, 206; A. Grynberg, 2001,'Des signes de résurgence de l'antisémitisme dans la France de l'après-guerre (1945–1953)', *Cahiers de la Shoah* 5, 196–97.

35. G. Leclerc, 1948, 'Fermez la porte aux navets américains, le Blum ne s'en charge pas!', *L'Humanité*, 8 January, 3.

36. A. Marty, 1948, 'Regardez-vous M.Blum!', *L'Humanité*, 9 January, 1.

37. P. Hervé, 1948, 'Blum ou le serpent caché dans la fleur de rhétorique', *L'Humanité*, 17 January, 1. For similar assertions see R. Garaudy, 1948, 'Silhouettes: Blum et Reynaud', *Cahiers du communisme* 9, 978.

38. 'Donga', cartoon for *L'Humanité*, 15 January 1948, 1.

39. J. Lacouture, 1977, *Léon Blum*, Paris: Seuil, 494–506.

40. G. Elgey, 1965, *La République des illusions, 1945–1951*, Paris: Fayard, 140.

41. B. Schulberg, 1941, *What makes Sammy run?*, New York: Random House; J. Vidal, 1947, 'Qu'est-ce qui fait courir Sammy', *L'Écran français* 126, 25 November, 2, 14.

42. C. Roy, 1946, 'Capitalisme et pellicule', *L'Écran français* 73, November, 14.

43. For scholarly analysis see S. Carr, 2001, *Hollywood and Anti-Semitism*, Cambridge: CUP, 228.

44. J. Renoir, 1999, *Cher Jean Renoir: Projet de film*, Paris: Gallimard, 138–39.

45. M. Winock, 2004, *La France et les juifs: de 1780 à nos jours*, Paris: Seuil, 287. See also M. Prazan and A. Minard, 2007, *Roger Garaudy*, Paris: Calmann-Lévy, 70.

46. M. Riffaud, 1969, 'Alerte aux "Bérets verts"!', *L'Humanité*, 31 July.

47. 'Protestations contre "Les Bérets Verts"', 1969, *Combat*, 11 August; 'Manifestation devant un cinéma du quartier latin qui affiche "Les Bérets verts"', 1969, *L'Humanité*, 2 September.

48. See M. Prazan, 2005, *L'Écriture génocidaire: l'antisémitisme en style et en discours*, Paris: Calmann-Lévy, 215; R. Brody, 2008, *Everything is Cinema: The Working Life of Jean-Luc Godard*, London: Picador, 620–24; de Baecque, *Godard*, 795–97.

49. Godard cited in A. Fleischer, 2009, *Courts-circuits*, Paris: Le Cherche midi, 289.

50. Truffaut, *Letters*, 387.

51. See M. Mourlet, 1962, 'Le cinéma', *Défense de l'Occident*, February. Bardèche's publication is advertised in Mourlet's film review, 1962, *Présence du cinéma*, 12, 57; 'Les Juifs contre la liberté d'expression', 1959, *Défense de l'Occident* 61, 70–73.

52. M. Bardèche and R. Brasillach, 1948, *Histoire du cinéma*, Paris, A. Martel.

53. M. Bardèche and R. Brasillach, 1964, *Histoire du cinéma* vol. 2, Paris: Poche, 73. See also M.J. Green, 1992, 'Fascists on Film: The Brasillach and Bardèche *Histoire du cinéma*', in R.J. Golsan (ed.), *Fascism, Aesthetics, and Culture*, Hanover: UP New England, 164–78.

54. Jean Cocteau wrote to Riefenstahl in May 1954. He had contacted Bonn to find a copy of the film for Cannes where he was president of the jury. See *Film Culture*, 56–57, 1973, 92–93. Marmin states that Cocteau provided the French subtitles for the 1954 *Tiefland*, see his 1976, 'Une femme: Leni Riefenstahl', *Éléments* 13, 30.

55. D. Chabrol, 2001, *Michel Audiard: 'C'est du brutal'*, Paris: Flammarion, 230.

56. M. Audiard, 1973, *Vive la France*, Paris: Julliard, 16.

57. P. d'Hugues, 2000, 'La droite et le cinéma', in Guyot-Jeannin (ed.), *Aux sources de la droite: pour en finir avec les clichés*, Lausanne: L'Age d'Homme, 34.

58. Chabrol, *Audiard*, 266

59. 1995, *Le Film français* 2566, July, 1.

60. P. Durant, 2009, *La Bande à Gabin: Blier, Audiard et les autres*, Paris: Sonatine, 102–3.

61. Durant, *La Bande*, 54.

62. P. Jardin, 1975, *Vichy Boyhood: An Inside View of the Pétain Regime*, London: Faber, 40–41.

63. S. Signoret, 1979, *Nostalgia Isn't What it Used to Be*, London: Penguin, 120. At the time of writing, two new titles discuss the well-known 'reactionary' figures: actor Maurice Ronet is discussed in J-A. Fralon, 2013, *Maurice Ronet, Le splendide désenchanté*, Paris: Equateurs; while scriptwriter and director Paul Gégauff is treated in A. Le Guern, 2013, *Une âme damné*, Paris: PGDR. Although both are original works, neither adds any substantial new evidence. While the subculture entertained its own members, their reputations were sometimes questioned or subject to rumour or hostile attack – not least in left-leaning periodical *Le Temps Modernes*. It is also the case that not everyone betrayed their politics so clearly (e.g. Eric Rohmer) and that attitudes changed over time.

64. See P. Ory, 1976, *Les Collaborateurs, 1940–1945*, Paris: Seuil, 203; D'Hugues, 'La droite', 33.

65. Jacques Audiard's father's historical deception is ignored in most of the commentaries made on the film.

66. For context see T. Elsaesser, 1996, *Fassbinder's Germany: History, Identity, Subject*, Amsterdam: Amsterdam UP.

67. 1977, 'Fassbinder's Pic's Offense to Israel', *Variety*. No date on microfiche.

68. J. Bojilow, 1977, 'Le Néo-Fascisme Travesti', *Libération*, 21 February.

69. G. Deleuze, 1977, 'Le juif riche', *Le Monde*, 19 February, 26.

70. R. Chazal, 1977, '"L'Ombre des Anges" Un théâtre de symboles', *France Soir*, 9 February; R. Marientstras, 1977, 'Modestes propositions', *Positif*, April, 54–59.

71. J-P. Bloch, 1977, 'La Controverse sur "L'Ombre des Anges"', *Le Monde*, 22 February, 24.

72. C. Lanzmann, 1977, 'Nuit et brouillard', *Le Monde*, 23 February, 23.

73. J. Tulard, 1997, *Dictionnaire du cinéma: les réalisateurs*, Paris: Robert Laffont, 44, 788.

74. See L-F. Céline, 1991, *Lettres à la NRF 1931–1961*, Paris: Gallimard, 582.

75. Truffaut, *Letters*, 250.

76. de Baecque, *Godard*, 122.

77. H. Le Bortef,. 1986, *Robert Le Vigan: le mal-aimé du cinéma*, Paris: France-Empire, 116; Le Bortef and M. Ronet, 1977, *Le métier de comédien, entretiens avec Hervé Le Bortef*, Paris: France-Empire, 129. Madeleine Renaud, Jean-Louis Barrault, Pierre Frenay, Marc Dantzer, Ronet and Le Bortef supported Le Vigan in his old age.

78. A. Riding, 2011, *And the Show Went On: Cultural Life in Nazi-Occupied Paris*, London: Allen Lane, 187–206, 333–34.

79. See N. Hewitt, 2003, 'Céline, the Success of the Monstre Sacré in Postwar France', *Substance* 32.3, 29–42.

80. 'Chantons sous l'occupation est retiré de l'affiche du circuit parafrance,' 1976, *Le Monde*, 11 May.

81 'Raid parisien contre "Entebbé"', 1977, *L'Est Républicain*, 13 January.

82. 'Pétitions pour défendre Tsahal', 1994, *Le Monde*, 12 November.

CHAPTER SEVEN

The Cinema and the Extreme Right-wing Undercurrent

A little later than the period discussed in this work, the film critic Serge Kaganski wrote in *Libération* that the international hit film *Amélie* (Jeunet, 2001) had a dangerous ideological subtext. The charming romantic comedy set in Montmartre provided an erroneous picture of the state of the nation. It was an all white, picture-postcard version of Paris that chimed with Jean-Marie Le Pen's rhetoric on what France meant.[1] With the benefit of hindsight, Kaganski's judgement was a little misplaced and overstated, not least because as this chapter discusses there are several far more convincing historical examples of complex intersections between cinema and the nationalist extreme right-wing than Jeunet's saccharine film. As I explored in the previous chapter of this book, in 1989 veteran filmmaker Autant-Lara used the politics of anti-Semitic scandalmongering to gain media attention for Le Pen's cause. That is just one significant film event where hard right-wing nationalism and the cinema have been intertwined. The following pages of this chapter will piece together where the cinema has had further explicit and implicit associations with the FN's form of nationalism. One therefore needs to discuss (1) how film stars have expressed coded and not so coded support for the FN and, in some limited cases, made films espousing hard nationalist political myths. And (2) when Martin Scorsese's *The Last Temptation of Christ* (1988) was released in France, how far-right-wing thugs stopped many screenings, as well as attacking Claude Chabrol's *Une affaire de femmes* (1988). These are distinctive and quite different phenomena. Nonetheless, themes do recur and can in conclusion be traced through works of right-leaning cinema, from director Gérard Blain to the protests against Scorsese. Closed defensive nationalism, memories of the Algerian war and shared perceptions of the scale of national decline are the linking themes.

The Fellow Travellers of the Right: Delon, Bardot and Blain

By most accounts, Alain Delon's dalliance with the FN began in April 1984 with an interview he gave for glossy magazine *VSD*. There, Delon spoke about his political preferences and mooted his own thinking on contemporary France.[2] Talking to Catherine Nay he explained his disappointment with President François Mitterrand and mused about the up-and-coming political extremist Jean-Marie Le Pen. Delon explained that he had known Le Pen for a long time and that he was a friend. He then remarked that Le Pen was dangerous for the political in-crowd because he was the only one who was sincere. Delon suggested that Le Pen's strength was that he said very loudly what lots of other people thought.[3] Next, Nay asked Delon if he was perturbed by Le Pen's offensive comments? For instance, he had declared on television that France should not be 'a brothel' for six million immigrants. Delon replied that the left and the centre-right had treated Le Pen like a pariah and therefore one could not expect him to be friendly. He suggested, 'Le Pen, avec tous ses défauts et ses qualités, est peut-être le seul qui aujourd'hui pense d'abord aux intérêts de la France avant les siens propres' ['Le Pen, with all his qualities and his faults, is maybe the only person today who thinks firstly of the interest of France rather than of his own concerns'].

Delon's commentary was a 'windfall' for Le Pen.[4] Maximizing the publicity he asserted that Delon and other unnamed celebrities might represent his party at the forthcoming European parliamentary elections. *Paris-Match* picked up the story and its reporter Arthur Conte visited Delon for another interview. Delon was ambivalent, stating that he would not vote for Le Pen but rather for Gaullist-conservative Raymond Barre. Also he underlined that he had never dreamt of standing for the European Parliament. All he had meant to articulate was that Le Pen was a helpful provocateur. Delon added that he believed that immigrants had a right to be respected and that they should be welcomed in the manner in which they deserved and that they should have their rights. But immigrants should not stop French workers from doing their jobs.[5]

When Delon was interviewed on the television channel Antenne 2 about his new film *Notre histoire* (Blier), his politics were again a talking point. Christine Ockrent asked Delon to clarify whether he was for the right wing or for the extreme right wing. Delon was irritated by Ockrent's question. He commented that there was not enough time to offer a sufficient answer. Then, he concluded that everyone knew he was a man of the right and he would never deny it, stating too that if he turned to the extreme right, it was still the (family of the) right. Speaking to *L'Express* magazine in 1977 he had been less coy than in this television performance. Then he had described his outlook quite explicitly, though of course it could have subsequently altered: 'Fasciste, disons le mot' ['Fascist, say the word'], and went on, 'Je suis profondément anticommuniste, c'est tout. Dès qu'on dit quelque chose, on est étiqueté. Alors bon, je suis fasciste, si vous voulez, tant pis' ['I am profoundly anticommunist, that's all. As soon as one says something one is labelled. So, good, I am fascist, if you like, never mind'].[6]

Delon's interventions in 1977 and 1984 were especially powerful because to an extent they chimed with an aspect of his wider public star persona. Through the 1970s Delon starred in a trilogy of films that were adaptations from extreme right-wing novels and which maintained traces of right-wing ideological subtexts. Thus, he had worked on versions of Félicien Marceau's *Creezy*, shot as *La Race des seigneurs* (Pierre Granier-Deferre, 1974), Paul Morand's *L'Homme pressé* (Édouard Molinaro, 1977) and Raf Vallet's *Mort d'un pourri* (Lautner, 1977). Grosso modo, these films represent France as corrupt and dysfunctional, a country in decay. By implication, in these films Republican France is in need of radical reform from a party perhaps like the FN. The descriptions of society offered in the works are a warrant for an authoritarian leader to take over the nation.

Let us look at some more detailed examples which illustrate Delon's political ambiguity. In *La Race des seigneurs*, Delon plays a left-liberal politician, Julien Dandieu, president of the Parti Républicain Unifié. He is a scheming and ambitious figure who is willing to sell his political values to enter into a coalition government. The film suggests that politics is a corrupt milieu peopled with ruthless men and women. In addition, Julien Dandieu is shown to be unable to decide between his career and his newfound love, Creezy (Sydne Rome). Ultimately, he prefers political power to romance. When winning his place in a coalition government he is invited to meet the President, and consequently is unable to keep a tryst with Creezy. As a consequence she commits suicide. Pascal Jardin's script for *La Race des seigneurs* is a strong piece of work with a political subtext. It subtly highlights the hypocrisy of an average centrist politician. Throughout, Delon is used to exemplify a hyper-ambitious man, addicted to power and love, as well as material possessions. One can read the film to see him as a negative exemplar of the political class, and the implied message is that this elite is failing to govern appropriately. Director Granier-Deferre explained the fundamental attitude and was open about part of his film's negative depiction of the state of French politics, 'I don't like politicians and it's a world that I find unattractive, that's why all the characters are unpleasant'.[7]

L'Homme pressé depicts a similarly pessimistic and negative modern world. Therein Delon plays a bourgeois antique dealer, Pierre Noix, who is obsessed with making money and gaining new acquisitions for his collection. The implication of the work is that the new capitalist elite, which Noix represents, is a decadent class and that it will be self-destructive. The subtext of the novel and the film is that modernity is dangerous compared with existing tradition. Delon puts in an admirably frenetic performance. For example, he is seen running from one meeting to another, cancelling his honeymoon in Venice to return for more business in Paris. In a neocolonialist subsection, he flies to Africa to obtain tribal masks, returning quickly to Paris to try to purchase an ancient vase. Meanwhile, he encourages his pregnant wife to give birth in seven months, rather than nine because speed is of the essence in his modern life (she leaves him). The only justification for his behaviour is that he is a loner, passionate about his ambitions. The film concludes with his death, a heart attack taking him precisely when his delegate at an auction house has outbid competitors for the precious vase. Based on the novel by Paul Morand, the film's politics are somewhat ambiguous. As stated, the character of Delon can be read as a personification of decadence, however, a right-wing audience would also no doubt appreciate the characters vital dynamism and self-belief. The work to an extent captures a French far-right-wing literary trope that hangs around the idea of the hero being at once exemplary of modern decadence, but also somehow in conflict with it and thus heroic. Here I am summarizing very generally from readings of Morand, de Montherlant, Nimier and others.[8]

Another deeply sceptical view of the state of democracy is provided in *Mort d'un pourri*. Delon plays a political advisor, Xavier Marchal, a veteran of the Algerian war, as is his boss, the politician Dubaye (Maurice Ronet). The film begins when Dubaye visits Marchal in the early hours of the morning. He confesses that he has murdered a colleague and has stolen a secret dossier of information relating to political and industrial corruption (a plot line possibly inspired by Gabriel Aranda's real life accusations of corruption made in parliament in 1972). Shortly after this scene Dubaye is himself killed. Through the rest of the film Marchal tries to protect the secret dossier, as well as Dubaye's young mistress who is in possession of it. As the plot thickens, it is revealed that all of politics in contemporary France is corrupt. A foreign tycoon, the sinister Tomsky (Klaus Kinski) controls most of Europe. Tomsky, hosting a shooting party at his French chateau, takes pleasure in informing Marchal how the modern world works. He declares that there is an 'l'Internationale du Pognon', and now 'le capital ne connaît plus de frontière' [money no longer understands national borders]. Everyone portrayed in *Mort d'un pourri* is involved in the secret machinations that run the state and the economy. Ministers from the government are friends of Tomsky. The law is tainted too with the *Procureur* [Prosecutor] being guided by the same conspirators, as is a leading police officer. The only figure who is presented as acting honourably is Marchal (Delon). Compared to the corruption and conspiracies that surround him, his position is refreshingly clear and honest: he wishes to protect his friends and to discover who murdered his former military comrades. Among the skyscrapers of the 'La Défense' business district, where much of the film is set, the only man with any principles is Delon's Algerian war veteran, who is loyal to his friends and able to defend himself against the politico-financial conspiracy.[9] If anything, this then is the most explicitly reactionary of Delon's work discussed here. It combines the repeated notion of mainstream politics being corrupt and adds to that the conspiracy theory of a mystery elite running France and Europe. As readers appreciate, such tropes were common in late-nineteenth-century and twentieth-century anti-Semitic writings (though of course that aspect is not rendered directly in the script of *Mort d'un pourri*.)

The matter at hand is complex. Delon's direct and relatively explicit forays into the political are limited to those of 1977 and 1984, and alongside the films discussed above he has made many sophisticated works that have little if any connection to extreme right-wing values. On the contrary, *Monsieur Klein* (directed by Losey, with production assistance by Delon himself, 1976) is the most significant reference point to reveal how the actor's body of work is paradoxical when explored for political meaning. This film depicts the horrors of the Vichy period and explores how Klein lives under threat of death because of the state's anti-Semitism. For its time it includes some of the most explicit and direct depictions of French complicity in the Holocaust, and as such it is a more subtle and refined work than Malle's *Lacombe Lucien* (see chapter 6).

Moreover, *Monsieur Klein* was made in between Delon's contributions to *La Race des seigneurs* and *L'Homme pressé*. Similarly, the film Delon was promoting at the time of his remarks about Le Pen in 1984, *Notre histoire*, was a powerful deconstruction of his own star persona. In *Notre histoire*, Blier uses him to imagine a film star as being a failure and a drunkard.[10] Furthermore, when Delon chose to direct a political thriller himself he turned to the work of leftist crime writer Jean-Patrick Manchette to adapt for his script.[11]

In contrast to the star's relative ambivalence, Le Pen has repeatedly cultivated Delon. In 1999 in a political pamphlet, *Lettres françaises ouvertes*, Le Pen asked him to return to the fold and to publicly support him once again. A decade later, in the two hundredth edition of Le Pen's online video blog, hosted on the FN's website, the leader announced that only Delon would be capable of depicting him in a biopic. Mischievously, he mused that Delon's lifestyle would make him the best qualified to portray him on the big screen.[12] That Le Pen should make such an overt bid for the star's attention evidences the value that he placed on him as a symbolic ally. Delon has encouraged some of this because he has not severed contact with the man he described as a friend. For example, when Jack Lang awarded Delon the 'Insigne de Commandeur des Arts et des Lettres', Le Pen was among the actor's guests.[13] Nevertheless, in the 2007 presidential election, Delon supported Nicolas Sarkozy. In September 2010 he travelled with President Sarkozy and his wife Carla Bruni to China to promote France abroad.

The public interventions of Brigitte Bardot on themes of animal rights have if anything meant that she has become more closely associated with extreme right-wing nationalism than Delon. According to the press clippings held at the BFI London, it was in 1989 and 1990 when Brigitte Bardot expressed concerns about Muslim slaughter of livestock that her opinions started to drift from purely animal rights issues into anti-immigration and anti-foreigner statements. As the 1990s wore on Bardot's politics became more radical. The key turning point was in 1996 when she published a piece for the opinion column in *Le Figaro*, two days before Aïd-el-Kébir [Eid al-Adha]. Titled, 'Mon cri de colère', she vented her fury at the presence of Muslim French in the country and the culture that they had brought to the nation.[14] According to Bardot, France was overrun with immigrants. When her memoirs, *Initiales BB*, were published later in 1996, Bardot continued her polemic. When recalling a visit to Beirut in the late 1960s, she wrote:

A cette époque, l'Islam n'avait pas encore envahi l'Europe, ni la France. Les musulmans avaient encore la discrétion de ne pas nous imposer leur moeurs, leurs costumes souvent barbares et archaïques, leurs mosquées et tous ces rituels sanglants et révoltants, telles l'Aïd el-Kebir. Au contraire, ils nous copiaient, essayant de s'européaniser, de se moderniser à notre image. Ça n'était pas toujours réussi, mais au moins leur démarche était pacifique.[15]

[At that time, Islam had not yet invaded Europe or France. The Muslims still had the discretion not to impose on us their often barbaric and archaic values and customs, their mosques and all their bloody and revolting rituals, like Eid al-Adha. On the contrary they copied us, trying to become European and modernize in our image. It wasn't always a success but at least their approach was peaceful.]

In addition, Bardot clarified her attitude towards the political leadership of France. She praised de Gaulle and criticized the student protesters of May 1968. She was a Gaullist and she recalled voting in favour of the General in the referendum of 1969. The French people had been ungrateful towards de Gaulle and all that he had achieved. She considered that his resignation had left France abandoned.[16] She wrote too about Le Pen. They had first met in 1958 when Bardot had visited injured soldiers returned from the war in Algeria. Years later they had chatted at a dinner party in 1992. According to Bardot, Le Pen is a charming man, bright, erudite, revolted by some things, passionate and entertaining company.[17]

Interviews, political publications and commentaries in the press continued apace in the period where this book's focus ends and the realm of 'instant history', or political science, begins. Through the 1990s, Bardot maintained that Eid al-Adha was a barbaric ritual that should be stopped in France. Throughout the second volume of memoirs, *Le Carré de Platon: mémoires*, she repeatedly explained that her actions were not politically motivated. She justified the *Le Figaro* piece (of 1996) on the grounds that she had written at a time of extreme pressure, cattle were being massacred in England because of the 'mad cow disease' and in Canada seals were being killed in their thousands.[18] Woven in between these explanations, she expresses further hostility towards Islam. Writing about her honeymoon to Agadir, Morocco, she commented that she was afraid of the 'Arabs' she saw and could not help thinking of their enemies, the tourists and the Catholic monks, whom they had killed. She stated that she observed them with contempt.[19]

For what it is worth, Bardot's essay, written after 9/11, *Un cri dans le silence* (2002), is filled with further nationalist rhetoric. Therein she attacks feminism, May 1968, television, globalization, changes to the French language, ugly modern art and the functioning of democracy. She complains that France is facing 'Islamization' and that for the last twenty years there has been an uncontrolled and dangerous infiltration of this force.[20] The Muslim youths who live in the Parisian inner-city estates are described as a force ready to take up arms against the French. She compares them to the 11 September 2001 terrorists and the murderers who held hostages in a Moscow theatre in 2002. Bardot feared a 'worsening decadence in society'. In retrospect, she preferred the 1950s, the days of Jacques Tati. They were a golden time for France – church bells rang, the Mass was read in Latin.[21]

Bardot remained popular in the media and through the early 1990s was often treated as a grand lady of the nation. Her politics and several court convictions for racism have not blocked her work in mainstream media. *Initiales BB* came out during the lucrative back-to-college autumn publishing season. At the time the British newspaper *The Daily Telegraph* reported that 'France is falling in love again with Bardot'. This was an exaggeration, but it is true that the star, then aged sixty-two, was granted numerous interviews. In the week of the publication of the memoirs, the TF1 television channel devoted its Friday evening to celebrating Bardot. The show was a biographical treatment with famous people coming to greet the star and congratulate her on her life and the publication of her memoirs.[22] At least until the mid 1990s, Bardot remained a national icon, for instance, still used by Air France for publicity campaigns. One can speculate that her high public status was assisted by the general mood to commemorate the greats of French cinema during the 1995 Centenary of Cinema year (see chapter 1).

Like Delon, Bardot plays a coy game regarding her political loyalties and it is important to offer her comments here in a fair and full way. On the one hand, she praises Le Pen, on the other hand, she keeps away from him by never declaring her outright support for the FN. Bardot is married to a leading member of the FN, Bernard d'Ormale. However she has explained that she does not share his commitment to the party. She was quoted in the British press: 'He looks after the politics and I look after the animals' … 'I don't give a damn about the Front National. I've had it up to here. My husband loves me and I love him.'[23] This is a position that is advantageous for everyone. Bardot maintains an implied position of independence while the FN in the 1990s is bolstered because a freethinking star of Bardot's status has some genuine sympathy for aspects of its ideology. When the FN has used Bardot, she expresses embarrassment and discontent. For example, following the publication of *Intiales BB* when the FN mayor of Toulon Jean-Marie Le Chevallier invited her to be guest of honour at the Toulon book fair, she was most unhappy. Journalist Kirsty Lang takes up the story:

> The Fair's organizers had planned to give a prize to Marek Halter, a Jewish author, but Chevallier said he wanted the prize to be given to Bardot for her memoirs. He said Halter, 'has an internationalist, global view of the world. I think our book fair should be honouring someone with local connections, with an attachment to the French nation'. Upset by the uproar, Bardot telephoned Halter and offered to share the prize with him. He declined.[24]

A third actor, also with roots in the Nouvelle Vague, represents the exceptional case of an artist working relatively directly on filmic material sharing FN ideology. Here I am underlining and drawing attention to the career of the actor-turned-director, Gérard Blain. Thus, Blain's explicit ideological statement in support of FN-thinking is his direction of the film *Pierre et Djemila* (1987). Working with Michel Marmin and Mohamed Bouchibi on the script, Blain films a love story between a young French man, Pierre (Jean-Pierre André), and an Algerian girl, Djemila (Nadja Reski), living in the industrial northern city of Roubaix. He slowly narrates their relationship as it grows. Meanwhile, Blain's camera observes the more general interactions between the two ethnic communities who share the Roubaix suburbs. For example, early in the film a woman observes the Algerian Muslims going to prayer; subsequently she comments: 'C'est toute un monde de voir ça. ... Ils sont plus nombreux que la dernière fois' [It's a whole world to see there ... there are more of them than last time]. Djemila's parents and older brother plan to send her back to Algeria, in preparation for an arranged marriage. Her father remarks that he does not want his children following French ways. In a parallel scene, Pierre speaks with his father about his fondness for Djemila. The father asks if she is an 'Arab' girl and Pierre replies that, 'She is as French as we are'. His father warns him that it will be complicated and there will be difficulties because 'the Arabs are not like us'. He highlights that they have already made a mosque in the town and that during the Algerian war he had found it odd to try to make Algerians French. Pierre replies, it is implied naïvely, that this was twenty-five years ago. The father does not retract his opinion and states calmly and with authority, 'They have things that are sacred'.

Slowly, Blain manipulates the audience towards a tragic conclusion. Tensions mount between locals and migrants to Roubaix and the mosque is attacked. Djemila's father informs her that she is to live in Algeria where she will marry his brother's son. In response, she writes to Pierre calling for his help, and together they briefly escape their torment, taking a pleasure boat around the industrial harbour of Dunkirk. On their return to Roubaix, Djaffa, Djemila's brother, stabs Pierre to death. Blain concludes his film with Pierre's funeral and of images of Djemila walking to the bridge where she and Pierre had once met. She throws herself into the water. The film therefore uses a romantic plot line, close in tone to *Romeo and Juliet*, to imply that immigration is a threat to the French and the Algerian migrants. One can add for further information that Blain shoots his morality tale on the dangers of interethnic romance in a clinical but naturalistic style that is reminiscent of work from Robert Bresson.

The work is a bleak commentary on Franco–Algerian relations and immigration. Blain implies that individuals from each community may fall in love with each other, but that any such relations are impossible because of the fixed cultural differences that exist between the two groups. The key scene is between Pierre and his father because it is here that Blain sets out the political philosophy of the film. The young man's father explains that French and Algerians will always be different from each other and he is proven correct when tragedy ensues for Pierre and Djemila. Pierre's relationship with Djemila is doomed because it transgresses the rule that the two communities should remain separate from each other because they are so different. In other words, throughout the film Blain and the scriptwriters Marmin and Bouchibi suggest that modern France cannot function as a multicultural society. Serge Daney's review of the film for *Libération* identifies precisely this central ideological purpose. He warns that, 'the Father and Djemila's brother are in agreement on one point: no mixing between the cultures', and that the film celebrates the idea of the 'right to difference', which the 'left-wing had believed to be its own idea without realizing too late that they should have spoken about the right to be alike'.[25]

It is worth spending longer on this work and considering its reception, its status as a film event and how this played into extreme right-wing intellectual goals. *Pierre et Djemila* was an official French entry to the Cannes Festival (May 1987). This was a publicity coup for the makers, encouraged by Blain who held a press conference after the premiere. There, a journalist from the right-leaning *Valeurs actuelles* questioned Blain as to whether the Algerian's murder of Pierre was respectable because it was an expression of his culture. Blain replied obliquely that the French were often incapable of understanding and respecting religion, as well as other people's traditions and cultures. Expanding on his subject, Blain commented that he was not 'judging the Arabs in his film'. This caused indignation among some of the journalists because it suggested that Blain happily conflated Moroccans with Algerians and with Egyptians into the reductive label 'Arab'. One journalist remarked that Blain's film was a failure because there too he had used the generic term 'Arab', a pejorative catchall stereotype. Blain defused the situation by stating that he wanted everyone in the world to get along.[26]

In printed interviews made to promote his film, Blain was more outspoken. He explained that he did not want to make judgements about different cultures, but he did want different groups and nations to preserve their distinctiveness. He believed that the temptation of money too often undermined long-established national traditions. For example, French cinema was wrong to be making films in the English language. He noted that he would prefer that peoples could live happily together, but that he feared that world affairs meant that this was impossible. He commented:

Mais regardez comment au Liban, les sunnites, les chiites, les druzes et les chrétiens se massacrent. Et ici, les Français considèrent toujours les Arabes comme des bougnoules. Je ne fais pas de films-solutions. Dans 20 ans peut-être, tous ces gens seront intégrés. Je fais un film contemporain. Je ne suis pas sur que l'Islam puisse étre intégré. Je suis plutôt pessimiste sur l'humanité et encore plus sur les rapports entre cultures différentes.[27]

[But look how in Lebanon the Sunnis, the Shiites, the Druze and the Christians are slaughtering each other. And here, the French still consider the Arabs as dirty. I am not making films to find solutions. Maybe in twenty years all these people will be integrated. I am making a contemporary film. I

am not sure that Islam can be integrated. I am more of a pessimist about humanity and even more on the relationship between different cultures.]

The controversy that Blain stirred up at Cannes made for good copy. It had been an otherwise dull festival with Wim Wenders winning best director and Maurice Pialat's adaption of Bernanos's *Sous le soleil de Satan* taking the Palme d'Or. When the critics wrote up more extensive reviews of Blain's work they were often relatively sympathetic to his film and its political subtext. The communist press defended *Pierre et Djemila*, perhaps because Blain had supported the party in public, and his longstanding anti-Americanism also went down well with the PCF. Writing for *L'Humanité*, Gilles Le Mattot explained that immigration was only the backdrop to a poetic film made in the tradition of Bresson. For him it was 'une simple histoire d'amour'.[28] Michel Perez reassured readers of *Le Matin* that the film was not a new version of the Nazi melodrama, *Juif Süss*. He pointed out that Blain's intentions were peaceful and that, in Roubaix, local branches of the FN had protested about the film being made because it did not do them justice. He wholeheartedly recommended it, writing, 'un film superbe dans sa rigueur et dont l'émotion et la pureté tragique font oublier l'agitation irréfléchie de la polémique' [a superb film because of its rigour and how its emotion and purely tragic style makes one forget about the unthinking agitation of polemic]. Claude Baignères also lauded the work in *Le Figaro*, where he highlighted the subtle style adopted by the director.[29] Thus, the public were encouraged to watch a xenophobic work as if it were a sample of high art.

Pierre et Djemila projects an extreme right-wing vision of the threat of immigration onto the big screen. As such, the work fully supports Le Pen's political project. Its visual representation of interethnic violence was a dramatic confirmation that the French were suffering insecurity because of migration from Algeria. Throughout its ninety minutes, it raises the spectre that the French are in the process of losing their identity and that by implication this must stop. This is an FN-ideological position regularly espoused in speeches, newspapers and other forms of political communication. It functions based on a Manichean view of the world, a sense that the French are embattled, besieged and on the brink of irreversible social change.

In its day, we can suggest too that Blain's intervention works as a riposte to Roger Hanin's *Train d'enfer* (1985). In that film the leftist director had narrated how extreme right-wing thugs had killed a young man by throwing him from a train window while he was travelling on the Ventimille–Paris line. Using an episode drawn from news headlines, Hanin had critiqued how France was in danger of becoming a violently racist society and how the rise of xenophobic nationalism, promoted by the FN, was a genuine threat. The extreme right wing accused him of being simplistic, essentially anti-French. When the film was rebroadcast on television during a period of elections (1995), Jean-Marie Le Pen called it a propaganda film worthy of Goebbels.[30] The centre right were also sceptical about the value of the movie. At *Le Figaro*, Alain Griotteray denounced it because for him it oversimplified what was happening in society and was filled with liberal self-loathing. In the same paper, François Chalais questioned if a film in which an Arab character killed a Frenchman would ever be allowed to be made in Mitterrand's socialist, antiracist, new France.[31] Two years later *Pierre et Djemila* proved that this was very possible and even to be rewarded with screening at Cannes. It seems plausible to say that Blain had replied to *Train d'enfer* by showing in his film a decent young French boy being stabbed to death by a Muslim Algerian immigrant. His solution to the perceived immigration crisis was for new immigration to stop, not for nationalists to reflect or to moderate their values.[32]

Finally, *Pierre et Djemila* is marked by the politics of scriptwriter Michel Marmin. Marmin is far more than a fellow traveller of the extreme right: he is an eminent member of their main intellectual movement. Since 1973, working with political philosopher Alain de Benoist, Marmin has contributed extensively to the New Right periodicals *Éléments* and *Nouvelle Ecole*. In the 1970s and 1980s, it was this school of thought that had first developed the idea that European nations had a right to protect themselves from mass culture, emanating from the U.S.A., and from non-European culture, arriving into the continent through immigrants. They moved nationalist prejudice away from the grounds of race to the territory of culture. Richard Wolin summarizes,

> Under the banner of preserving the sanctity of and integrity of cultures the Nouvelle droite *argued against immigration, the mixing of cultures, and cosmopolitanism. For the sake of reaching a broader audience, it cynically appropriated the universalist values of tolerance and the right to difference for segregationist ends. Thus it was the cosmopolitans who were the true racists, insofar as they forced immigrants to submit to the brutal rites of assimilation.*[33]

This was the intellectual backdrop to the FN's discourse against immigration and the underlying philosophy of *Pierre et Djemila*.

After attending the film school IDHEC, Marmin worked in the research department of the national broadcasting company the ORTF, run at the time by Pierre Schaeffer.[34] Over the years, his essays on French and European cinema are a mainstay of the *Nouvelle droite* magazine, *Éléments* (his cinema review column features on the cover of the first ever issue of the publication, dating from 1973). Numerous issues of the magazine include his essays and interviews, and he serves as an editor. These reviews have discussed Blain's cinema and works from Pierre Schoendoerffer.[35] In 1974, he even interviewed British director Michael Winner for *Éléments*. His latest film *Death Wish* chimed with the *Nouvelle droite*'s belief that capitalist society, the U.S.A., was crumbling into chaos. It also corresponded to the French intellectual group's attachment to traditional macho violence, with Charles Bronson's vigilante character a figure to be greatly admired. Thus, Marmin considered it an important sociological statement as much as an action picture. In the published interview, Marmin asked Winner why he thought that New York and America was facing such crime. Winner replied:

> *L'Immigration. Il y a trop d'étrangers dans les grandes villes qui ne peuvent être intégrés. Aussi ont-ils tendance à devenir des criminels. ... Pourtant, pour échapper à l'accusation de racisme, j'ai encore atténué la réalité. Les assassinats, les viols et les vols sont, à New York, à 95% le fait des Noirs et des Porto-Ricains. J'ai ramené cette proportion à 50%.*[36]

> [Immigration. There are too many foreigners in the major cities, who cannot be integrated. Also they have a tendency to become criminals. ... Even so, to escape from being accused of racism I attenuated the reality. The murders, rapes and thefts in New York, 95% are committed by Blacks and Puerto-Ricans. I reduced this proportion to 50%.]

Marmin, presumably, persuaded one or two other famous filmmakers to contribute to *Éléments*. Coinciding with the release of his medieval drama *Perceval le Gallois* (1974), Eric Rohmer gave an interview to the periodical. Rohmer avoided discussing the content of his film and instead responded to questions about technical issues, the script, the casting and the form of his work. Marmin included notes next to photographs from the film. He considered it a masterwork that celebrated French and European heritage. It was an example of the indigenous Franco-European tradition to be promoted, the precise opposite image of the modern Americanized world, captured onscreen in the likes of *Death Wish*. Marmin asserted that *Perceval* and other recent French and European medieval history films were the beginning of a recovery of positive national and European values, standing against the tide of Hollywood-inspired decadence.[37]

When analysing the career of Marmin, we are not limited to discussing relatively low-circulation publications. Besides *Éléments* Marmin also wrote for mainstream conservative magazines *Valeurs actuelles* and *Spectacle du monde*. In 1978, he worked briefly for *Le Figaro*, later resigning from that post because he claimed that the paper was pressured to publicize films from the American majors. He went on to become Secretary General of the weekly *Magazine Hebdo*.[38] At the time of making *Pierre et Djemila*, he and Blain were neighbours, living in nearby Parisian apartments.

Certainly, many members of the French film community are on the left, liberals, republicans, socialists and communists. There are others with more radical right-wing nationalist opinions: Delon, Bardot, Blain and Marmin. Their perception of modern society overlaps with ideas common among supporters of the FN. In particular, they seem to portray France, and indeed often the Western world, as being in a state of terrible peril. The forces ranged against the nation differ: corruption, Islam, immigration causing 'clashes of civilization', liberalism, the end of the good old days – nostalgically sited as the late 1940s and 1950s. Analysing this political myth one is struck by the passion of the rhetoric, the fear that the nation is being irreparably destroyed, especially regarding Blain and Marmin who are plainly more extreme than Delon, who as we have noted contributes differently. This catastrophist mythmaking turns politics into a bitter war and sharply divides the world into good and evil. Intriguingly, precisely what is French that is worth defending is not always fully adumbrated. In its most pessimistic mode, à la Blain, it is as if the battle has already been lost and that France is already finished.

To add context, Bardot, Blain and Delon made their careers at the time of the New Wave breakthrough. Antoine de Baecque writes on the links there with right-wing politics. He explains that, from the 1950s onwards, right-wing novelists contributed to cinema and influenced New Wave directors as inspiration or as scriptwriters. As is well known, the so-called Hussard novelists, or right-wing anarchists, (Roger Nimier, Jacques Laurent, Antoine Blondin and Michel Déon) took great interest in cinema.[39] For example, Roger Nimier worked with Louis Malle on his debut film, *Ascenseur pour l'échafaud*, and Antoine Blondin inspired Henri Verneuil for *Un singe en hiver* (see also chapter 2 herein) and returned in the 1970s by scripting *Le Dernier saut* (Édouard Luntz, 1970). Roland Laudenbach, the influential right-wing literary editor, provided the script for Alexandre Astruc's interpretation of Gustav Flaubert's *L'Éducation sentimentale* (1962). The young François Truffaut published film criticism across the right-wing press, including work that chastised and mocked communist critic Georges Sadoul.[40] In addition, he entered into correspondence with the politically disgraced critic and former collaborator Lucien Rebatet. Eric Rohmer contributed to Hussard literary periodicals, for example, when he provided film reviews for the issue of *La Parisienne* dedicated to 'The Right'.[41] Film critic Philippe d'Hugues wrote for *Cahiers du cinéma* at the same time as contributing his weekly column for the royalist and Algérie française, *La Nation française*. Michel Marmin's career as a film critic and scriptwriter developed out of this world, coauthoring a study of Cecil B. de Mille with Michel Mourlet.[42] Simply for context, one should add the well-known biographical detail that in his youth Chabrol knew Le Pen when the two men were in the same student club, Le Corpo. This was the milieu that the director mined to make his second film, *Les Cousins* (1959), which features some of the most politically ambivalent sequences in a New Wave work. It seems also that Le Pen had attended film screenings at the Ciné-Club de Saint Maxient. It is known that he was outraged at the predominance of Soviet films being screened there, even telephoning the Minister of Defence, Pleven, to complain that subversion was occurring in Parisian cinemas while the troops fought communism in Indochina.[43]

This was a milieu that cinema revisited in the 1980s when the critic and filmmaker Pascal Kané focused on it in his retro-drama *Liberty Belle* (1983). Therein, Kané suggests that a film critic, possibly Michel Mourlet, was connected to the OAS. The film and this idea provoked controversy. Bertrand Tavernier, who as a young man had published in Mourlet's film-review periodical, *Présence du cinéma*, defended him by recalling that he could barely light his own pipe let alone engage in paramilitary bombings.[44] Nonetheless, because of French film's propensity for making films about cinema, the New Wave's loose and undirected associations with the extreme right-wing anarchist counterculture was first acknowledged onscreen, years before the more recent scholarly attention it has received.

The War Against *The Last Temptation of Christ*

The release of Martin Scorsese's *The Last Temptation of Christ* in France was marked by new reactionary protests comparable to those that welcomed *La Bataille d'Alger* in 1970. Mainstream and extreme right-wing integrist Catholic groups campaigned against the film being released because they considered it blasphemous. Integrism is the word used in France to describe ultratraditional Catholics, some of whom have left the official Church because it is considered too liberal. Several of these integrist lobby groups are linked to the FN. Bernard Antony, the leader of the main anti-Scorsese faction, Alliance Générale contre le Racisme et pour le respect de l'Identité Française (AGRIF), was also a prominent member of the FN, representing it in the European Parliament and running the only daily paper that supported it, *Présent*. He and fellow FN figures, such as Jean Madiran, had already voiced conservative antipathy to radical cinematic treatments of Christianity, protesting against Godard's *Je vous salue Marie* (1985).[45] Scorsese's film provided a further opportunity to campaign for a return to ultraconservative Catholicism and for renewal of national pride.

The protests that were mounted went in rapid stages, moving from official condemnation by mainstream clergy to violence that ended in one fatality and several casualties. In early September 1988, representatives of the Catholic Church publicly denounced the film. Cardinal Decourtray, archbishop of Lyons, and Cardinal J-M. Lustiger, archbishop of Paris, wrote that it was an insult to millions of Disciples of Christ. They called for screening to not take place in France.[46] Cardinal Decourtray expanded further. He argued that the dignity of France was threatened if respect was not shown to its Catholic community. Spokesperson for the French Episcopat, Father Di Falco, repeated similar remarks.[47]

The integrists took direct action against *The Last Temptation*. AGRIF, 'Le Credo', and the Association de Saint-Pie-X brought a legal case against the film. Their barristers, Wellerand de Saint-Just, Jean-Marc Varaut and Anny-Claude Roissard, respectively, argued that *The Last Temptation* was blasphemous. Their claim was that the film should not be shown because the law of 1 July 1972 prohibited public defamation of a religious community. Wellerand and Varaut asserted that the film was as offensive as remarks made by Jean-Marie Le Pen about the Holocaust, and that the same law that had seen the extreme right-wing leader punished should now protect viewers from *The Last Temptation of Christ*. Varaut petitioned that if the film were to be permitted for release then it should be screened alongside a warning text guiding that it was neither an adaptation of the Bible, nor of Jesus of Nazareth, 'as he was historically known'.[48] The case concluded on 22 September 1988 with the judgement that the request to censor the film was unfounded. Citizens had a right to enjoy works of art and this had to be maintained. Jean-Marc Varaut's intervention that screenings be accompanied with an explanatory text was however upheld. This compromise did not stop the plaintiffs from appealing but this hasty appeal was rejected. Myriam Ezratty, presiding over the Court of Appeal, ruled that no additional text should be added to the screenings of the film because Scorsese had included a title at the beginning of the film asserting that it was a work of fiction. Jean-Marc Varaut's gambit was therefore now blocked, despite its initial success. However Ezratty requested that posters for the film feature the statement: 'Ce film est tiré du roman de Nikos Kazantzakis *La Dernière tentation*. Il n'est pas une adaptation des Evangiles' ['The film is taken from the novel by Nikos Kazantzakis, *The Last Temptation*. It is not an adaptation of the Gospel'].[49]

After legal action failed and the film was released, there were widespread public disturbances outside theatres. On 28 September 1988, AGRIF gathered its supporters at the Place de l' Opéra. Simultaneously, the integrist worshippers of the Church of Saint Nicolas de Chardonnet met at the Place de l'Odéon outside the UGC cinema. These protests turned violent and a police officer was injured. A tear-gas bomb was thrown into the cinema and masked youths, armed with Molotov cocktails, started a running battle. A journalist sardonically pointed out that this was quite an opening night for a movie. Another highlighted that it was Abbé Laguerie, of Saint Nicolas de Chardonnet, who had been prominent in 1985 in the campaigns against Godard's *Je vous salue Marie*, who had started the violence.[50]

The disturbances escalated in scale when two Parisian cinemas were attacked (10 and 11 October 1988). In the midst of the violence, attacks were also mounted against a second film that the extremists similarly hated. Thus on 8 October 1988, an extreme right winger targeted Claude Chabrol's *Une affaire de femmes*. It was a historical melodrama set during the Vichy regime and starring Isabelle Huppert. It focuses on an abortionist (Huppert) who is ultimately tried and convicted to death for her actions by the Vichy state. As she is about to be executed, she recites a blasphemous version of the prayer 'Je vous salue Marie'. The combination of historical setting (Vichy), abortion, and what some considered a blasphemous script was sufficient to be met with further violence. Thus, in Paris a reactionary threw a tear-gas bomb into the Miramar in Montparnasse that was showing Chabrol's film. As the audience escaped on to the streets, a 61-year-old man, M. Yves Butault, was taken seriously ill. Local pharmacists cared for him but to no avail, and he was pronounced dead. The intimidation that had been organized against *Last Temptation*, and which had quickly also turned on Claude Chabrol's film, had resulted in a member of the public losing their life.

The tragedy in Montparnasse did not stop the hate campaigns and police were unable to protect cinemas showing *The Last Temptation* from renewed attacks. In the early hours of the morning of 23 October 1988, the Saint Michel cinema in the Latin Quarter was burned out. A British man watching a different film in the auditorium next to where Scorsese's work was being screened was severely hurt, falling into a stage-3 coma. Members of the emergency services who arrived on the scene and who helped people escape the cinema were also injured. The Saint Michel was rendered inoperable, and the casualties totalled thirteen.[51]

There were demonstrations and criminal violence all over France. Tear-gas bombs were released in front of cinemas in Lyons. In Marseilles, screenings were stopped because of tear gas and stink bomb attacks. Violence broke out in Nice between spectators waiting in line for the film and people declaring their hostility towards it. In Besançon, the 'Building' cinema was completely destroyed by an incendiary device. Also in the south west, an attempted firebombing of a cinema occurred in Pau. Catholic conservatives marched on the streets to demonstrate their anger. Scenes of this type were repeated in the cathedral and university towns Angers, Avignon and Poitiers. In Aix-en-Provence and in Lourdes the municipal councils banned the film. Neither was *The Last Temptation* screened in Strasbourg because the Alsace region was hosting a visit by the Pope. Other towns in the region held the film back from release for one week.[52]

Anonymous threats were sent to cinema owners. Such texts evidence an anti-Semitic tone to the campaign. The crude message that one contained implied that the French Jewish community was protected from insults but that the Catholics were not.[53] That is the same rhetorical theme that barrister Varaut used in court where he erroneously compared Scorsese's film with Le Pen's statement that the Nazi gas chambers were a detail in the history of the Second World War.

Left-leaning journalists implied that, while three young Parisians were the main perpetrators of some of the worst of the violence in the capital, responsibility also fell at the door of senior extreme right-wing leaders, especially Bernard Antony and his AGRIF organization. The police held documents that showed that AGRIF had offered legal support to Dousseau's organization in the case of anyone being arrested. Among Dousseau's documents, he had a telephone number that journalists linked to Antony. François Caviglioli, writing for Le Nouvel Observateur, suggested the phone number was that of an extreme right-wing think tank, Cercle Charlier, which Antony also directed. Agence France Presse offered greater clarity: the note the police discovered had contained Antony's phone number but the address of the Centre Charlier.[54] The Centre Charlier had some sixty members and it organized an annual pilgrimage to Chartres. Its public aim was to defend the national and religious identity of France. Antony reacted to these allegations by stating that Scorsese's film was 'indigne' but that he was not the instigator of the 'excesses that may have been committed'.[55]

The FN-supporting Parisian radio station, Radio Courtoisie, had also probably contributed to the atmosphere of violence and intimidation (according to some contemporary press reports). In his slot on the station, Serge de Beketch suggested that tear gas would be one effective means of forcing audiences to leave cinemas that were programming Scorsese's film. In the same tirade he remarked that cutting up seats was also a useful strategy. This broadcast came under public scrutiny when the protests against Scorsese's and Chabrol's films resulted in a fatality. Station patron Jean Ferré admitted that there had been a vigorous broadcast about The Last Temptation but that nothing had been said about Chabrol's Une affaire de femmes.[56]

The state was unprepared for the scale of the protests and it was incapable of defending cinemas. Left-wing politicians were surprised and unable to control events on the streets. After the fatality in Montparnasse, Jack Lang declared that a minority of extremists would not stop the freedoms of the majority. Following a visit to the Miramar-Montparnasse, Lang very publicly went to a cinema where Scorsese's film was screened. On 12 October 1988, Jérôme Clément, the Director General of the Centre National de la Cinématographie (CNC), declared his fears that censorship was taking over the country. Cinema owner's livelihoods were being undermined, with the severe vandalism meaning many auditoria already required renovation. All who respected freedom of expression needed to speak out to protect their human rights.[57] The socialist and communist parties, along with the Société des Réalisateurs de Films and the Société des Auteurs, organized a rally for freedom of speech. Intellectual Max Gallo spoke to the crowd that gathered outside what remained of the burned-out Saint-Michel cinema. There he denounced the Mayor of Paris, Jacques Chirac, for his silence about what was happening in the capital. The socialists mooted the idea that Scorsese's film be broadcast on public television. This did not take place but Antenne 2 did interview Scorsese, where he commented that his film was profoundly religious and that he was sorry that people who had not watched it condemned it. Some prominent filmmakers publicly defended the work, with Jacques Rivette, Claude Sautet and the elderly Marcel Carné offering supportive statements.[58] However, there was an air of melancholy about all the belated interventions against the far-right-wing violence. Speaking in his capacity as vice-president of the SACD (Société des Auteurs et Compositeurs dramatiques) Jean-Claude Carrière noted that everyone had been too quick to bury their heads in the sand when they had been confronted with the fascistic acts of aggression.[59]

The campaign against Scorsese's work was a restaging of the protests mounted against *La Bataille d'Alger* that were inspired by the Algérie Française movement (Bernard Antony had been a supporter in his youth). French integrists had historic links to the milieu of officers and veterans who were unrepentant about French colonialism and who had fought long and hard to stop decolonization. As Harvey Simmons suggests, fundamentalist Catholicism had been a part of the AF and OAS. It was from this world that a number of integrist groupings had emerged in the 1960s. For example, Cité Catholique, an intellectual circle composed of pro-Algérie Française soldiers, had 'justified the use of torture in the war'.[60] The riots were also an echo of earlier extreme right-wing violence against films considered to be unacceptable because of their blasphemous or antipatriotic content. As was noted in the previous chapter of this book, a film critical of French action during the Vichy years had been attacked in the 1970s: that is Halimi's documentary *Chantons sous l'occupation*. The first comparable protests can however be traced back to 1930. Then fascistic bands of youths who were members of the Jeunesses Patriotes attacked the cinema Studio 28 in Paris, because it was premiering Luis Buñuel's *L'Âge d'or*. They considered Buñuel's film blasphemous and a threat to the nation's morality.[61] Similarly, in 1939 Renoir's *La Règle du jeu* was stopped on its opening night when a member of the audience at the Colisée cinema, 'set fire to his newspaper and tried to ignite the back of his chair, declaring that any cinema that showed such a film ought to be destroyed'.[62] Released in the weeks preceding the outbreak of the Second World War, it offered too bleak a vision of France for people of extreme nationalist sentiments to accept. When war broke out it was censored on the grounds that it was demoralizing the fight. Just as the French left takes to the streets to protest, so too does the nationalist right and the extreme right, and on some occasions directly against cinemas because of the works they are projecting.

Furthermore, it seems to me that at the heart of the extreme right's antipathy to the film there was a sentimental nostalgia for a world of tradition that the Church had already moved away from in the 1960s. Thus, the attack on *The Last Temptation* was a belated critique of liberal theology espoused in Vatican II. The brutal film event also exemplifies the hugely defensive nature of organic nationalism. In the imaginations of the anti-Scorsese faction, the country was placed in moral jeopardy by just one film. They believed that modern culture like Scorsese's work was ruining their society, literally eradicating the pure France of their imaginations.[63] In effect, the attacks were a lightning conductor for the belief that France was on the brink of annihilation because of its liberal decadence and slack modernist theology. Through much of the 1970s and 1980s, it had been popular to believe that conservative Catholic France had been reshaped into a liberal, multicultural, multifaith society. The extreme right considered that its values had been marginalized because of this process and they resented this deeply. The protests were a popular public, violent demonstration that their vision of society, national identity, continued to have currency. It also shows how a minority political group can use reactions to a work of cinema (what we have called film events) to gain publicity and impose a de facto censorship.

In part, the mainstream Church's position against *The Last Temptation* corresponded to the interpretation taken up by the integrist, and the wider FN movement. The speeches from the Bishop of Lyons repeated the extreme right-wing trope that French, traditional, values, were no longer being appreciated and were under threat because of the arrival of the film in the country. The mainstream conservatives played with a softer version of the resentful, catastrophist belief that modernity was destroying all that had been noble and sacred. Others on the right, Mayor of Paris Jacques Chirac, had been complacent, as had the mainstream film industry, which was acknowledged at the time.

Conclusion

The hard nationalist political mythmaking is highly defensive, the far rightists' campaigning to stop the literal destruction of France. The perceived attacks change – blasphemy, liberal theology, Islam, immigration, political-financial corruption – but they are always threatening devastation, the end of France itself. Clearly, this political myth ran through the integrist campaign against *The Last Temptation*. It is also evident to some lesser degree in Bardot's writings, and features too in a softer format in the cinema from Granier-Deferre and Blain. What maybe links the high-profile fellow travellers with the violent protests described in the second part of this chapter is the pessimistic version of their nationalism, in which France is repeatedly placed in mortal peril but is then protected or awaiting protection by figures from the extreme right wing. The vision is a Manichean one in which forces for the good, traditional, organic, Catholic nation are always ranged against enemies who are different: foreign films, exponents of alternative religions and theologies, international business people exploiting the nation, hyper-individualists out for their own ends (Delon's character in both *La Race des seigneurs* and *L'Homme pressé*).

Through the different material one can identify too that the religious identity of France was important in each main example. For the extreme right-wing French, nationhood is identified as being contingent on the dominance of conservative Catholicism. Hence, any revision of that tradition is likely to be criticized. For example, several of Bardot's writings have raised religion and identity for debate. Her campaigns for animal rights appear to have inexorably led her to a position of hostility towards Muslim citizens of France. Like Bernard Antony, Bardot implies that France is at its best when its Christian 'roots' are protected. Tellingly, Blain's *Pierre et Djemila* highlights the fault line of religion too, when the key character in the work, Pierre's father, tells his son that the migrants are different and that connection with them is impossible: 'They have some things that are sacred'.

The ghosts of the Algerian war (1954–1962) also loom large across much of the cases discussed above. Prominent FN campaigners, including Le Pen himself, had served the military and had supported Algérie Française. This tone permeates extreme right-wing film culture too. FN integrist Bernard Antony had been in the AF movement, and AGRIF'S work against *The Last Temptation* built on protests against the films that depicted the Algerian war in a critical, 'anti-French', manner (see chapter 5). The war features too in the background to the Delon films of the 1970s that critiqued the political class. *Mort d'un pourri* made the point quite clearly. Its hero, a veteran from the war, was a fighter who would defend his comrades from the conflict as they are swept into intrigues of modern political and industrial corruption. At the beginning of the film the hero (Delon) scans black and white photographs of himself and others in military uniform. It is implied that it is out of loyalty to these memories that he stands up against the conspiracies ranged against him. The history of the Algerian war features too in *Pierre et Djemila*. The main Christian French character, Pierre's father, is another veteran of the war and his memories of it inform his thinking. He is no longer a colonialist but rather an ethno-religious separatist: Algeria for the Algerians and by implication the old nationalist chant, France for the French.[64]

Finally, Delon, Bardot and Blain have been criticized for their contributions to politics and, in the case of Bardot, been tried under the law by antiracist groups. They are aware that when they have spoken out, albeit only implicitly, in favour of Le Pen that they have been courting controversy. These interventions are examples of carefully prepared and managed film events, by powerful actors, highly experienced in working with the media and presenting an image. Few if any other contemporary figures have dared to copy them. Filmmakers like Pierre Schoendoerffer have made conservative films on the decline of Empire, but have not become embroiled in controversy by expressing opinion on Le Pen, à la Delon or Bardot. Only the character actor Jacques Dufilho has made known comparable views to those discussed above. He espouses royalist political beliefs and has a preference for the Latin Mass (the integrist disposition) but has otherwise kept away from public politics.[65]

Notes

1. Drazin, *French Cinema*, 384–85.
2. C. Nay and A. Delon, 1984, 'Interview', *VSD*, 12 April; B. Violet, 2000, *Les mystères Delon*, Paris: Flammarion, 402–5.
3. Violet, *Delon*, 402–5.
4. See G. Besson and C. Lionet, 1994, *Le Pen, biographie*, Paris: Seuil, 412.
5. A. Conte and A. Delon, 1984, *Paris-Match*, 18 May.
6. Violet, *Delon*, 374; 1977, *L'Express*, 17–23 January.
7. E. Gion, 1974, 'Pierre Granier Deferre', *Combat*, 16 April.
8. The right-wing critic Paul Sérant emphasized part of this aspect in his defensive account, 1960, *Le Romantisme fasciste*, Paris: Fasquelle. Examples can be found across numerous texts. A good starting point is de Montherlant, 1935, 'Chevalerie du néant', in *Service inutile*, Paris: Grasset. Such work can be compared with, for example, Drieu La Rochelle, 1931, *Le Feu follet*, Paris: Gallimard. After the war another key work is also Antoine Blondin, 1962, *Un singe en hiver*, Paris: Table Ronde. But it would be wrong to think there is a single definitive novel of the type or that this sentiment is crafted in comparable ways by the different authors.
9. Dehée, *Mythologies politiques*, 203–4.
10. In 1985, the Delon cop thriller *Parole d'un flic* identified extreme right-wing terrorists as the social threat in Lyons. See discussion in chapter 5.
11. *Pour la peau d'un flic* (Delon, 1981).
12. J-M. Le Pen, 1999, *Lettres française ouvertes*, Paris: Objectif France; see also www.letelegramme.com/ig/generales/france-monde/france/front-national-le-pen (accessed October 2012).
13. 'Jean Marie Le Pen ami de Alain Delon', www.centerblog.net/politique/153249-5349991-jean-maire (accessed December 2012). Le Pen and Delon were also pictured together when Delon was awarded the 'Commander of Arts and Letters' in 1986.
14. B. Bardot, 1996, 'Mon cri de colère', *Le Figaro*, 26 April.
15. B. Bardot, 1996. *Initiales BB*, Paris: Grasset, 621.
16. Bardot, *Initiales*, 624–25, 676, 679.
17. Bardot, *Initiales*, 246–47.
18. B. Bardot, 1999, *Le Carré de Pluton: mémoires*, Paris: Grasset, 431–32, 632–33, 660–61.
19. Bardot, *Le Carré*, 281.
20. B. Bardot, 2002, *Un cri dans le silence*, Paris: Editions du Rocher, 133.
21. Bardot, *Un cri*, 135.

22. J. Nundy, 1996, 'Why France is Falling in Love again with Bardot', *The Sunday Telegraph*, 29 September, 28.
23. See Bardot quoted in G. Aziz, 1993, 'BB's Beasts', *The Guardian* – Section 2, 15 December, 7
24. K. Lang, 1996, 'France Ends its Love Affair', *The Sunday Times*, 1 December, 18.
25. S. Daney, 1987, 'Cannes: Blain, Beur, et polémique', *Libération*, 12 May.
26. See G. Lefort, 1987, 'Je voudrais que tout le monde s'aime', *Libération*, 12 May.
27. G. Blain, 1987, 'Par-delà...', *Libération*, 27 May.
28. Anon, 1987, 'L'Art du simple', *L'Humanité*, 12 May.
29. M. Pérez, 1987, 'Les enfants de l'intolérance', *Le Matin*, 27 May; C. Baignères, 1987, 'Pierre et Djemila', *Le Figaro*, 11 May.
30. See J. Tardi and M. Boujut, 1995, *Un Strapontin pour deux*, Tournai: Casterman, 158.
31. A. Griotteray, 1985, '"Train d'enfer": M. Roger Hanin déraille', *Le Figaro Magazine*, 19 January; F. Chalais, 1985, 'Une tranche de mort', *Le Figaro Magazine*, 19 January. Hanin's film was not shown in the region where the racist attack took place. Barristers for the youths who had been arrested brought out an injunction against its display.
32. Blain's later films underline his ideology. In 2000, he starred in his own work, *Jusqu au' bout de la nuit*. In the publicity pack produced for the film he noted his admiration for Robert Brasillach and Maurice Bardèche.
33. R. Wolin, 1998, 'Designer Fascism', in R.J. Golsan (ed.), *Fascism's Return: Scandal, Revision, and Ideology since 1980*, Lincoln: Nebraska UP, 54.
34. F. Charpier, 2005, *Génération Occident*, Paris: Seuil, 201.
35. *Éléments* included a brief debate on Schoendoerffer's film *Le Crabe Tambour* (1977). See, for example, the criticism from J. Mabire, 1977, 'Le Crabe Tambour', *Éléments*, no 24/25, 79–80; and the defence of the film, F. Durand, 1978, 'La vertu d'orgueil', *Éléments*, no. 26, 37–8.See also chapter 5 above for further discussion of this director's work.
36. Winner in M. Marmin, 1974, 'Un justicier dans la ville', *Éléments*, 8/9 (November), 1, 31; see also M. Marmin, 1974, 'Un justicier dans la ville', *Valeurs actuelles* (28 October) reprinted in Marmin, 1976, *Fausto, Vania, Kaspar et Véronique. Chroniques cinématographiques, 1972–1976*, Lausanne: Éd T'Annay, 157.
37. M. Marmin, 1978, 'Légendes, histoire et cinéma', *Éléments* 27 (Winter), 7–9; E. Rohmer, 1978, 'Perceval le Gallois', *Éléments* 27 (Winter), 10–13.
38. C. Durante, 1987, 'Raciste, disent-ils...', *Le Quotidien de Paris*, 13 May.
39. A. de Baecque, 2008, *L'Histoire-Caméra*, Paris: Gallimard, 142–68.
40. de Baecque and Toubiana, *François Truffaut*, 168–73.
41. E. Rohmer, 1956, 'Films de vacances, films de rentrée', *La Parisienne* (October), 631–32; P. d'Hugues, 1962, 'Two Rode Together', *Cahiers du cinéma* 127 (1962).
42. M. Mourlet and M. Marmin, 1968, *Cecil B. De Mille*, Paris: Seghers.
43. See Besson and Lionet, *Le Pen*, 86–87.

44. See S. Grassin, 1998, 'La légende du Mac-Mahon', *L'Express* 2469, 29 October.

45. See de Baecque, *Godard*, 628–33; see also P-A.Taguieff, 'Nationalisme et réactions fondamentalistes en France: Mythologies identitaires et ressentiment antimoderne', *Vingtième siècle* (1990) 69.

46. 'La dernière tentation: un communiqué des cardinaux Decourtray et Lustiger', *La Croix*, 7 September 1988.

47. J. Bourdarias, 1988, 'Film de Scorsese: le non indigne des catholiques', *Le Figaro*, 14 September.

48. M. Peyrot, 1988, 'Le procès de Satan', *Le Monde*, 22 September.

49. P. du Tanney, 1988, 'Film de Scorsese: la mise en garde', *Le Figaro*, 23 September; Agence France Presse, 1988, 'Justice-Cinéma', 27 September.

50. J. Bourdarias, 1988, 'Trois manifestations contre le film de Scorsese', *Le Figaro*, 28 September; T.R. Lindlof, 2008, *Hollywood Under Siege: Martin Scorsese, the Religious Right and the Culture Wars*, Lexington: University Press of Kentucky, 293–94.

51. 'La police soupçonne des extrémistes de droite d'avoir incendié le cinéma Le Saint-Michel', 1988, *Le Monde*, 25 September; Taguieff, 'Nationalisme', 59.

52. F. Eskenazi, 1988, 'Scorsese crucifié', *Libération*, 14 October, 34.

53. Eskenazi, 'Scorsese', 34.

54. F. Caviglioli, 1990, 'Le bûcher de Saint-Michel', *Le Nouvel Observateur*, 15 March; AFP, 1988, 'Comment Roman Marie a décroché un rôle dans "la Dernière tentation du Christ"', *Libération* 31 October.

55. The formal denial is cited in H. Tincq, 1988, 'Les soldats perdus de la tradition catholique', *Le Monde*, 1 November, and was also widely circulated in other public reporting.

56. See J-P. Cruse, 1988, 'Enquête difficile après la mort d'un spectateur "d'Une affaire de femmes"', *Libération*, 11 October.

57. J. Clément, 1988, 'La censure par la peur', *Libération*, 12 October.

58. See 'Une manifestation pour la libre projection du film de Martin Scorsese', 1988, *Le Monde*, 26 October; 'Cinéma Saint-Michel: Un manifestant écroué', 1988, *La Croix*, 29 October; 'Croyants et non-croyants', 1988, *L'Humanité*, 26 October.

59. J-L. Macia, 1988, 'Trois questions à Jean-Claude Carrière', *La Croix*, 25 October.

60. Simmons, *French National Front*, 200.

61. P. Hammond, 1997, *L'Âge d'or*, London: BFI, 60–64.

62. A. Sesonske, 1980, *Jean Renoir: the French films, 1924–1939*, Cambridge Mass: Harvard UP, 384–85.

63. Taguieff, 'Nationalisme', 60.

64. For intellectual sample of argumentation see A. de Benoist, 1986, *Europe-Tiers Monde: Même Combat*, Paris: Robert Laffont.

65. J. Dufilho, 2003, *Les Sirènes du bateau-loup*, Paris: Fayard, 237.

Conclusion

Before turning to a discussion regarding the 'bigger picture', it seems useful to first underline that one aim throughout this work has been to suggest an intellectual gain from a different kind of writing on film history: the micro-histories of reception and the expansion on Marc Ferro's idea of the film event. Excellent academic articles focusing on individual films have of course already more than adequately demonstrated the importance of context in better understanding the cinema, but such an approach has only rarely been undertaken in a very thematically focused book. Readers are invited to reconsider the material offered in this book and, one hopes, be encouraged to continue new thinking on the role of film events and their political function.

For now, one can conclude that the debates about film and the controversies inspired by individual works in France in the modern period were a highly dynamic phenomenon. Thus, in the course of the many polemics around films, rarely did one political side win out. Yet what the evidence discussed in this work hopes also to illustrate is that such events were recurrent, even a relatively common part of ordinary everyday life; if not for everyone, then certainly for cineastes, critics, state officials, politicians, actors, craftspeople, intellectuals and cinephiles. Intriguingly this quite repetitive nature of film events was overlooked by the participants, with the outburst of each new controversy overruling a sense of its own repetitiousness. Only the Blum–Byrnes dispute (1946–1950) forged a deeper mark on future discussions of American influence and market share. Reviewing the material raised in each chapter, we can add further to our present knowledge of film events with the following remarks. Such disputes were often about the control of meaning and its mediation; however, that was rarely ever fixed or pinned down to a dominant position. Among many instances, the example of *Danton* evidences very clearly how expectations for a film can change and its reception spin out of control. Furthermore, the public mediation of cinema in press reviews (if not necessarily more specialist periodicals) was often about making coded political comment on wider issues, either being debated at around the time of a film's release or subtly implied in its content. This means that reviewers used cinema to write about politics, and reviewing was a metaphorical mode for discussing broader sociopolitical issues in an elegant if coded style. In other words, here one can refine Ferro's position of seeing cinema sparking social change. This no doubt did occur on occasions but this study has also examined several cases where it is an existing social question (for example, loyalty to de Gaulle; how to approach newly independent former colonies) that feeds into how a film becomes a public issue. This was the case with reception of Lelouch's *Un homme et une femme* in Paris in 1966, when responses to the work provided a space to offer up attitudes on de Gaulle's governance. Film events though were never localized only to Paris; again *Danton* is a good example because of its internationalism and the lines it drew between Paris and Poland, but so are the many film events discussed in chapter 6 that pertain to neocolonialism. Finally, because this work has been about expression of nationalism, it has meant that extreme right-wing scandalmongering in the late 1980s has had greater focus than in any more general survey. One can note that reactionary groups used cinema and film-people as a means to gain publicity, claim to set politically taboo ideas onto the public agenda and generally cause mischief and offence in the name of national honour. When these reactionary groups sought to use the cinema to their own violent ends, the state and the film industry were required to make a response. In other words, the extreme right wing deliberately provoked debate about themselves. The book has underlined that state groups and individuals did provide counter-protests to the extreme right wing's actions, with cinema owners often even risking their lives and livelihoods by showing controversial works. However, there was often a lack of coherent and unified effort between agents (state; industry; cinema chains; intellectual commentators), not least because the threat of public disorder always posed the difficult ethical question as to whether films should continue to be screened to uphold freedom of speech, even at the risk of fatalities. The state was consistently uneasy and unable to insure screenings of works that were also an irritation to maintenance of social order (Pontecorvo's and Scorsese's films).

One should add very briefly that the film events described in the chapters of this book developed in relation to institutions. On a basic level there is of course the lively world of the daily and weekly press. Yet important too are the government bodies (general political leadership, the Ministry of Culture; censorship boards, and many other offices), film festivals, the Cinémathèque, IDHEC, the industry, its spokespeople, and of course specialist reviewing and trade periodicals. In the postwar period, these are institutions that are structured along mainly national lines, while also being open to internationalism, the Festivals especially so. Beyond the usual suspects listed above, and given our main thematic interest, I would like to draw attention to the role of the military and its film units. Through the 1950s it was there that several prominent directors discussed in this book cut their teeth: Schoendoerffer, but also Lelouch, Enrico, Coutard, de Broca, not to mention Cousteau (with the navy) or the brief sabbatical Dupont and Decaë took with UN forces in Korea. All such institutions were also far more hierarchical than today's digital, transnational, flat forms of management of reception (internet etc).

In the introduction to this work, I noted that the writing and research was informed by my residual admiration for structuralism. It is appropriate to note here that the completion of the work has thrown that affinity into some question. It remains attractive to me to want to offer a complete picture of the nationalist-cinema nexus; however, this is plainly increasingly problematic because the same structural approach tends towards overgeneralizations and the placing of many different types of evidence and political attitudes into a single system, rather than accepting variations and patterns that are cut loose from one mooring place. In particular, searching for the core of where cinema and nationalist mythmaking are strong tends towards generalizations that can ignore left–right wing variation and contestation. It also means that rightly or wrongly political extremes are considered inside a notional whole system, and this is potentially problematic as by definition they are on the edge or even outside the nominal mainstream. Regarding the cinema, such an implicitly structuralist outlook also has the tendency to underplay differences between genres and their relative status as higher or lower cultural forms, as well as the role of the specifics of aesthetics. It has also meant that I have only fleetingly pointed out examples from outside France that show comparative political phenomenon. This study has sought to work with these genuinely difficult fissures in the quasi-structural approach and here it acknowledges them (and, today one is less enamoured with structuralism than once before). It is hoped that my insistence on discussing very detailed and specific historical evidence has at least in part mitigated against some of the above concerns. Also, because of this newfound scepticism, it means I will not be attempting to put forward any expanded 'total description' of the phenomenon. Readers are invited to return to each thematic chapter to think through how in a series of different ways, the cinema and nationalism worked together at specific times and locations. Nonetheless, if one still wants a few red threads that connect national mythmaking into a greater whole they appear to me now to be as follows. (1) Its very contested nature, with several different nationalisms being articulated in different works of cinema and then relayed and further disputed through the complex film debates. (2) Between the 1940s and the early 1990s cinema provided a national sense of belonging around myths of independence and resistance (from Hollywood, from Nazism) and myths of cultural primacy in cinema, but also in bourgeois lifestyle. These were balanced with expression of myths of deep concern around, and fear of, perceived outsider groups, including significant traces of late-nineteenth-century racism and anti-Semitism. (3) Expression of hard nationalism occurred, then, but this was wrapped up as provocation, ironic humour, counterculture – a so-called anarchism from the right wing. And, this was a significant attitude among some film people, including some famous stars and their directors. Such perspectives are not necessarily a bridge to the FN but they are commonly held among intellectuals in that political family. However, as my earlier remarks underline, it is with scepticism and reluctance that I even begin to draw up parameters for any such wider picture of connected facets in a system. At the least, that quintessentially French idea of finding structures, when applied to France, nationalism and cinema, starts to look too general and in danger of cliché because it so forces complex ideas and cultural expressions into too closed a single bundle, ultimately not that dissimilar in tone from Siegfried Kracauer's work on Germany from over fifty years ago.

What this book has sketched in to play are the varieties of nationalism pursued in cinema and it has underlined how these run from banal constructs of the ideal bourgeois couple, their house and swimming pool, his sports car, her clothes, to more overtly exclusionary discourses that are cruel and supportive of the extreme right wing. It has aimed to give students of French history, politics and film, as well as the more general reader, a greater understanding of the proximity of cinema to the advocacy of nationalism. It has not claimed cinema originated these political ideas, but it has intended to analyse when and how films and film debate circulated them, maybe only in coded ways, and only in the selected instances. It has also underlined that, in the period covered, the so-called film event brought subtexts and content of films from the screen away from the purely symbolic and into a network of living encounters between different social actors, ranging from the state and the presidency to quasi-terrorist organizations. In recent times, one can read with dismay that non-Western peoples are offended by cartoons or works of cinema. Yet, it was not so long ago in late 1980s France that the nationalist right shared conceptually comparable attitudes towards visual forms.

Periodically, and often with much furore and discussion, prominent intellectuals have bemoaned what they believe to be the reactionary nationalism of their own society. One thinks for example of the once much-discussed work of Bernard-Henri Lévy or more recently writings from Daniel Lindenberg or in a different register essays from Alain Badiou. I suppose therefore that one should not be surprised that the world of the cinema was marked by some of the harder varieties of nationalist ideology and that film events were sometimes violent. Nevertheless, and it should be underlined very strongly here, there were many examples of where the cinema provided a counterposition, or a more complex expression of nationalism. These instances have been underlined in this book, albeit often only briefly because they were not its primary subject. Resnais, Tavernier, Ophuls, Lanzmann and others stand out anew as being especially distinctive because it seems to me that their cinema consistently provides a different political imaginary to the focus of this work. (At times I have wondered to myself why I did not decide to write a book about these brilliant people. Quickly I remind myself that at the start of the research I did not know where the nationalist–cinema intervention would so clearly fall.) At the least, this book can assist future scholars to think further about these figures. In light of the analysis offered throughout the work, I consider that it is also plausible to return to Audiard, Bardot, Blain, Blier, Clément, Clouzot, Delon, Lelouch, Pagnol, Tati, Thomas, Truffaut, Verneuil, and the many others, to discern new facets in their cinema too. My excavations of where some of their works aligned with forms of nationalism are not intended to ruin the celebration of some of their filmmaking as an international art form. What the content of this book reveals is when and where they were integral to the nationalist politics of their own time and place.

Jean-Marie Le Pen and Alain Delon celebrate together on the occasion of the latter's award of 'Insignes de Commandeur des Arts et Lettres' (26 May 1986). Image courtesy of Paris Match/Getty Images, with kind permission.

Bibliography

Adler, K.H. 2011. 'Nation and Alienation: Retrievals of Home in Post-war French Film'. *History*, 326–53.

———. 2013. 'Indigènes after *Indigènes*: Post-war France and its North African Troops'. *European Review of History* 20.3, 463–78.

Aknin. L. 2012. *Mythes et idéologies du cinéma américain*. Paris: Vendémiaire

Alekan, H. 1999. *Le Vécu et l'imaginaire*, Paris: Sirène.

Anderson, B. 1991. *Imagined Communities. Reflections on the Origin and Spread of Nationalism*. London: Verso.

Andrew, D. 1987. *Breathless: Jean-Luc Godard, Director*. New Brunswick: Rutgers University Press.

Assouline, P. 1993. *Germinal: l'aventure d'un film*, Paris: Fayard.

Audiard, M. 1973. *Vive la France*. Paris: Julliard.

Autant-Lara, C. 1989. *Le Bateau coule*. Paris: Liberté.

de Baecque, A. 2002. *La Cinéphilie*. Paris: Fayard.

———. 2008. *L'Histoire-Caméra*. Paris: Gallimard.

———. 2010. *Godard, biographie*. Paris: Gallimard.

de Baecque, A. and S. Toubiana. 2001. *François Truffaut*. Paris: Gallimard.

Baetens, J. 2013. 'Writing the "Making of", a New Literary Genre?' Research paper presented L'Aquila, 17/11. Forthcoming.

Balladur, E. 2009. *Le Pouvoir ne se partage pas*. Paris: Fayard.

Bardèche M. and R. Brasillach. 1942. *Histoire du cinéma*. Paris: Denoël.

———. 1948. *Histoire du cinéma*. Paris: A Martel.

———. 1964. *Histoire du cinéma*. Paris: Poche.

Bardot, B. 1996. *Initiales BB*. Paris: Grasset.

———. 1999. *Le Carré de Pluton: mémoires*. Paris: Grasset.

———. 2002. *Un cri dans le silence*. Paris: Éditions du Rocher.

Barré, J-L. 2005. *Dominique de Roux: Le provocateur, 1935–1977*. Paris: Fayard.

Barrot, O. 1979. *L'Écran français 1943–1953, histoire d'un journal et d'un époque*. Paris: Les Éditeurs Français Réunis.

Barthes, R. 1970. *Mythologies*. Paris: Seuil.

Bazin, A. 1997. *Bazin at Work*. London: Routledge.

de Beauregard, C. 1991. *Georges de Beauregard: Premier sourire de Belmondo...dernier de Bardot*. Nimes: Lacour.

Bellos, D. 1999. 'Tati and America: *Jour de fête* and the Blum-Byrnes Agreement of 1946'. *French Cultural Studies* X/29, 145–59.

———. 2001. *Jacques Tati: His Life and Art*. London: Vintage.

Belot, R. 1994. *Lucien Rebatet: un itinéraire fasciste*. Paris: Seuil.

de Benoist, A. 1986. *Europe-Tiers Monde: Même Combat*. Paris: Robert Laffont.

Bertin-Maghit, J. 1986. "'La Bataille du rail": de l'authenticité à la chanson de geste'. *Revue d'histoire moderne et contemporaine* 33, 280–300.

Besson, G. and C. Lionet. 1994. *Le Pen, biographie*. Paris: Seuil.

Betz, M. 2001. 'The Name above the (Sub)Title: Internationalism, Coproduction, and Polyglot European Art Cinema'. *Camera Obscura* XVI/1, 3.

———. 2009. *Beyond the Subtitle: Remapping European Art Cinema*. Duluth: Minnesota UP.

Beylie. C. 1986. *Marcel Pagnol ou le cinéma en liberté*. Paris: Atlas.

Bickerton, E. 2009. *A Short History of the Cahiers du Cinéma*. London: Verso.

Billig, M. 1995. *Banal Nationalism*. London: Sage.

Birnbaum, P. 1993. *La France aux Français: histoire des haines nationalistes*. Paris: Seuil.

Bosséno, C-M. and Y. Dehée. 2004. *Dictionnaire du Cinéma populaire français*. Paris: Nouveau Monde.

Bourdieu. P. 1988. *L'ontologie politique de Martin Heidegger*. Paris: Éditions de Minuit.

———. 1991. *Language and Symbolic Power*. Cambridge: Polity.

———. 1993. *The Field of Cultural Production*. Cambridge: Polity.

Brion, P. 2005. *Cinéma français, 1895–2005*. Paris: ADPF.

Brody, R. 2008. *Everything is Cinema: The Working Life of Jean-Luc Godard*. London: Picador.

Carr. S. 2001. *Hollywood and Anti-Semitism*. Cambridge: CUP.

Carrière, J-C. 2003. *Les Années utopies, 1968–1969*. Paris: Plon.

Caute, D. 1994. *Joseph Losey: A Revenge on Life*. London: Faber.

Céline, L-F. 1943. *Bagatelles pour un massacre*. Paris: Denoël.

Celli. C. 2011. *National Identity in Global Cinema*. Basingstoke. Palgrave.

Chabrol, D. 2001. *Michel Audiard: C'est du brutal*. Paris: Flammarion.

Chapier, H. 2012. *Version originale*. Paris: Fayard.

Charpier, F. 2005. *Génération Occident*. Paris: Seuil.

Chéron, B. 2012. *Pierre Schoendoerrfer: un cinéma entre fiction et histoire*. Paris: CNRS.

Clerc, J-M. 1998. *Littérature et cinéma*. Paris: Nathan.

Cointet. M. 1993. *Vichy Capitale, 1940–1944*. Paris: Perrin.

Collins, L. and D.L. Pierre. 1966. *Is Paris Burning?* London: Penguin.

Cottaz, M. 1962. *Les Procès du putsch d'Alger*. Rennes: NEL.

Crisp, C. 1993. *The Classic French Cinema, 1930–1960*. Bloomington: Indiana University Press.

Crittenden, R. 1998. *La Nuit américaine*. London: BFI.

Curchod, O. 2012. 'Avant La Bataille'. *Positif* 612, 92.

Darnton, R. 1990. *The Kiss of Lamourette*. London: Faber.

Davidson, J. 1954. *Correspondant à Washington, 1945–53*. Paris: Seuil.

Decoux, J. 1949. *A la barre de l'Indochine*. Paris: Plon.

Dehée, Y. 2000. *Mythologies politiques du cinéma français, 1960–2000*. Paris: PUF.

Deray, J. 2003. *J'ai connu une belle époque*. Paris: Christian Pirot

Diop, B.B., O. Tobner, and F-X. Verschave. 2005. *Négrophobie*. Paris: Les Arènes.

Douin, M. 1998. *Dictionnaire de la Censure au Cinéma*. Paris: PUF.

Drazin, C. 2011. *The Faber Book of French Cinema*. London: Faber.

Dreyfus. M. 2009. *L'antisémitisme à gauche*. Paris: La Découverte.

Dufay, F. 2006. *Le soufre et le moisi. La droite littéraire après 1945*. Paris: Perrin.

Dufilho, J. 2003. *Les Sirènes du bateau-loup*. Paris: Fayard.

Dumas, R. 2007. *Affaires étrangères: 1981–1988*. Paris: Fayard.

Dunn. K.C. 2003. *Imagining the Congo: The International Relations of Identity*. New York: Palgrave.

Durant, P. 2009. *La Bande à Gabin: Blier, Audiard et les autres*. Paris: Sonatine.

Duranton-Crabol, A-M. 1995. *Le Temps de l'OAS*. Brussels: Complexe.

Ehrlich, E. 1985. *Cinema of Paradox: French Filmmaking under the Occupation*. New York: Columbia University Press.

Elgey, G. 1965. *La République des illusions, 1945–1951*. Paris: Fayard.

Elsaesser, T. 1996. *Fassbinder's Germany: History, Identity, Subject*. Amsterdam: Amsterdam UP.

Faulkner, W. 1984. *Faulkner, Brodsky Collection Volume Three: De Gaulle Story*. Jackson: University Press of Mississippi.

Fenby, J. 2002. *On the Brink: The Trouble with France*. London: Little Brown.

Ferro, M. 1993. *Cinéma et histoire*. Paris: Gallimard-Folio.

Fleischer, A. 2009. *Courts-circuits*. Paris: Le Cherche midi.

Flood, C. 1996. *Political Myth: A Theoretical Introduction*. New York: Garland.

Forbes, J. 1992. *The Cinema in France after the New Wave*. London, BFI.

Fralon, J-A. 2013. *Maurice Ronet. Le Splendide désenchanté*. Paris: Equateurs.

Frey, H. 2004. *Louis Malle*. Manchester: Manchester University Press.

———. 2011. 'Cannes 1956/1979: Riviera Reflections on Nationalism and Cinema', in S. Berger, L. Eriksonas and A. Mycock (eds), *Narrating the Nation: Representations in History, Media, and the Arts*. Oxford: Berghahn, 181–206.

Frodon, J-M. 1995. *L'Âge moderne du cinéma français*. Paris: Flammarion.

Garreau, L. 2009. *Archives secrètes du cinéma Français*. Paris: PUF, 230–31.

Gaulle, C. de. 1954. *Mémoires de guerre*, Paris: Plon.

Gellner, E. 1997. *Nationalism*. London: Weidenfeld.

Girardet, R. 1957. 'L'Héritage de l'Action française'. *Revue française de science politique* 7 (4), 765–92.

Gobard, H. 1976. *L'Aliénation linguistique*. Paris: Flammarion.

———. 1979. *La Guerre culturelle*. Paris: Copernic.

Green, M.J. 1992. 'Fascists on Film: The Brasillach and Bardèche *Histoire du cinéma*', in R.J. Golsan (ed.), *Fascism, Aesthetics and Culture*. Hanover: UP New England, 164–78.

Grynberg, A. 2001. 'Des signes de résurgence de l'antisémitisme dans la France de l'après-guerre (1945–1953)', *Cahiers de la Shoah* 5, 171–223.

Halimi, A. 1985. *Touche pas à l'Amérique*. Paris: Plon.

Hammond, P. 1997. *L'Âge d'or*. London: BFI.

Harris, M. 2008. *Pictures at a Revolution: Five Movies and the Birth of the New Hollywood*. London: Penguin.

Hayward, S. 2005. *French National Cinema*. London: Routledge.

Hewitt, N. 1996. *Literature and the Right in Postwar France*. Oxford: Berg.

———. 2003. 'Céline, the Success of the Monstre Sacré in Postwar France'. *Substance* 32.3, 29–42.

Historia-Paris Match. 2012. *1945–1975. La France Heureuse*. Paris: Paris-Match.

Stuart Hughes, H. 1968. *The Obstructed Path: French Social Thought in the Years of Desperation, 1930–1960*. New York: Harper.

d'Hugues, P. 1999. *L'Envahisseur américain: Hollywood contre Billancourt*. Geneva: Favre.

———. 2000. 'La droite et le cinéma', in Guyot-Jeannin (ed.). *Aux sources de la droite: pour en finir avec les clichés*. Lausanne: L'Age d'homme.

———. 2005. *Les Écrans de la guerre. Le cinéma français de 1940 à 1944*. Paris: De Fallois.

Insdorf, A. 1994. *François Truffaut*. Cambridge: CUP.

Jackson, J. 2009. *La Grande illusion*. Basingstoke: BFI.

Jardin, J. 1975. *A Vichy Boyhood: An Inside View of the Pétain Regime*. London: Faber.

Jeancolas. J-P. 1998. 'From the Blum–Byrnes Agreement to the GATT Affair', in G. Nowell-Smith and S. Ricci (eds). *Hollywood and Europe*. London: BFI, 47–62.

Jobs, R.I. 2007. *Riding the New Wave: Youth and the Rejuvenation of France after the Second World War*. Stanford: Stanford University Press.

Joseph, D. 1972. *Guerre et cinéma. Grandes illusions et petits soldats, 1895–1971*. Paris: Armand Colin.

Judt, T. 1992. *Past Imperfect: French Intellectuals 1944–1956*. Berkley: California UP.

Kaplan, A.Y. 1987. *Relevé des sources et citations dans 'Bagatelles pour un massacre'*. Tusson: Lérot.

Kaplan, S.L. 1993. *Adieu 89*. Paris: Fayard.

Kauffer, R. 2002. *OAS. Histoire d'une guerre franco-française*. Paris: Seuil

Kedward, R. 2005. *La Vie en bleu: France and the French since 1900*. London: Allen Lane.

Kennedy, P. 1988. *The Rise and Fall of the Great Powers*. London: Fontana.

King, N. 2000. 'Eye for Irony: Eric Rohmer's *Ma nuit chez Maud* (1969)', S. Hayward and G. Vincendeau (eds). *French Film: Texts and Contexts*. London: Routledge, 202–12.

Kracauer, S. 1947. *From Caligari to Hitler: A Psychological History of the German Film*. London: Dennis Dobson.

Kuisel, R.F. 1997. *Seducing the French: The Dilemma of Americanization*. Berkeley: University of California Press.

———. 2000. 'The Fernandel Factor'. *Yale French Studies* 98, 119–34.

———. 2012. *The French Way*. London: Princeton University Press.

Labro, P. 1975. 'L'armée des ombres: de tous ses films, c'est celui que Melville préférait'. *France Soir*, 21 June.

Lacouture, J. 1977. *Léon Blum*. Paris: Seuil.

Lang, J. 2009. *Demain comme hier*. Paris: Fayard.

Langlois, G. 2002. 'La bataille d'Alger'. *CinéAction* 103.

Le Bortef, H. 1986. *Robert Le Vigan: le mal-aimé du cinéma*. Paris: Éditions France-Empire.

Le Bortef, H. and M. Ronet. 1977. *Le métier de comédien, entretiens avec Hervé Le Bortef*. Paris: Éditions France-Empire.

Le Guern, A. 2013. *Une âme damnée. Paul Gégauff*. Paris: PGDR.

Lelouch, C. 2000. *Journal d'un enfant très gâté*. Paris: Pocket.

Le Pen, J-M. 1999. *Lettres française ouvertes*. Paris: Objectif France.

Lev, P. 1983. *Claude Lelouch, Film Director*. London: Fairleigh Dickinson UP.

———. 1993. *The Euro-American Cinema*. Austin: University of Texas Press.

L'Herbier, M. 1979. *La tête qui tourne*. Paris: Pierre Belfond.

Lindeperg, S. 1997. *Les Écrans de l'ombre*. Paris: CNRS.

Lindlof, T.R. 2008. *Hollywood under Siege: Martin Scorsese, the Religious Right and the Culture Wars*. Lexington: University Press of Kentucky.

Looseley, D. 1995. *The Politics of Fun*. Oxford: Berg.

Loti, P. 1886. *Pêcheur d'Islande*, Paris: Calmann-Lévy.

Manchette, J-P. 1997. *Les Yeux de la momie: chroniques de cinéma*. Paris: Rivages.

———. 2008. *Journal, 1966–1974*. Paris: Gallimard.

Marmin, M. 1970. *Raoul Walsh*. Paris: Seghers.

———. 1976. *Fausto, Vania, Kaspar et Véronique. Chroniques cinématographiques, 1972–1976*. Lausanne: Ed T'Annay.

Marrus, M. and R. Paxton. 1981. *Vichy France and the Jews*. New York: Basic Books.

Martin, L. 2008. *Jack Lang: une vie entre culture et politique*. Paris: Complexe.

Massu, J. 1971. *La Vraie bataille d'Alger*. Paris: Plon.

Mazdon, L. 2000. *Encore Hollywood. Remaking French Cinema*. London: BFI.

Mckinney, M. 2011. *The Colonial Heritage of French Comics*. Liverpool: Liverpool University Press.

Mirzoeff, N. 2011. *The Right to Look. A Counterhistory of Visuality*. Durham: Duke University Press.

Mitchell, W.J.T. (ed.). 2002. *Landscape and Power*. Chicago: University of Chicago Press.

Monaco, J. 1976. *The New Wave*. New York: Oxford University Press.

Morrey, D. 2005. *Jean-Luc Godard*. Manchester: Manchester University Press.

Mosse, G.L. 1985. *Nationalism and Sexuality: Respectability and Abnormal Sexuality in Modern Europe*. New York: H.Feritg.

Mourlet, M. and M. Marmin. 1968. *Cecil B. De Mille*, Paris: Seghers.

Murray, A. 2000. 'Le Tourisme Citroën au Sahara (1924–1925)'. *Vingtième siècle* 68, 95–107.

Ory, P. 1976. *Les Collaborateurs, 1940–1945*. Paris: Seuil.

———. 1985. *L'Anarchisme de droite*. Paris: Grasset.

———. 1992. 'Mister Blum goes to Hollywood', in M. Boujut and J. Chancel (eds). *Europe-Hollywood et retour*. Paris: Autrement, 100–111.

O'Shaughnessy. M. 1995. '*La Bataille du rail*: Unconventional Form, Conventional Image', in H.R. Kedward and N. Wood (eds). *Liberation: Image and Event*. Oxford: Berg, 15–28.

———. 2009. *La Grande illusion*. London: IB Tauris.

Pagnol, M. 2008. *Carnets de cinéma*. Paris: Éditions Privé.

Peer, S. 1998. *France on Display: Peasants, Provincials and Folklore in the 1937 Paris World's Fair*. Albany: State University of New York Press.

du Plantier, D.T. 1995. *L'Émotion culturelle*. Paris: Flammarion.

Pollock, G. and M. Silverman (eds). 2011. *Concentrationary Cinema*. Oxford: Berghahn.

Prazan, M. 2005. *L'Écriture génocidaire: l'antisémitisme en style et en discours*. Paris: Calmann-Lévy.

Prazan, M. and A.Minard. 2007. *Roger Garaudy*. Paris: Calmann-Lévy.

Quilès, P. 1985. *La politique n'est pas ce que vous croyez*. Paris: Robert Laffont.

Raskin, R. 1987. *Nuit et brouillard: On the Making, Reception and Function of a Major Documentary Film*. Aarhus: Aarhus University Press.

Rebatet, L. 1941. *Les Tribus du cinéma et du théâtre*. Paris: NEF.

Renoir, J. 1994. *Letters*. London: Faber.

———. 1999. *Cher Jean Renoir: Projet de film*. Paris: Gallimard.

Riding, A. 2011. *And the Show Went On: Cultural Life in Nazi-Occupied Paris*. London: Allen Lane/Vintage.

Rioux, J-P. 1987. *The Fourth Republic, 1944–58*. Cambridge: CUP.

de la Rochère, A-E. D. 1998. *Les Studios de la Victorine, 1919–1929*. Nice: AFRHC.

Roger, P. 2004. *L'ennemi américain*. Paris: Seuil.

Ross, K. 1996. *Fast Cars, Clean Bodies*. London: the MIT Press.

Rothberg, M. 2009. *Multidirectional Memory*. Stanford: Stanford University Press

Rousso, H. 1987. *Le Syndrome de Vichy*. Paris: Seuil.

de Roux, D. 1973. *Ne traversez pas le Zambèze*. Paris: L'Age d'Homme.

Roy, J. 1972. *J'Accuse le Général Massu*. Paris: Seuil.

Saadi, Y. 1962. *Souvenirs de la Bataille d'Alger*. Paris: Julliard.

Sadoul, G. 1938. *Ce que lisent vos enfants*. Paris: Bureau d'éditions.

———. 1953. *French Film*. London: Falcon Press.

———. 1979. *Chroniques du cinéma français*. Paris: Union Générale d'Editions.

———. 2009. 'Les Quais des brumes 1960', in P. Graham and G. Vincendeau (eds), *The French New Wave: Critical Landmarks*. London: BFI, 235.

Sand, S. 2004. *Le XXᵉ siècle à l'écran*. Paris: Seuil.

Scarpetta, G. 1981. *Éloge du cosmopolitisme*. Paris: Grasset.

Schulberg, B. 1941. *What makes Sammy run?* New York: Random House.

Schwartz, V. 2007. *It's So French!: Hollywood, Paris, and the Making of Cosmopolitan Film Culture*. Chicago: Chicago UP.

Sérant, P. 1960, *Le Romantisme fasciste*. Paris: Fasquelle.

Sesonske, A. 1980. *Jean Renoir: the French films, 1924–1939*. Cambridge Mass: Harvard UP.

Sherzer, D. 1996. 'Race Matters and Matters of Race', in Sherzer (ed.). *Cinema, Colonialism, Postcolonialism*. Austin: University of Texas, 232–52.

Sibelman, S.P. 2000. 'Jewish Myths and Stereotypes in the Cinema of Julien Duvivier', in E. Ezra and S. Harris (eds). *France in Focus: Film and National Identity*. Oxford: Berg, 79–95.

Siclier, J. 1997. 'Le cinéma', in J.F. Sirinelli (ed.). *Les Droites en France*, Vol.2. *Culture*. Paris: Gallimard, 293–324.

Signoret, S. 1979. *Nostalgia Isn't What it Used to Be*. London: Penguin.

Simmons. H.G. 1996. *The French National Front*. Oxford: Westview Press.

Simsi, S. 2000. *Ciné-Passions*. Paris: Dixit.

Smith, A. 2005. *French Cinema in the 1970s: the Echoes of May*. Manchester: Manchester University Press.

Solinas, P. 1973. *Gillo Pontecorvo's The Battle of Algiers*, New York: Scribner.

Soria, G. 1948. *La France deviendra-t-elle une colonie Américaine?* Paris: Éd. du Pavillion.

Spenle, A. 1946. 'La Bataille du rail'. *La Revue de cinéma* 1.1, 73.

Spoto, D. 1984. *The Dark Side of Genius: The Life of Alfred Hitchcock*. New York: Plexus.

Stoner Saunders, F. 2000. *Who Paid the Piper? The CIA and the Cultural Cold War*. London: Granta.

Stora, B. 1999. *Le Transfert d'une mémoire. De l'Algérie française au racisme anti-arabe*. Paris: La Découverte.

Taguieff, P-A. 'Nationalisme et réactions fondamentalistes en France: Mythologies identitaires et ressentiment antimoderne'. *Vingtième siècle* (1990) 69–103.

Tardi, J. and M. Boujut. 1995. *Un Strapontin pour deux*. Tournai: Casterman.

Tavernier. B. 2011. *Le cinéma dans le sang*. Paris: Écriture.

Thibau, T. 1979. *La France colonisée*. Paris: Flammarion.

Thorez, M. 1963. *Oeuvres*. Paris: Éd. Sociales.

Truffaut, F. 1989. *Letters*. London: Faber.

———. 2000. *La Nuit américaine, scénario, suivi de Journal de tournage de Fahrenheit 451*. Paris: Cahiers du Cinéma.

Tulard, J. 1997. *Dictionnaire du cinéma: les réalisateurs*. Paris: Robert Laffont.

Turk, E.B. 1992. *Child of Paradise: Marcel Carné and the Golden Age of French Cinema*. Cambridge: Harvard UP.

Ulff-Moller, J. 2001. *Hollywood's Film Wars with France: Film Trade Diplomacy and the Emergence of the French Film Quota Policy*. Rochester: Rochester University Press.

Vadim, R. 1986. *Bardot, Deneuve, Fonda: The Memoirs of Roger Vadim*. London: New English Library.

Van der Knaap, E. (ed.). 2006. *Uncovering the Holocaust*. London: Wallflower Press.

Vautier, R. 1998. *Caméra citoyenne: mémoires*. Paris: Apogée.

Vignaux, V. 2005. *Suzanne Simonin ou La Religieuse de Jacques Rivette*. Liège: Éditions du CEFAL.

Vincendeau, G. 1992. 'France 1945–1965 and Hollywood: the *policier* as International Text'. *Screen* 33.1, 50–80.

———. 2000. *Stars and Stardom in French Cinema*. London: Continuum.

———. 2003. *Jean-Pierre Melville: An American in Paris*. London: BFI.

Violet, B. 2000. *Les mystères Delon*. Paris: Flammarion.

Walton, W. 2010. *Internationalism, National Identities and Study Abroad: France and the United States, 1890–1970*, Stanford: Stanford University Press.

Wharton, S. 2006. *Screening Reality: French Documentary Film during the German Occupation*. Oxford: Peter Lang.

Weber, A. 2007. *La Bataille du Film*. Paris: Ramsay.

Wild, F. 1996. 'L'Histoire ressucitée: Jewishness and Scapegoating in Julien Duvivier's *Panique*', in S. Ungar and T. Conley (eds). *Identity Papers: Contested Nationhood in Twentieth Century France*. Minneapolis: University of Minnesota Press, 178–92.

Winock, M. 1996. 'Qu'est-ce qu'une nation?'. *L'Histoire* 201, 8.

———. 2004. *La France et les juifs: de 1780 à nos jours*. Paris: Seuil.

Witt, M. 2000. '"Qu'était-ce que le cinéma, Jean-Luc Godard?" An Analysis of the Cinema(s) at Work in and around Godard's *Histoire(s) du cinéma*', in E. Ezra and S. Harris (eds). *France in Focus: Film and National Identity*. Oxford: Berg, 23–41.

Wolin, R. 1998. 'Designer Fascism', in R.J. Golsan (ed.). *Fascism's Return: Scandal, Revision, and Ideology since 1980*. Lincoln: Nebraska UP, 48–62.

Index